SURF
TRAVEL

THE COMPLETE GUIDE

orcapublications

SURF TRAVEL
THE COMPLETE GUIDE

Published by Orca Publications
Berry Road Studios
Berry Road
Newquay
Cornwall
TR7 1AT
United Kingdom
(+44) 01637 878074
www.orcasurf.co.uk

EDITOR: Roger Sharp
DESIGNER: David Alcock
PROOFREADER: Hayley Spurway
PRODUCTION: Louise Searle

CONTRIBUTING WRITERS: Roger Sharp, Ben Mondy, Chris Power, Gabe Davies, Brendan Bosworth, Owen Pye, Rob Barber, Alan van Gysen, Skip Snead, Mick Fanning.

CONTRIBUTING PHOTOGRAPHERS: Bastien Bonnarme, Bosko, Sam Breeze, Chris Burkard, Chus Carvajal, Diogo d'Orey, Greg Ewing, Joe Foster, Pete Frieden, Alan van Gysen, Victor Gonzalez, Pete Hodgson, Tobias Ilsanker, Andrew Kilfeather, Greg Martin, Laurent Masurel, Manu Miguelez, Edwin Morales, Bill Morris, Tim Nunn, Rodd Owen, Pacotwo, Marcus Paladino, Chris Power, Jason Reposar, Epes Sargent, Danya Schwertfeger, Cory Scott, Sean Scott, Mike Searle, Sharpy, Andrew Shield, Hugo Silva, DJ Struntz, Bernard Testemale, Kiefer Thomson, Ben Thouard, Alex Williams, Simon Williams, Corey Wilson.

PRINTED BY:
Prosperous Printing Co. Ltd., China

COPYRIGHT © 2018 ORCA PUBLICATIONS

ISBN 978-0-9930383-2-7

DISCLAIMER

While every effort has been made to ensure that the information contained in this guide is accurate and up-to-date, the publishers cannot accept responsibility for any errors it may contain. Before travelling, it is advisable to check all information locally, including information about accommodation, transport and the suitability of surf breaks. Surfing can be a dangerous sport and you are responsible for your own safety at all times. The writers and publishers accept no responsibility or liability for any inconvenience, loss, injury or death sustained by anyone a a result of any advice or information contained in this guide.

COVER PHOTO: BRYCE YOUNG AND THE DREAM WE ALL SEEK, REMOTE INDONESIA. **PHOTO:** ANDREW SHIELD
BACK COVER PHOTO: NORWAY PUMPING. **PHOTO:** TIM NUNN. COOKING CANARIES. **PHOTO:** MANU MIGUELEZ,
AWESOME AUSTRALIA. **PHOTO:** ANDREW SHIELD **OPPOSITE:** MICK FANNING AND THE ULTIMATE AIM OF SURF TRAVEL: SCORING A SICK, EMPTY, MYSTO LINEUP TO YOURSELF. THIS IS 'THE SNAKE' WHICH STILL REMAINS A DELIGHTFUL MYSTERY AS TO ITS LOCATION.

THE SEARCH

RIP CURL

CONTENTS

SECTION THREE: INFORMATION

foreword

BY **MICK FANNING**

I've lived most of my life on the road, and the older I get the more I understand just how much it has shaped me into who I am today. All of the different places, different waves, unique cultures, interesting people … everywhere I've been over the years has left an imprint. And for those of us on Tour, going back to the same places year after year, we suddenly have family all over the world. That is invaluable.

And at the same time that routine of travel makes those moments when we break out into a new place, those times when we go Searching, all the more exciting.

It's so important to enjoy the comforts of home, and embrace those times when you are actually home. But without travel, life is small – you don't learn and grow and expand your horizons. And because we surf, we have the gift of travelling with purpose – of bonding with people in a foreign land, who might not speak the same language, but share the same craft.

Flip through the pages of this book over and over again, and be inspired to get out of your comfort zone and go Searching. **– Mick**

MICK HAS TICKED OFF MORE SPOTS THAN MOST…

introduction

From the moment you first feel the rush towards the beach on a surfboard your life has taken a new path. It's the good path you've embarked upon, one with broader horizons and adventure guaranteed. By deciding to become a surfer you've stoked the innate explorer that's been simmering inside of you all along. Coastal curiosity is now your thing.

Once you've mastered the nuances of your home beach you wonder what's around the next corner. From there you figure out your coast and as your surfing experience builds you wonder about other regions, other countries and continents. Luckily we're living in the most economical and easiest time to explore the world looking for waves and good times.

Pretty much anywhere in the world open to a decent stretch of sea gets surfable waves at some point in the year. Which makes deciding where to explore a delightfully varied proposition. It comes down to the time you've got free, the cash you've set aside for the adventure and how deep you want to go down the surf travel rabbit hole.

Do you want a quick strike on a niche spot that only works twice a year, a week of near guaranteed waves, ten days on boat, a fortnight of surf and culture or a year long around the world bender? Whichever you choose the Complete Guide to Surf Travel can help you get there.

We've selected a smorgasbord of the world's finest surf destinations to tease and tempt you with. From the easy European runs to deep Indonesian missions there are more options than you could sample in most lifetimes … unless you won the lottery. Which if it does happen please bring us along for the ride.

The key to scoring is planning and research. There's no point going to the North Shore with dreams of Pipeline glory in August. All you're going to get at that time of year is a mirror calm ocean and sublime snorkelling. Figuring out where to go is one side of the equation, the when is the other vital factor. Somewhere in the world is going off pretty much all the time. Being there in peak season, or if a popular destination, shoulder season when it can still be good but less busy, is what you need to aim for. Research well and you up your chances of all time waves, we've got prime seasons mentioned for all the key areas. Having the right visas, inoculations, boards, wetsuits and more is the planning side, it's better to prepare too much than to be caught short on arrival. We've got loads of handy tips and information for that too.

So wherever you're thinking of going dive into the guide, get some inspiration and get looking at flights, forecasts and surf camps. There's no better feeling than knowing you've got a surf trip locked in.

It's a big old world full of waves, you owe it to yourself to experience as many of them as possible. Good luck!

– Sharpy

LEFT: CAN'T BEAT A BOAT TRIP.
RIGHT: HARLEY INGLEBY AND FRIENDS SOAK UP SCOTLAND.

SECTION ONE:

PREPARATION

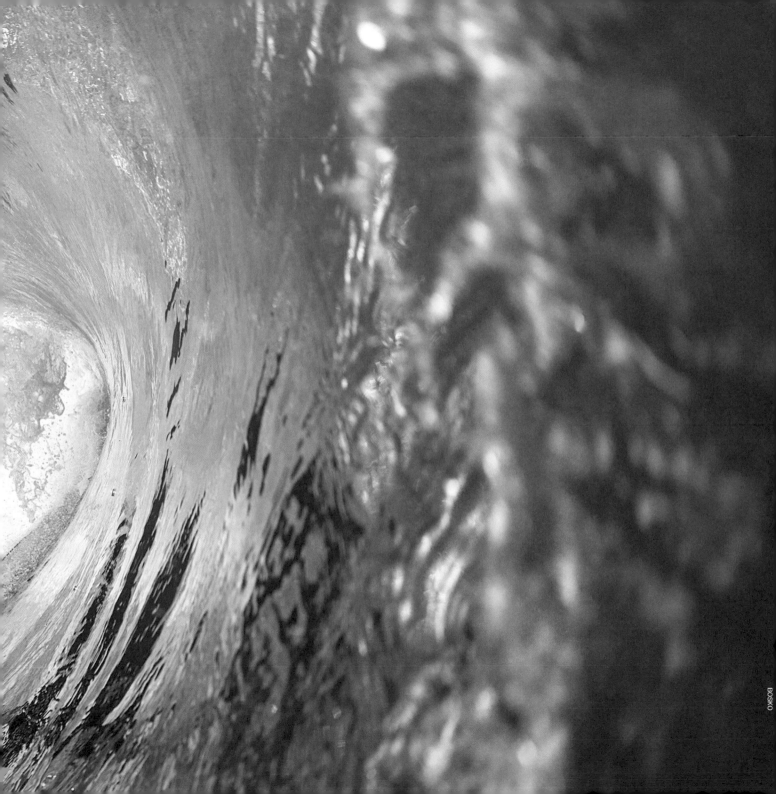

PLANNING YOUR TRIP

Okay, so you're frothing to go on a surf trip. But what kind of trip? Where to? And when? Well, to answer the first of those questions, turn to page 30 and check out some of the trip options open to you (boat trips, road trips, and so on). Then have a browse through the Destinations section (starting on page 46), which will give plenty of ideas about where to go. As for the timing of your trip, well, once again you've got options...

Every destination has a prime season for waves, when you're likely to score consistent swells and optimum wind conditions. Trouble is, just as you're eyeing up the charts, so the rest of the world will be doing likewise, and they'll be ready to pounce on the same cheap flights and head to the same primo camps. Before you know it, you'll be sharing the lineup with 50 other dudes. Which is why it's sometimes worth taking a gamble on the off-season; while sick waves aren't guaranteed, the lineups will be uncrowded, and when the waves turn on you'll be seriously stoked.

It could be worth jotting down your aims, so you can plan the kind of trip that should (hopefully!) nail your priorities. If you really want to surf a specific spot and you don't mind waiting in a busy lineup to get that one barrel you've always dreamed of, then going in the peak season is probably your best bet. Conversely, if you hate crowds and don't mind putting up with a bit of unfavourable weather between the good days, then the off-season could be the winning ticket for you.

Flights and accommodation are almost always cheaper outside of holiday periods and peak times. If you can book cheap off-season flights, chances are that you'll be able to find discounted rates on apartment rentals too. You'll often find that the earlier you book flights, the cheaper they'll be. Then again, it's often possible to grab some insane last-minute bargains.

If you're on a tight budget, it's worth considering the countries whose peak swell season coincides with their off-season tourist industry, so you can score the cheapest prices. Ticking both boxes is sure to yield some great waves without breaking the bank. For example, if you went to Portugal in November, you'd probably pay half as much as you'd pay in August – and probably get twice the number of days with sick waves.

Another factor to consider when planning a trip is how many guys you're thinking of going with, if any. Flying solo has some major advantages. You're less likely to get hassle from locals, since you won't be part of a mobile rent-a-crowd. You won't have to make any compromises for the good of the group. You'll meet more people, and you'll be free to take off on all sorts of impromptu local trips which will inevitably crop up once you're over there.

If you plan to go with a mate (or a bunch of mates), the most important thing is to be absolutely certain you will get on well with them. Travelling, surfing and living with the same person, 24 hours a day, can test even the strongest of friendships. Your mate might be a brilliant tube-rider and a great bloke, but what's he like after eight beers? The last thing you want is to get embroiled with a dozen local heavies because your boozy loudmouth mate tried it on with the wrong girl.

When you're planning a trip with a group of mates, talk about what you want to achieve – for example, surfing certain spots or visiting certain places. Do your research and find out what non-surfing activities are on offer, in case it goes flat. Many surf camp websites claim 'incredible, consistent waves', but you can't rule out the fact that Mother Nature might not play ball during your stay. Having a range of backup activities is always a good thing.

If you have mates at home who've previously travelled to your destination of choice, tap them up for info about surf spots, accommodation, and most importantly, any friendly locals they're still in contact with. If you can, get in touch, ask them some questions and see if you can hook up with them. One of the best things about travelling is meeting people and making friends all over the globe. Do enough of it and you'll never have to pay for a room on a trip again! It's incredibly useful (and a privilege) to leave a country having made new friends who'll welcome you back. Having local knowledge of an area is unbeatable, and being able to bro-down with a local crew could be the golden key to your next trip.

OPPOSITE THE SURF WORLD HAS EXPANDED INTO NEW COLD FRONTIERS. THEY'RE THERE TO BE EXPLORED AT YOUR LEISURE.

FITNESS AND TRAINING

If you're lining up the trip of a lifetime you'll obviously want to make the most of the waves, and that means being at the top of your game, both physically and mentally. A well-planned fitness programme will help you achieve peak condition before you board the plane, rather than when you return home. Yes, it'll involve grunting and sweating every day for weeks on end. But all that hard work will pay off when you see your mates calling it quits after a few hours surfing each day, while you paddle back out for more like some kind of surfing cyborg!

For overall fitness improvement nothing beats getting in the water as often as you can, but there are certain complimentary workouts that are well suited to the start-stop nature of surfing and its stamina requirements. Circuit training, for example, is an ideal dry land workout. By performing a series of exercises for a minute or so in a circuit-based format you can really build up your all-round fitness.

Surf-specific 'strength and conditioning' workouts are also becoming popular. These employ a range of full body exercises (core exercises, squats, lunges, balance exercises and so on) and make use of inexpensive equipment like weights, pulleys and Swiss balls.

If you're serious about improving your fitness, get your hands on a copy of Advanced Surf Fitness For High Performmance Surfing by Lee Stanbury. This book is not only comprehensive, it's inspirational. You'll have abs like Slater in a couple of months!

CORE

FRONT PLANK

The front plank is a static exercise that will strengthen your abdominals, back and shoulders. It specifically strengthens the transverse abdominals – the deepest layer of abdominal muscles that wrap around your mid section. NB This exercise should be done on a cushioned non-slip surface to avoid injury.

• Start by lying face down with your hands either side of your head. Then lift your body completely off the ground, transferring your bodyweight onto your elbows and toes. Contract your abdominals and relax your shoulders.

• Try to maintain a good straight body alignment. Keep breathing easily and relax your neck.

• Hold the exercise for as long as you can, and contract your abdominals constantly throughout the exercise.

BALANCE TRAINING

INDO SQUAT

Cracking your board off the lip can be as demanding as you make it. At any level this requires balance and proprioception skill. In many surfing movements you won't always have eye contact with your board, and this is where training in this area can help.

• Try standing on your Indo Board with feet about a hip width apart, knees slightly bent, then once you feel stable try closing your eyes.

• Closing your eyes will heighten your proprioceptive skills. (This exercise is best done using a partner for safety!)

EXPLOSIVE POWER

SIDE STEPS AT PACE

The Reebok side step is also a basic exercise but can be used to boost aerobic and anaerobic fitness and improve coordination when done at speed.

• Simply start the exercise with feet both sides of the step then, slowly to start, step one foot up on the box followed by the other. As your coordination improves increase speed. As you progress with your fitness and the exercise speeds up, intensify your step over with a jump.

• Work at intervals, improving your fitness by increasing your duration. (20, 30, 40 seconds etc.)

HIT THE POOL

A basic swimming programme will allow you to cover all areas and types of aerobic training needed for surfing. Low and high range aerobic training is important for overall fitness. Anaerobic fitness is also important for those days when your duck diving just goes on and on. Follow these programmes and feel the benefits within just a few weeks.

Here are two examples of basic swimming programmes, each based on a 60-minute session.

BASIC SWIMMING PROGRAMME

• Warm up with six to eight minutes of light swimming, getting faster every minute.
• Depending on your ability (adjust the distances as necessary) swim 400 metres (16 x 25m lengths) front crawl with 15 seconds rest at the end of each length. The pace of this should be low-end aerobic; quite light swimming at about 65-75% effort. Your breathing should be light, meaning you're doing low-end aerobic exercise.
• Now swim 400 metres (16 x 25m lengths) front crawl

at a faster pace, at about 80-85% effort. This will put you up into high-end aerobic swimming; your breathing should be quite fast. Only rest for 15 seconds or less between each length.
• For your last 400 metres go for the highest output – anaerobic swimming. There's a fine line between high-end aerobic swimming and anaerobic swimming, and this type of training will achieve the sort of fitness levels you're aiming for. (Imagine you're surfing and you face a long hard paddle out through heavy waves; after half-a-dozen duck dives in a row you'll be in the anaerobic zone!) Try swimming at just under your maximum speed; if you were running this would be a sprint. Give yourself 30 seconds between each length to recover. You may not be up to doing 16 lengths straightaway, but 10 is a good starting block to work from.
• At the end of the session, warm down with six to eight minutes of gentle swimming.

HYPOXIC LOW OXYGEN SWIMMING PROGRAMME

• Warm up with six to eight minutes of light swimming, slowly getting faster every minute.
• Depending on your ability (adjust the distances as necessary) swim 400 metres (16 x 25m lengths) front crawl, taking a breath every five strokes; this will mean keeping your head down slightly more than you're used to. This form of hypoxic swim training helps your breath holding for those nasty hold-downs!
• Now swim 400 metres (16 x 25m lengths) front crawl breathing every seven strokes. This is much more demanding and you may need to give yourself a longer rest after every 25m.
• The final set is straightforward – try sprinting for as long as you can with your head down. This will be tough. When you've gone as far as you can, take a deep breath, recover, and swim slowly to the end of the pool. Try this 10 times, and as you get fitter just increase the distance.
• At the end of the session, warm down with six to eight minutes of gentle swimming.

Photo credit (vertical): GUSTAVO MIGUEL FERNANDES / SHUTTERSTOCK.COM

GET INTO STRENGTH AND ENDURANCE TRAINING

Strength training offers many benefits for surfers, including increases in muscle mass and connective tissue thickness, with associated increases in muscle strength and endurance. Strength training isn't just about lifting weights. Yes, weight training can be used to increase surfing strength, however, there are a range of other strength training regimes that can also be of great benefit. To increase your paddling strength, start a land-based resistance band workout using a PowerStroke cord.

> "REGULAR SURFING IS THE KEY, FOR SURE. IF YOU CAN'T GO SURFING, THEN SWIMMING IS THE NEXT BEST THING – FOR FITNESS AS WELL AS BASIC WATER AWARENESS. CORE TRAINING IS ALSO REALLY GOOD FOR SURFING."
>
> – FERGAL SMITH

POWERSTROKE CORD TRICEPS EXTENSION

This exercise will improve paddle strength, by working the triceps.

- Start by standing with your legs hip-width apart. Grasp the cord with your left hand behind your back at waist height, and with your right hand behind your head over your right shoulder.
- Keeping your left arm locked in position, extend your right arm upwards, taking care not to lock your right arm out fully.
- It's important to maintain a good body position throughout the exercise.
- Repeat this 12 to 15 times, then switch arms.

PADDLE SPRINT TRAINING

This exercise will improve your endurance and allow you to paddle faster for longer, enabling you to catch more waves.

- Start by finding a good area to work out with your PowerStroke cord. Warm up by doing ten minutes of mobility exercises, such as arm swings.
- Place your hands in the PowerStroke cord handles, engage your core and tighten your abdominal muscles; this will maintain stability. Then begin paddling with slow and controlled movements, just as you would on your board. After about 20 strokes, speed up sharply for 10 seconds before slowing back down again into a light recovery paddle.
- Continue this for three or four minutes. Rest for a minute or two and then repeat. Six to eight sets of this exercise will be enough to start improving your paddling speed. Try doing this two or three times a week, and increase the time of each workout by a few minutes to add progression to your sessions.

POWERSTROKE REVERSE FLY

- Standing with feet firmly on the cords, grab both handles, then with a relaxed neck, slowly draw the arms outwards.
- From here squeeze the shoulder blades together, repeat 8-10 times .
- Rest before attempting another 10.

TRAVEL ESSENTIALS

If you're going on a surf trip organisation is key. Simple as that. If you're not on the ball then you're heading for a one way trip to Stress Town – population: 1.

Do you really want to be the person who's mislaid their passport at the border crossing? The leash free loser when the swell kicks in? The car charger free navigator who's phone has just hit 1%? Or a first aid kit short when a trip to Boots before you left would've sorted most ailments? Nope? Us neither.

Take a leaf out of an aeroplane pilots, way of doing things and make a check list of all the stuff you need. Check lists are the key to aviation and they work just as well for your vacation. Make a solid one for warm water trips and one for cold. Keep them safe, and use them every time you go on a trip. It's simple these days as most smartphones have list making apps built in so you can check things off as you pack.

Here's a basic list of travel essentials to get you started. Or course packing as light as possible is desired, but this is a good base kit. There's more about gadgets and cameras on the following pages.

• **Boards** It's simple: take a quiver. There'll be sick days, big days, weak days and stick-snapping days. Cover yourself. Two is minimum unless it's a real quick trip.
• **Boardbag** Check out the options and get the best quality boardbag you can afford. Wheeled bags are your friend if there's going to be airport terminal changes or much cross town missioning.
• **Wax** Goes without saying, wax is essential and incredibly hard to get hold of in some parts of the world. Ensure it's the right temperature and you've cleaned your boards before you go.
• **Leashes** You can never have enough leashes, especially if you're heading on a big-wave trip. Bring leash strings too. Always pack leashes carefully, you don't want new unintentional go faster dents in your precious sticks.
• **Ding repair kit** The travelling surfer's best friend. Solarez style one tube products are a good fix for minor dings.
• **Spare fins** If you snap a fin off and don't have a spare it can ruin your trip. So bring a spare set ... plus a few fin keys and grub screws or fin plates.
• **Roof straps** The most forgotten item in every surfer's travelling life. Don't be the 'lets leash them on' crew.
• **Boardshorts** Make sure they fit before you go!
• **Rashie/tee** Keep the sun off your back. Tans are nice, melanoma isn't.
• **Wetsuit** If you're going cold, make sure your wetty is the right thickness for the sea temps.
• **Booties** For warmth or for rock hopping. Toughening your feet up by walking around barefoot also helps to stop reef cuts.
• **Sunblock** You only have one skin. Look after it.
• **Hat** To protect your noggin from the sun or keep you warm. Depending on destination.

• **Sunnies** Your eyes are really useful. Protect them.
• **First aid kit** Keep it small, comprehensive and waterproof. Include plasters, bandages, gauze, antibiotic cream, malaria tablets, water purification tablets, toothbrush and paste, soap, Vaseline, pain-killers, tweezers, and diarrhoea tablets. If you're going really remote take spare syringe needles so you know they're sterile and learn how to do stitches.
• **Inoculations** Check which ones you need and get jabbed with plenty of time to spare before you fly.
• **Mozzie net and spray** Essential for malarial destinations. Keep the little feckers off at all costs.
• **Ear plugs** If you suffer from surfer's ear, don't forget your ear plugs or Blu-Tac. Night time ones handy for shared accom too.
• **Passport / visas** Get these checked out months before you fly wherever you're going. Nothing sucks more than getting turned back on arrival. Make a photocopy of your passport's info page and keep it somewhere separate, just in case you lose it.
• **Tickets / travel documents** You won't be going far without these and if they're on your phone make sure you have a...
• **Phone charging brick** Keep those boarding passes alive if it's a long way between plug sockets.
• **Driving licence** An absolute shocker to forget.
• **Travel insurance** If you're going deep, check the level of cover carefully. Medivac is essential for adventurous missions.
• **Credit cards** Keep 'em safe and if poss keep one away from another in case your wallet/bag gets nabbed.
• **Cash** Local dosh always useful. US dollars work most places also.
• **Phrasebook** Essential in case you run into difficulties.
• **Guidebook / maps** So you know where to go.
• **Books to read** Keep your mind active on flat days or between sessions. A Kindle saves weight.
• **Clothes** Don't load yourself up with tons of clothes. Pack light. You can always wash a few things.
• **Duct tape** There's nothing it can't fix, nothing.
• **Socket adaptor** Essential for re-charging electrical gadgets and you can get UK convertor plugs with bonus USB charging holes these days.

PREPARATION

GADGETS

Gadgets and gizmos come in all shapes and sizes. Their usefulness and value on a trip obviously varies and depends on the kind of place you're going. Most people would agree that a multi-tool is an essential piece of kit for any kind of surf trip, anywhere. But pricey electronic items like smartphones and tablets are probably not the sort of things you'd want to take on a backpacking trip around Central America or Indo. At the end of the day it's all down to personal preference and the amount of stuff you want to carry around!

Here are nine gadgets you might want to pack.

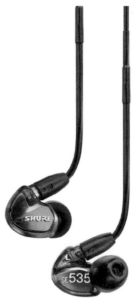

SMARTPHONE

Phones are now more powerful than some laptops and are now priced reflecting that. So as useful as they are, you need to look after your precious while travelling. Especially if your model isn't waterproof.

All the big name manufacturer phones are much of a muchness these days, featuring fantastic cameras, 4K video, GPS mapping and access to satellite views that are really handy for searching for the next spot. Battery life isn't that great so make sure you've got your cables, a car charger and a power brick just in case. If you're going off the grid then a solar charger could be handy. It's also worth considering going old school and taking a cheap festival phone (just in case) and enjoying being off the internet for a bit!

BINOCULARS

When you're exploring a new area it's good to have a decent pair of travel binoculars. Pentax, Nikon and Bushnell all make compact lightweight models ideal for horizon-scanning surf explorers. Good to know whether it is worth the hike to that spot or not.

TORCH

Sure there is one on your phone smartie pants but a decent head torch is really handy. New LED models have awesome battery life and are super bright. And you're less likely to drop it down the bog in that jungle toilet you've just dodged snakes to get to.

NOISE-CANCELLING HEADPHONES / EARPHONES

Noise-cancelling headphones or earphones are essential for any travelling, especially long-haul flights. For audiophiles who crave top-end sound quality on the go, Bose's QuietComfort 35 headphones are superb – they're expensive (£300+ / $460) but you'll travel in your own bubble of peace. Cheaper and smaller, but just as effective, are in-ear phones like those made by Etymotic Research. They're perfect for planes, ferries or buses, allowing you to completely silence the screaming baby on the row in front and listen to your music naturally at safe volume levels. They're also way less bulky to travel with. Bluetooth headphones are getting better but are yet another thing to charge on the road.

IPOD

If you shun smartphones but need your tunes, an iPod is a must, otherwise you'll be listening to screaming kids, the drone of jet engines and other aural atrocities throughout your entire trip. Thankfully you can get old school ones for a steal on eBay. And it's a lot cheaper to lose a secondhand iPod than a shiny new iPhone.

MULTI-TOOL

A decent multi-tool is an is an indispensable piece of kit for any kind of surf trip. Whether you're under the bonnet of an overheating Toyota Land Cruiser or deep in a Fijian jungle cutting down vines to lash together a raft, you'll have a tool for every job. Gerber, Leatherman and Victorinox are among the best brands. Prices for a basic multi-tool start at around £30 / $45, but if you've got cash to splash there are some uber-cool, lightweight titanium models for around £135 / $200. Be aware you'll have to pack in your hold bag or risk losing your precious tool.

IPAD

Laptops are heavy and a pain while travelling, if you need your Netflix fix or have to do a bit of work on the go then an iPad is the ideal solution. And they're rad for travelling as your own entertainment system.

KINDLE

Being on a surf trip can involve down time, be it travelling or flat days. You're on holiday so it's meant to be relaxing and what better way to chill than hanging in a hammock or on a beach with a cold beer and a good book? Traditional books, lovely as they are, ain't travel friendly. A Kindle can have years worth of reading matter on it and takes up the space in your carry on of a one small paperback. Battery life is also superb, outlasting your phone by weeks and you can actually see the screen in the sunshine.

PLAYING CARDS

A low tech gadget for sure but an essential surf trip bonding ritual. What better way to make new friends than a game of 'Shithead'? Get everyone out of their phone bubbles and engage with each other with mere bits of printed card!

SHOOTING YOUR TRIP

Everyone is a photographer these days. How are you supposed to keep your Insty game strong without a decent camera? While phone cameras are increasingly amazing the jump to a better camera has its benefits … as does knowing what to do with it.

EQUIPMENT

Phone cameras have killed off the compact camera market and rightly so, as the marriage of quality and convenience is just too perfect. Whilst phone snaps are enough for most folks, stepping up your equipment game is only going to make for even better images. There are still some awesome high-end compacts, that while they aren't cheap, can take your photos to the next level and are brill for travelling. The Sony RX100 series is a perfect example.

If you want even better quality images without having to lug around a bulky DSLR, go for one of the mirrorless options like a Panasonic GH or Sony A series. Both companies are producing insane cameras that produce incredible images and video and don't shout 'Hey! Mr Thief! I've got a really big expensive camera here.'

If you're really into photography and are considering buying a DSLR from Canon or Nikon, make sure you have enough cash left over for a couple of good lenses. It's all about the glass in the end. For travel a 24-70mm zoom and a 70-200mm are a good pairing. When you buy a new camera, play around with it at home to familiarise yourself with the controls. That way you won't miss a thing when you're on a trip and the perfect shot pops up.

CHOOSE YOUR LIGHT

Photographers refer to the time after dawn and before sundown as 'golden hour'. This is the best light for outdoor shots with golden glows and surreal sky colours. From midday to late afternoon the sun is just too harsh to get pleasing results. That said, midday sun is good for underwater shots.

CREATE AN IMAGE

The difference between pro photographers and everyone else is that they 'create an image', rather than just taking a snap of what's there. Look around for rocks, trees, a shack on the beach or a boat on the horizon, and try to incorporate them in the shot. Framing a peeling lineup with some palm trees may be an old trick, but it's a good one.

WORK THE ANGLES

Move around and look for a more striking angle. See how the light changes as you change position. Get low, or see what happens when you shoot from a high viewpoint. Photography is a creative art, so use your imagination. Think of your holiday album as a portfolio, so mix it up to get some good variety. Modern digital compacts have amazing macro settings (usually shown on the control dial by a flower logo) which means you can get in really close and shoot details like leaves, flowers, insects and textures. Don't go mad, but these are the kind of shots that most people miss.

There are a few basic laws of composition which will help you take more pleasing shots. The most widely used one is the 'rule of thirds'. Divide the image into thirds with two imaginary vertical lines and two horizontal lines; then place the most important element/s of the image at the intersections of those lines. Slightly off-centre subjects work much better than centred ones, and horizons should normally never divide the image in half.

PEOPLE

When travelling in a strange land keep an eye out for interesting looking people to photograph. Smile and ask them politely if you can take their photo. If you don't speak their language, pointing to the camera is normally a good move. Frame your photograph, and then get closer. Most people stand too far back and don't fill the frame, but it's always worth getting closer, even if you're shooting the grizzled face of a gnarly Indo dude with one tooth. For street photography a 35mm or 50mm lens is your friend. For more shooting tips check out our Amazing Waves book.

VIDEO

If you want to shoot video of your trip it's so much easier than it used to be. For water footage a GoPro is the weapon of choice. The GoPro 6 or a Session are powerful units that take great footage, especially slow motion. They also take decent stills. The battery life isn't great, but spares are only £20 so you can have a few on hand to see you through a day. Practice before you go if you're going to get those rad inner tube shots. Board mounts are a bit passé and a good way of losing your rig. With a GoPro and your phone's video camera you can knock up cool little edits without much stress. Just remember to mix up the footage and angles. Lifestyles, lineups, action and time lapses all add to the mix.

DRONES

Unmanned aerial vehicles are all the rage. But be considerate as they're annoying to most. Follow the rules, learn basic air law and always think, 'Is this safe?' The DJI Mavic is the current travel drone of choice, as it's tiny yet powerful.

BACK UP

Finally, don't forget to download the images onto your laptop as soon as you get in. There's absolutely nothing worse than losing a card full of memories!

LEGENDS OF SURF TRAVEL

PETER TROY

Peter Troy put Bells Beach on the map in the early 1960s and then went on to become one of the all-time greatest surf travellers. The lanky Aussie introduced the sport to Indonesia (where he discovered waves such as Lagundri Bay on Nias), Brazil, Italy and Peru, to a name just a few. He also

hitchhiked from the world's southernmost township (Tierra Del Fuego) to its northernmost (Spitzbergen)… with a ten-foot balsa board. All in all he visited more than 140 countries in his lifetime. Makes your boat trip to Indo seem a bit tame doesn't it?

WAYNE LYNCH

After pioneering the big, cold waves of his native Victoria, on his own, Wayne Lynch was also among the first to surf Australia's classic desert waves. He travelled to France as a teenager, surfing Le Barre and the Basque coast in 1967, and later spent time in the US, exploring the northwest coast of California. He's spent the last couple of decades travelling, shaping boards, surfing and playing music. "These days I continue to explore this ocean and its coastlines under sail," says Lynch, "which has furthered my respect and appreciation of its uniqueness." Enough said.

BILL AND MIKE BOYUM

American brothers Bill and Mike Boyum were among a small band of Aussie and American surfers who found their way to Bali in the late '60s. For a few years they had it all to themselves, but as the lineups became busier they began looking around for new waves. In 1972 Bill made the arduous journey to Grajagan in East Java with his friend Bob Laverty, after Laverty had spotted incredible lefts peeling along a reef while on a plane journey from Jakarta to Bali. The pair lucked

into a three-day swell and the flawless waves they found blew them away. Mike was hot on Bill's heels for subsequent trips to G-Land, and two years later he set up the world's first surf camp there. In the '80s, after a stint in jail for drug trafficking, Mike moved to the Philippines where he set up base at another amazing wave, Cloud 9. He subsequently died there in 1989 after undergoing a self-imposed 50-day fast. Bill Boyum moved to Hawaii, but returned many times to G-Land as an honorary guest.

CRAIG PETERSON AND KEVIN NAUGHTON

In 1972 these two young Americans hit the road with their camera gear and surfboards. For a decade they chronicled the waves and the people they met in places like California, Mexico, El Salvador, Costa Rica, West Africa, Morocco, Ireland, France and Fiji. Surfer Magazine published numerous articles about their travels, and their 'just do it' philosophy motivated a whole generation of surfers to sack off the real world and broaden their horizons. Parents hated them, but for surfers they were the link to a bigger and better world.

TONY HINDE

When his yacht ran aground in the Maldives in 1973, halfway through a surfing and sailing exploration mission from Sri Lanka to Reunion Island, Aussie Tony Hinde realised he'd been shipwrecked somewhere

WAYNE LYNCH

special. In fact, it was so special that he never left – he became a Maldivian citizen, turned Muslim, and married a local girl. For the next 15 years he kept his discoveries quiet, only telling a few mates. But eventually other surfers came sniffing around and he succumbed to commercial pressures, opening a surf camp at Tari village (now Chaaya Dhonveli Resort) in the late '80s. Hinde died after suffering a heart attack while surfing Pasta Point in 2008, a wave he'd discovered and surfed on his own for two decades.

MARTIN DALY

"I couldn't believe it. I'd sailed and explored right across Indonesia, but the Mentawais was a whole new class. And we had it to ourselves, for about five years." That's how Aussie Martin Daly describes his early years in the Mentawais, which he first explored in 1983. Later, after building up a successful surf charter business in Indo, he embarked on The Crossing,

KEVIN NAUGHTON AND CRAIG PETERSON ROCK UP AT EASKEY, IRELAND, IN THE MID '70S.

a Quiksilver-funded exploration of the whole goddamn world. Suffice to say Daly lays claim to discovering more breaks than any other, and he ain't done yet.

TIMMY TURNER

Back in the '00s, Huntington Beach surfer Timmy Turner took the old Indonesian exploration theme and went a step further. He chose the outer frontier of Panaitan Island, off the western tip of Java, and with a mix of madness and talent, took to its shallow deadly perfection with obsessive dedication. Camping on the land, living off rice and dodgy water, he spent whole seasons getting 20-second tubes and fighting malaria. Timmy ended up with (and miraculously survived) a staph infection of the brain, and these days turns his wandering eye and camera to the freezing waters of Canada and Alaska.

KEPA ACERO

The Basque minstrel has made a career from going off the beaten path. Often by himself, Kepa has explored deep in South America and Africa and encapsulates the magic of travel perfectly in his films.

ANTONY 'YEP' COLAS

When asked about his travels, the French photographer replied: "I've been focusing on the three M's over the last decade. In the Mediterranean I've surfed Egypt, Tunisia, Algeria, Libya, Malta, Cyprus and Montenegro. In the Maldives I've scoured 20 out of the 26 atolls and completed 15 boat trips since 1998. And I've ridden the *mascarets* [tidal bores] of Brazil (Pororoca), China (Quang Cao), Malaysia (Benak) and Indo (Bono)." Apart from his M-based travels, Yep has also explored Pakistan, Hainan, India, Maluku, Philippines, Madagascar, Cape Verde and Gabon. We're

not sure what he'll run out of first, countries or letters of the alphabet.

TED GRAMBEAU

If there's a surf photographer with more stamps in his passport then we'd be very surprised. This gentle Australian legend is responsible for a generation getting the itch to explore. And anyone who thinks they're finding a new spot ... odds on Ted found it twenty years ago.

CHRIS BURKARD

While he didn't invent coldwater surf exploration, Chris has definitely earned his stripes as the leading modern exponent of going the extra mile for a chilly wave. His missions to Iceland, the Aleutians, Faroes and Norway have graced surf magazines worldwide and legitimised the cold fringe dweller lifestyle.

AIR TRAVEL

Believe it or not, you can make air travel an almost stress-free experience. You just need to be prepared, organised and punctual. If you get a decent seat, watch a film and grab a bit of sleep, flying can almost be relaxing! Try to think of it as a few hours to dream about the waves that you're about to score, or if you're flying home, a chance to replay the trip's best sessions in your head. Here are some ways you can make everything go as smoothly as possible…

• **Be early.** If you're flying long-haul, aim to be at the airport at least three hours before your flight is due to depart. The finer you cut it the more stressed you'll be.

• **Check the weight and dimensions of your luggage at home** to make sure they fall within your airline's limitations. Check the guide updated every year on carvemag.com

• **Double check your carry-on luggage before you pack it,** and make sure you remove any sharp objects, liquids or anything else that could potentially get you in trouble at the airport. The last thing you want is an aggressive Alsatian stuffing his nose in your crotch, or the security team finding a hardcore porn mag in your backpack courtesy of your hilarious mates.

• **Wear slip-on shoes.** You'll probably have to remove your shoes going through airport security, and during a long flight your feet will swell up a bit, so slip-ons beat lace-ups.

• **Get a neck pillow.** Yes, you'll look like a geek. But it'll save you getting a stiff neck and vastly add to your comfort. And stop you dribbling over fellow passengers.

• **Invest in some noise-cancelling headphones.** They're worth every penny on a long flight with a screaming baby two rows in front.

• **Sign up with frequent flyer programmes.** A lot of airlines are partnered so your airmiles will be transferable for upgrades.

• **Don't overlook the Executive Lounge.** Lounges aren't just for posh folk, and if you have one of those packages with your bank account that gives you travel insurance and breakdown, they often include free lounge passes too. So you can be on the free booze and grub gravy train!

• **Chill out.** If flying makes you nervous, go to a health food shop and buy some Pharma Kava (for anxiety) and / or some Melatonin (for sleeping). These non-prescription remedies can make a sketchy flight bearable for any health conscious, white-knuckle flyer. Valium or Ambien can also be prescribed by doctors; you could sleep through a loop-the-loop on that stuff.

• **Sail through security.** Laptops and Kindles need to be out. Pockets empty, liquids out, belt and shoes off. Done.

• **Remember your manners at the check-in desk.** They have to deal with grumbling fools all day long, so arrive early, smile and be nice. Upgrades can still happen.

"SOME PEOPLE PILE THEIR CLOTHES INTO THEIR BOARDBAGS, BUT I RECKON YOU SHOULD KEEP IT LIGHT. YOU'RE ALLOWED TWO BAGS AT CHECK-IN AND IF YOUR BOARDBAG IS REASONABLY LIGHT YOU'RE LESS LIKELY TO GET STUNG FOR EXCESS BAGGAGE."

- TAJ BURROW

BOAT TRIPS

If there's one type of trip worth saving up for, it's an all-out boat trip to somewhere exotic. Let's face it, the idea of waking up next to a pumping empty peak and getting shacked out of your mind is the ultimate dream.

While utopian destinations like the Mentawais and the Maldives have become more crowded in recent years, there are still plenty of waves to go around, simply because there's so many quality breaks. And, for the more adventurous, there are plenty of rarely (or never) surfed archipelagos out there just waiting for intrepid explorers to sample their treasures. So do your research, read the reviews, check the charts, and bite the bullet – it will be a trip worth waiting for. Here are some tips to help get you amped...

· **Pack meticulously.** You don't want to forget anything, from camera chargers to sunscreen. If you don't take it, you won't have it – simple as that. Above all, remember to take spare fins and leashes, and at least one spare board. The last thing you want is to be left high and dry with your only board in two pieces while perfect waves peel off 200 metres away.

· **Be fit.** On a boat trip, you'll be surfing much more than on any other type of surf trip. If all goes well you should be mooring up next to a break each day, and piling in for a session whenever you can. If it's pumping you'll want to be in the water a lot, so make sure your body is ready for it. Check the Fitness section on page 18.

· **Pack an open mind and a friendly attitude.** Unless you're mega rich or you've managed to organise a whole crew of mates for your trip, you're likely to be sharing the boat with other surfers. That means you'll be living in confined spaces with strangers and it's important that you get on from the outset, for the communal harmony of the boat. Some guys tell corny jokes, some guys whistle out of tune, and some guys chew raw garlic. Big deal. Just let those little niggles wash over you ... the last thing you need is a boat based Lord of the Flies.

· **Bring some snack bars if you're picky about food.** When you fork out for a luxury boat trip you'll be fed like a king and served the most divine fish suppers imaginable. If, however, you don't like fish, or are picky about what you eat, remember to pack some snack bars that will supply you with plenty of energy.

· **Choose your charter carefully.** You're going to be living at sea for a week or more, so choose the biggest, most comfortable boat you can afford. Check the safety record, and contact people who've chartered the boat before. Double check the boat's schedule, and if you particularly want to hit a certain spot, make certain the captain will take you there.

· **Creature comforts are essential.** Remember your tunes, movies, some good books, and so on. These are the things that can help you zone out during a spell of bad weather, or if you need a bit of time away from the rest of the gang on the boat.

· **Be first on board.** So that you get the pick of the cabins and the beds.

· **Don't be squeamish.** On some boats, especially in Indo, you may find there's livestock on board (usually poultry) that you will be eating at some point on the trip. If you'd rather not meet tomorrow night's three-course meal, it's best to avoid the cooped-up chickens and animals that you may see outside the galley.

· **Enjoy the whole boat trip experience.** Go snorkelling, catch a beast of a tuna, do a night dive. Enjoy the ocean in every way you can while you're living on it.

"YOU WANT A QUIVER OF GOOD BOARDS, SUNSCREEN, AND FISHING LURES. AMAZING WAVES, GREAT FISHING...WHAT MORE COULD YOU WISH FOR?"
– BEDE DURBIDGE

"ON A BOAT TRIP I THINK THE MOST IMPORTANT THING IS TO HAVE THE RIGHT SIX BOARDS WITH YOU. 'COS IF YOU SNAP ONE, YOU CAN'T JUST GO INTO YOUR GARAGE TO GET ANOTHER ONE!"
– MARLON LIPKE

ROAD TRIPS

If you're thinking about embarking on a serious road trip – to the deserts of Western Australia perhaps, or the wilds of Namibia – it's vital to have a reliable wagon. Travel addict and part-time motoring journalist Owen Pye offers some advice.

There are few greater pleasures in life than hitting the road with a few good mates and embarking on an epic surf trip. The mental image of finding some unridden gem in the middle of nowhere sure is an enticing one. But before you part with your hard-earned it's worth taking some time to get the right vehicle – it really could make the difference between life and death, especially if you're planning to go looking for waves in remote places.

Although you won't necessarily need to stray off the blacktop to find amazing waves, you're bound to be tempted to take a quick look down a rutted coastal track to see what secrets it might yield. With this in mind, it's worth getting a decent 4x4 – not just for the

extra ground clearance, but for the fact that it'll handle the rough stuff should the track get worse the further you go … as it invariably will!

When checking a second-hand vehicle, the first thing to do is assess the seller. If the person is shifty, doesn't look you in the eye, gives a limp handshake or seems vague about important questions, it's best to walk away. Similarly, if something appears too good to be true, it probably is.

Choosing a 4x4 which will get you through 10,000 kilometres of the harshest terrain on earth is something you don't want to rush. First off, find out about the history of the vehicle. Why is it being sold? How long has the seller owned it? What did he use it for? Get

as much information as you can about what parts have been replaced during its lifetime before you even turn the key.

CLOSE INSPECTION
If you're satisfied that everything seems legit at this stage, get out your fine tooth comb and check the following:

TYRES Each tyre should be nail and patch-free, with deep tread and no signs of the rubber cracking or perishing on the tread blocks or sidewalls. Also, check the spare tyre. If you need an extra spare, factor this into your budget (to drive in some areas of the Australian bush, for example, you're required to have

two spares).

BODYWORK Make sure there's no rust on structural areas (chassis rails, subframe, sills). And while you're underneath, check the chassis is dent-free – a big impact with a rock at some point may well have damaged other parts like the engine, gearbox or driveshaft.

DRIVESHAFT The prop-shaft, which runs from the front to rear diff housing, should rotate free and true. Check for signs of recent lubrication at either end – a failure of these U-joints (due to a lack of oil) can cause the shaft to snap, pole-vaulting the vehicle into a lengthways flip at 60mph quicker than you'd know what was

CV JOINTS Check the CV (constant velocity) joints, the rubber boots between the driveshafts and the wheels. Make sure they're not split or leaking grease. On the test drive, turn the wheel to full lock and do slow circles in both directions – there should be no clicks.

EXHAUST The exhaust pipe should be hung high and tight on rubber bushes which aren't cracking. When you turn the engine on, check for recently applied putty or blowing sounds caused by small holes; if you do hear blowing, the exhaust pipe is on borrowed time.

GEARBOX AND DIFF HOUSINGS These need to be leak free, and move without crunches, grinds and knocks. It's always worth changing the gearbox fluid before

done. On the test drive, try all the gears (including reverse) – make sure each gear change is slick, with no trouble engaging. Likewise with the high/low ratio gearbox, check each setting works without hesitations or problems. For full four-wheel drive you may need to manually lock the hubs on the front wheels; without these engaged you'll still only be spinning the rears. Some manufacturers have auto-locking hubs, some don't, so do your research on this before testing the vehicle. Bear in mind that the car should always be run in two-wheel drive mode until you physically need four-wheel drive due to lack of traction (and then only at low speeds, usually).

absorbers should level the car on each corner after a couple of bounces. If it continues to bounce and bounce you'll need to replace the shocks. If the shocks seem okay but the car has done a lot of off-road driving, it's worth checking them in case any are weeping. While you're looking under the wheel-arches, make sure the springs aren't cracked or even snapped (it does happen).

TOW BAR If the car has one, enquire for how long. If it's been towing two-tonne trailers all its life it could be due a clutch change or some big transmission bills, especially if it's an automatic.

BRAKES Check the pads and discs have plenty of life left in them. On the test drive, check that the calipers aren't sticking to the discs. If the car has ABS brakes, check them by trying to lock up the brakes on the test drive; if the car skids (rather than quickly juddering to a stop), the ABS isn't working.

ENGINE Get as much history as you can about the engine, including previous service intervals and dates when parts were replaced. All engines require regular oil and filter changes, and periodically bigger jobs need to be done, such as the cam belt being changed. Check to see that these have been done, and if so, when. Cross-reference the change dates to the mileage, and compare it to what the manufacturer-suggested mileage is for each part. If you snap an ageing cam belt it will destroy your valves and could potentially damage your pistons, requiring an expensive rebuild; so if a cam belt change is overdue, get it done. If there's no record of when it was changed, take off the plastic cover and see if there's any printed writing still visible on the back of the belt – if it's faded and gone, it's time for a change. Also, check for patches of oil or coolant on the ground, underneath the engine; if you see any, try to figure out which part of the engine the drips are coming from. If there's oil dripping from the oil filter it'll probably just be a cheap O-ring leaking, but leaky gaskets are another matter. When you turn on a petrol (gasoline) engine it should catch instantly – if it takes longer to start you may have a tiring battery, alternator, starter motor or ignition system. Diesel engines need a few seconds for the glow plugs to warm up before firing up; the requisite light on the dash should extinguish within a few seconds of turning the key a click. Once the engine is idling, listen out for whistles, knocks, taps or clunks. The engine should idle at about 750rpm (plus or minus 50rpm). If it's idling high there could be a problem such as a vacuum leak, carbon build-up, or a faulty ECU (engine control unit). Make sure the engine revs cleanly with no hiccups or flat points – if it's running rough you may have distributor or ignition issues (or worse!). On your test drive check that the car accelerates, brakes, changes gear and handles as you would expect. Make

sure the temperature gauge sits halfway when warmed up, and that the oil pressure isn't too high or low (it should vary from halfway to three quarters, depending on load). If anything seems out of the ordinary, bring it up — you may have room for haggling (or even a reason to walk away).

PAPERWORK Finally, you should also satisfy yourself that all the paperwork is in order and that the seller definitely owns the vehicle. And well before you set off on your trip, do some research into the legal requirements for vehicles in the country you're visiting, including things like insurance and the possible need for an emissions test certificate.

TUNE UP

Once you've bought your new ride it's time to get it ready for the road. Start by taking it to a garage for a full service. Get the air, fuel and oil filters changed; get the engine, gearbox and diff oil changed; get fresh coolant put in; get leads and plugs checked; and get the wheels balanced and aligned. Doing this will give you peace of mind, and it'll also improve the car's economy.

ROOF RACK

If the car doesn't have a roof rack, it's a good idea to fit one. With a roof rack you can carry all sorts of stuff:

• **Spare jerry cans of fuel,** which will extend your mileage range between filling stations by hundreds of kilometres.

• **Water containers** – you'll need plenty of water for drinking and you may need it to replenish the cooling system of an overheating engine after a split hose or busted radiator.

• **An extra spare tyre.**

• **Lockable roof box** – these provide useful external storage for a tent, wetties, tools and so on.

• **Roof spotlights** – these beauties will considerably improve your night vision and help spot highway obstacles.

BULL / ROO BARS

Your 4x4 may already come with bull / roo bars, but if it doesn't, see if you can get some cheap. Hitting a large animal like a cow or kangaroo is extremely dangerous for front seat occupants. As well as having bars, it's worth installing some big external spotlights (either on the front bars or the roofrack) so you can spot animals on the road or the hard shoulder. Kangaroos love to play at dawn and dusk, and roads seem a favourite hang out in certain places. It's obviously safer not to travel at night, but if you have to, take it easy and keep your wits about you. When you stop at service stations, ask truckers travelling the other way if they've seen packs of roos further along the road.

"WHEN YOU ROCK UP AT A NEW BREAK, TRY TO GET TO KNOW THE LOCALS AND LET THEM HAVE THEIR SPACE WHEN PADDLING FOR WAVES. WAIT YOUR TURN ... AND STAY HAPPY! ALSO, DON'T TRAVEL IN A BIG PACK – IMAGINE BEING ONE OF THE LOCAL GUYS AND SEEING TEN GUYS ALL PADDLING OUT TOGETHER."

– MICK FANNING

BRING PLENTY OF TUNES FOR LONG TRIPS.

ROAD TRIP KIT

Okay, so you've got yourself a set of wheels. Now you just need to gather up a few additional items and you'll be ready to hit the road.

- **Tool kit** Get a decent one. 'Buy cheap, buy twice' as the saying goes.
- **CB radio and giant antenna** Can be expensive, but if you plan to go deep into the bush it could be a lifesaver.
- **Fine plastic mesh** Wrap some plastic mesh over the middle section of the roo bars to protect your radiator from flying stone chips kicked up by passing trucks. The mesh will also intercept insects – you'd be surprised how quickly a radiator can get clogged with squished bugs, leading to overheating.
- **12v tyre compressor** Allows you to deflate your tyres (if you plan to drive on sand), and inflate them again afterwards – all from the cigarette lighter socket. (Check the socket actually works before setting off!)
- **Mozzie netting** You'll need mozzie netting to span any windows left open overnight. You've been warned!
- **Duct tape** Get a few rolls. The stuff can fix all but the biggest of problems.
- **Cable ties** As above.
- **WD40** Can unseize a bolt which hasn't been taken off in 20 years – saving you a lot of effort, swearing, and bleeding knuckles.
- **Screen wash** You'll need some serious stuff to cut through the inevitably thick glaze of splattered insects.
- **Tent** Bring one which zips up fully. And watch out for spiders / scorpions in your boots come morning.
- **Gas stove** Boils the water for the coffee needed to cope with those long sessions behind the wheel. And for hot meals of course.
- **Cooking utensils** Plates, cups, cutlery, pans, matches...
- **Mobile phone charger** You can buy chargers that plug into the cigarette lighter socket.
- **Maps** Get large scale maps for the coastal areas you plan to explore.
- **Dash compass** Always handy.

SURF CAMPS

Many an epic surf adventure begins when you check into a surf camp. Choose a good one and you can find yourself in surfing heaven for the duration of your stay, with nothing to think about other than the next session and the next swell. But it's important to do your research and choose wisely.

Occasionally you hear purist travellers denouncing the humble surf camp as a waste of money for the would-be surf adventurer. They claim surf camps are an easy option that take away 'real' travel experiences like finding your own way and learning from your mistakes. While this is true to an extent, surf travel has one main goal: scoring quality waves in far-off lands. And surf camps exist to make this easier.

Surf camps offer the option to hang out with like-minded individuals, share experiences, and make the most of your time abroad. The staff can help with advice about anything, from what board to ride at a certain break to where you'll find the coolest local bar. You can involve yourself in the group atmosphere as much or as little as you want to. Everything is set up with one main aim – scoring waves.

You can spend hours squinting at Google Earth and you can track approaching swells using all manner of online forecasting charts, but there's no way you can beat the knowledge of a local surf guide. As we all know, Mother Nature can be a fickle mistress; just because Anchor Point is usually good in November, and just because a certain website says that it's going to be six foot and offshore next Thursday, you could still roll up to find it flat or a hideous 15-foot onshore mess. This is when a local guide is worth his weight in gold. He'll direct you to the best spot for the conditions (and your ability level) on the day. And if the conditions change, he'll know a certain sandbank that works on a certain

tide, and the quickest way to get there. (Possibly via a village that sells some tasty local delicacy for a quick snack, or via a back road that doesn't have a police checkpoint.)

Most surf camps offer tiered accommodation to suit every budget. So, if you're a wedged-up investment banker flying in for a deluxe long weekend of waves, they'll give you the penthouse suite (or nearest thing). Likewise, if you're a dedicated round-the-world tripper who's keen to save every rupiah and peso possible, they should have safe, comfortable options to cater for you too. Check out the camp's website then drop them an email with your needs.

Since you're going to be surfing for several hours each day, you'll need fuel in your belly to make it happen. Most surf camps will have a local chef who sources the best local produce to supply you with carb-fuelled meals, so you'll get the most out of the waves every day. Sure, you don't have to eat at the camp, but the option of a hearty meal is there if you want it.

These days, many of us check travel review websites to see testimonials from other travellers. Surfers usually have lots to say about surf camps they've visited, so make a note of the camps that get the most recommendations. Similarly, ask your mates at home which camps they've been to: which to try, and which to avoid. Decent camps build up good reputations and have high proportions of return visitors. Bad camps soon drop off the radar.

The surf camp phenomenon is here to stay. There are hundreds of 'em now, all around the world, so your options are virtually limitless. The vast majority offer good waves and a good time at a fair price; they'll keep you safe, well fed and stoked.

SURF FORECAST

The simple act of standing on a board riding energy originally from the sun is mind bending. But where do waves come from and how to we predict them? Read on as we delve in to the inner workings of the surf.

A wave has a life cycle that's almost organic. From being born as the merest of capillary ripples in the midst of one of the great wave nurseries, the baby wave grows into adolescent chop. It then hits its straps travelling out into the world as an adult wave. Maybe wrapping around, perhaps breaking, on a mid-oceanic island chains as it traverses thousands of miles. Later, in the prime of its life, as a clean, well defined swell, an OAP in the metaphor, it will end its days with one last hurrah against some distant continental shore.

Wave generation starts with solar energy. The sun heats the earth unevenly. The equatorial regions get the lion's share of the energy and the poles a minimal amount. The redistribution of the warmth in the middle is the basis for our weather. Hot air rises and cooler air replaces it: the basis of convection. Add in the rotation of the earth that gives us the Coriolis force, the tilt of the earth causing seasons and the distribution of oceans, and continents that heat and cool at different rates to the mix, and you can see it's a complex beast. But the takeaway is all that convection means packets of warm and cool air and moisture are on the move.

It's the march of low pressure systems across the world ocean that gives us surfable waves. Where the warm air from the south meets the cold air from the north, and vice versa in the southern hemisphere, is known as the polar front. Any disturbance along its length can start the formation of a low pressure system (you'll know them as the onion rings on the pressure maps). Warm air is less dense than cold air and slides over the top and when a low forms this process becomes intense, with air being sucked into the vortex by the Coriolis force. As the polar front splits into individual warm and cold fronts, behind which the respective warm/cold air masses reside, (cold fronts have blue triangles and warm have red semi-circles on the pressure maps), it's the warm sector between the fronts where the surface winds are strong and blow for some distance in the same direction. This is the key to good surf.

Waves are the result of friction between the atmosphere and the ocean. A breeze under two knots will generate tiny capillary waves, but if the wind dies they die also, thanks to surface tension of the water. A breeze over two knots, sustained for any length of time, will generate 'gravity waves', and the ripples turn to waves as it becomes increasingly easy for the wind to act on the backs of the ripples. Ripples progress to 'chop' then to a 'sea'. The bigger the waves, the easier it is for the wind to transfer its energy to the waves; to a certain point. For wind waves to become swell there are three vital factors in the equation: the strength of the wind, the length of time it blows and the distance it blows over (fetch). If you've ever seen foot-high waves in a lake, you'll know it doesn't take vast tracts of ocean for waves to develop. Most models suggest the biggest swells ever seen can be generated with less than a thousand miles' fetch. Next time you watch the weather try and pick out the warm sector between the fronts, this is the fetch generating our waves.

So, it's the remote sensing, monitoring and modelling of the wind acting on the ocean that is the key to surf forecasts. Thankfully for us, the advent of satellites has made the acquisition of data way easier and forecasts in the digital age are way more accurate

than the home-brew ones we relied on last century. No more ship observations and wave buoy reliance.

Pressure maps are readily available online from the Met Office and other sources. WAM charts – both US and European models – show the wave size and period, and combined with the brilliant weather visualisation app, Windy.com, you can see the relationship between isobars, wind and surf on an ocean or local level. Tie this in with data from windguru.cz, surfline.com or magicseaweed.com, and observations of your local spot, and you can get a picture of the whole deal. The low spinning in the Atlantic indicates the groomed swell arriving a few days later, which is fierce at first then better as the period calms down.

Wherever you are in the world it's the same process. It's the key to understanding how it works that gives you a deeper insight into when and where to score better waves..

For more on the science and ninth dan forecast knowledge check out Tony Butt's awesome Surf Science: An Introduction to Waves for Surfing book.

"TO MAKE THE MOST OF YOUR SURFING YOU HAVE TO BE ON THE CASE WITH THE SURF FORECAST. WE HAVE UNBELIEVABLE DATA AT OUR FINGERTIPS AND IF YOU KNOW HOW TO PIECE IT TOGETHER YOU CAN MAKE SURE YOU SCORE. GOT TO LOVE THE CHASE, IT'S ALMOST AS GOOD AS THE SCORE!"

– OLI ADAMS

COLD WATER

Well, you've manned up. You've decided to ditch the boardies for a new pair of gloves and a hood, and somewhere cold and dark awaits. You might have to endure numb extremities, but one thing you won't be battling on a coldwater trip is crowds.

While most travelling surfers head for warm (and often crowded) destinations, there's nothing to stop you going in the other direction, to a surfing frontier most wouldn't even consider. It's really not as mad as it seems. The world's coldwater locations get just as much swell as the tropical ones, there are thousands of sick setups, and the scenery in places like Iceland and Canada is stunning.

Think about it – while your sweating brethren are copping aggro and jostling for a place in the hectic lineup at Padang Padang, hoping to snag the odd leftover shack every couple of hours, you could be getting repeatedly slotted in clear glass funnels for as long as you want. And afterwards you can warm up next to a toasty campfire. Plus, when you get back home you'll have some real stories to tell, not just the standard, 'went to Indo, surfed a bit'. So, go on, think about taking a trip to the far North, or the far South. It could be phenomenal.

HERE ARE SOME TIPS FOR COLDWATER FRONTIERSMEN...

• **Invest in the best rubber** Be sure to sort yourself out with a top quality 5/4/3mm or 6/5/4mm wetsuit, plus accompanying hood, gloves and boots (depending on the water temperature of your destination). Suits with built-in hoods are awesome if the water is super cold. Get gloves rather than mitts, they're much more practical. Never underestimate how crucial your kit is in cold climes.

• **Bring the right wax** Stock up on coldwater wax before you set off. Hard tropical wax will be about as effective as candle wax in sub-zero temperatures.

• **Pack a flask** Warm food equals a warm body. When you get out of the water have a hot flask of tea, coffee or soup ready to drink. You'll feel the benefit as soon as you get it inside you.

• **Check your gear carefully** Ensure that all your neoprene gear is up to scratch. A split wetsuit boot can potentially ruin a whole trip. Likewise, check your leashes for nicks or cracks; you don't want to be swimming for miles to retrieve a lost board when it's minus two degrees.

• **Bring everything you'll need** You don't want to find yourself in some remote part of Alaska asking the local bear hunters if they have an FCS fin key.

• **Double up** If your baggage limit allows, try to travel with two wetsuits. The simple logic here is that you can let one dry out as you surf in the other, so you'll (hopefully) never have to put on an icy suit.

• **Find out if you can buy surf gear locally** Depending on your destination, you may be able to buy surf gear locally. Places like Scotland, Ireland, Canada and even Norway have surf shops, so there's every chance you'll be able to buy a nice thick wettie when you arrive (check online first to be sure). That way you won't have to lug too much heavy gear halfway around the world.

• **Bring sunscreen** Sounds crazy, but windburn can be almost as bad as sunburn. So protect your face, or you might end up in an Icelandic bar looking like a beetroot.

• **Get your timing right** The amount of time you can spend outside in freezing temperatures is limited, so try to time your session to hit the optimum conditions. You don't want to be sitting around for ages in freezing conditions waiting for the swell to pick up, or the tide to drop.

• **Wrap up warm** Thick, warm, loose fitting clothing is the best clobber to wear when you're on a coldwater surf trip. It's also the easiest to get in and out of when you're standing half-naked in a snow flurry. Think trackie bottoms, Ugg boots and a hoodie, rather than skinny jeans, trainers and a button-up shirt. It's survival, not a fashion show. If you're going somewhere really cold, bring thermal underwear. Oh, and don't forget a beanie.

WAVE POOLS

Man-made wave pools aren't new, although considering the recent coverage, you'd be forgiven for thinking they were.

The race to beat nature at its own game is reaching the end point, with Kelly Slater's Surf Ranch producing the kind of waves you'd gnaw your own arm off to surf. The quality is there, now it's a case of figuring out the interval.

As with the WaveGarden design that clearly inspired Kelly's pool, the central pontoon hides a plough being dragged by what is in essence chairlift cable technology. So one wave is produced per drag, two if the pool has two sides, and then at the end it can go back the other way. So there's not that many waves to go round. This is also an issue with the Dubai style water dump generated wave pools. Waves ridden per hour is a key metric when it comes to balancing the books for any project, as the wonderful, but now sadly defunct, Ocean Dome in Japan proved.

The new WaveGarden Cove design supposedly nails this conundrum by producing endless waves, but as of the time of going to press, there's only a small test one in the Basque hills, so it remains to be seen how it will scale up. Greg Webber also has an unproven design which may alleviate the interval issue.

It's interesting times; wave pools are fun, especially when there's been no waves for a month. They will, of course, never replace the ocean, but it's going to be an interesting decade as the tech becomes more widespread and available to the masses to session.

Here's where you can get a freshwater fix right now on your travels:

SURF SNOWDONIA

The world's first commercial WaveGarden is one of the gems of the amazing Snowdonia region in North Wales.
ADDRESS: Conway Rd, Dolgarrog, Conwy, LL32 8QE, UK.
PHONE: 01492 353 123
WEB: surfsnowdonia.com

NLAND

If you're ever in the lively city of Austin, Texas, then you get a slide at the biggest WaveGarden built so far.
ADDRESS: 4836 E. Highway 71, Del Valle, Texas, 78617, USA.
PHONE: 512-806-1900
EMAIL: questions@nlandsurfpark.com
WEB: nlandsurfpark.com

WaveGardens are also proposed for Edinburgh, Seattle, Perth, Sydney and Melbourne.

AL AIN SURF PARK

The desert pool made famous by Dion Agius, incredible short film, *Electric Blue Heaven,* is handy if you ever find yourself in the wave starved UAE.

ADDRESS: Jebel Hafeet, Al Ain - Abu Dhabi

PHONE: 971 3 781 8422

EMAIL: reception@wadiadventure.ae

WEB: wadiadventure.ae

KUALA LUMPUR

The pool that started the modern fascination with wave pools, thanks to Parko and Taj having jet ski assisted fun in it.

ADDRESS: 3, Jalan PJS 11/11, Bandar Sunway, 47500 Selangor Darul Ehsan, Malaysia.

PHONE: 603 5639 0000

EMAIL: ask_lagoon@sunway.com.my

WEB: sunwaylagoon.com

TENERIFE

Similar style pool to Dubai, in one of Europe's biggest water parks.

ADDRESS: Av. Siam, s/n, 38660 Costa Adeje, Santa Cruz de Tenerife, Spain.

PHONE: +34 822 07 00 00

EMAIL: rp@siampark.net

WEB: siampark.net

KELLY SLATER'S SURF RANCH

At present Kelly's phenomenal wave isn't open to the public, but there is one planned for Palm Beach in Florida for 2019.

ADDRESS: 18556 Jackson Ave, Lemoore, CA 93245, USA.

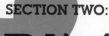

PRIME SURFING DESTINATIONS

Arctic Circle (66°33')

Tropic of Cancer (23°27')

Tropic of Cancer (23°27')

Equator

Equator

Tropic of Capricorn (23°27')

Tropic of Capricorn (23°27')

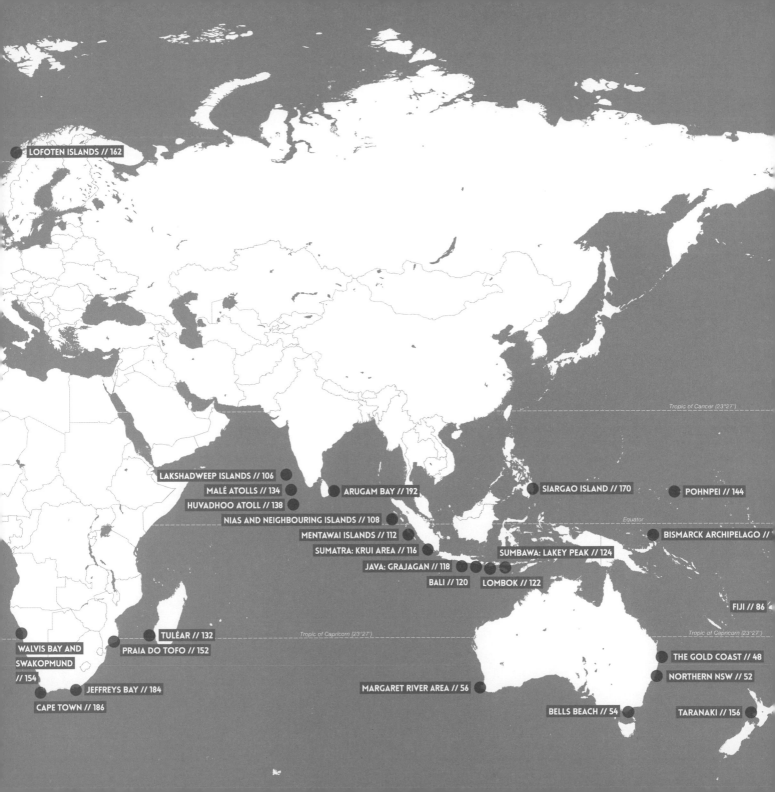

LOFOTEN ISLANDS // 162

LAKSHADWEEP ISLANDS // 106

MALÉ ATOLLS // 134

HUVADHOO ATOLL // 138

ARUGAM BAY // 192

SIARGAO ISLAND // 170

POHNPEI // 144

NIAS AND NEIGHBOURING ISLANDS // 108

Equator

MENTAWAI ISLANDS // 112

BISMARCK ARCHIPELAGO //

SUMATRA: KRUI AREA // 116

SUMBAWA: LAKEY PEAK // 124

JAVA: GRAJAGAN // 118

BALI // 120

LOMBOK // 122

FIJI // 86

Tropic of Cancer (23°27')

TULÉAR // 132

Tropic of Capricorn (23°27')

Tropic of Capricorn (23°27')

WALVIS BAY AND
SWAKOPMUND
// 154

PRAIA DO TOFO // 152

THE GOLD COAST // 48

NORTHERN NSW // 52

JEFFREYS BAY // 184

MARGARET RIVER AREA // 56

CAPE TOWN // 186

BELLS BEACH // 54

TARANAKI // 156

AUSTRALIA

THE GOLD COAST

LOVE REELING RIGHTHAND POINTS? YOU'RE NOT ALONE!

ANDREW SHIELD

Since the 1960s, Australia's Gold Coast has been a honey pot of surfing treasure, attracting the best surfers from far and wide to its warm, sticky goodies. A blessed combination of geography, coastal morphology and cultural hedonism makes this stretch of coast a true (if you'll excuse the locational pun) surfers' paradise.

For starters, the water and weather retain a blissful heat all year round. Locals get away with boardshorts for nine months of the year, and only need to wear cling-film thin wetsuits for the brief winter season. On top of that, the Gold Coast gets a consistent supply of swell: macking cyclone swells from the east in the summer, Southern Ocean swells in the autumn and winter. When a lined-up swell hits the Gold Coast's plethora of point breaks, there really are world-class waves wherever you look.

It's no wonder then that this corner of Queensland has churned out champion surfers by the dozen, from Michael Peterson, Peter Townend and Rabbit Bartholomew in the '70s, through to the likes of Mick Fanning and Joel Parkinson today.

For three decades starting in the '70s, the Gold Coast was world famous for its five distinct and perfect point breaks: (from south to north) Snapper Rocks, Greenmount, Kirra, Currumbin and Burleigh Heads. To those world-class spots you could add the hollow wedges of Duranbah and the grinding pits of South Stradbroke Island. These waves, and the surfers they

helped produce, were already enough to sustain a surfing folklore for the rest of time.

Then, in the early 2000s, the creation of the Superbank added a peacock-sized feather in the cap of this already legendary stretch of coast. A dredging project at the mouth of the Tweed River dumped kilotonnes of sand at the tip of Snapper Rocks, and the relentless waves distributed it evenly all the way past Kirra. Three individual breaks were thus joined, and the resulting two-kilometre stretch of sand now boasts some of the world's longest, hollowest, most crowded and most photographed waves in the world. More than 15 years later, the sand is still being pumped out of the Tweed River, and the Superbank still pumps out ridiculous waves. The only thing that taints this man-made marvel is the loss of Kirra, once an insanely long and hollow wave.

Of course, waves of the highest quality attract surfers of the highest quality, and today the Gold Coast is home to more pro's than any other stretch of coast on the planet. All the recreational surfers rip too, and thanks to the wonders of modern surf forecasting, every surfer on the Goldie knows when a decent swell is coming, and every one of them will be on it. Yes, the points get *seriously* crowded. And don't kid yourself that you →

OPPOSITE D-BAH – THE GOLD COAST FUN PARK.
ABOVE RIGHT TAKING OFF BEHIND THE ROCK AT SNAPPER ISN'T ALWAYS EASY.

WHEN TO GO: Whenever a tropical cyclone appears in the Coral Sea, usually between January and April.
AIRPORT: Brisbane (BNE) for international flights; Gold Coast Airport (OOL) for domestic flights.
ACCOMMODATION: There's everything from five-star penthouses to basic

motels, all within walking distance of the Superbank. Bear Rentals have a fleet of fully kitted out Land Rovers for OZ road trips in most cities.
WATCH OUT FOR: A ruthless attitude from locals at the prime spots.
BOARDS: Anything by local shapers Darren Handley or Jason Stephenson.

RUBBER: Most of the year you'll only need boardshorts.
AFTER DARK: Head to the local surf lifesaving clubs for arvo beers, the nightclubs of Coolangatta for cocktails, and Surfer's Paradise for early morning debauchery.

ABOVE THIS IS WHY FOLKS LOVE THE GOLDIE, CROWDS AND ALL, THE REGION IS NOW A WORLD SURFING RESERVE. **BELOW AND RIGHT** BEDE DURBIDGE, ONE OF THE MANY PROS THAT CALL THE GOLDIE HOME.

might be able to snag a whole bunch of waves if you get up at 5am for a dawnie; even in the pre-dawn near blackness you'll be paddling out with hundreds of others.

But if the crowds and drop-ins at the points are too much for you, there's good news. You don't have to go far to find waves with a bit more elbow room. To the north, South Stradbroke Island offers peak after peak of grinding beach break barrels. To the south, there are a dozen more super fun spots just a short drive into northern New South Wales. Fingal Point, Cabarita, Norries Head, Bogangar Beach, Pottsville Beach, Hastings Point, Black Rock and Brunswick Heads offer a smorgasbord of waves for all abilities; the further you drive, the fewer other surfers you'll encounter.

The Gold Coast also offers a myriad of ways you can spend money and have fun, fun, fun on dry land. Bars, nightclubs, casinos, theme parks...it's all here whenever you want it. If, however, you've just made the most of a five-day cyclone swell and you're finally relaxing with a cold beer at one of the surf club bars that overlook the points, you'll know that life cannot get any better than this. **– Ben Mondy**

AUSTRALIA

NORTHERN NEW SOUTH WALES

LAID-BACK BYRON BAY AND A PLETHORA OF POINTS

The small town of Byron Bay in northern New South Wales has played a pivotal part in the history of surfing Down Under. The once sleepy fishing and whaling town was transformed by surfers back in the '60s when a ragtag bunch of hippies, draft dodgers and city runaways found their way there, looking for an alternative way of life. Byron Bay provided the waves, the pot and the freedom for creative thinking that would change surfing forever. Bob McTavish, Gary Keyes and Chris Brock moved to Byron in the winter of '68, and their tales of organic produce and epic waves encouraged the likes of George Greenough and Nat Young to follow. All shapers and supremely talented surfers, their radical experiments in surfboard design led to boards dropping in length from eight feet to under six feet in just 12 months. This momentous period of change, now known as the shortboard revolution, led to a whole new way of surfing – a combination of dynamic expression and surfing aggression that became the blueprint for modern surfing.

Today some things have changed and some

haven't. While the hippies and draft dodgers have been replaced by TV moguls and Swedish backpackers, the waves, the source of it all, remain the same.

Cape Byron is the easternmost point in Australia. As a result it captures every ounce of swell going, including intermittent northwest swells and cyclone swells from the Coral Sea, and more consistent south swells from the Tasman Sea.

On the north side of the Cape, along the town's beachfront, southerly winds blow offshore. Here you'll find Byron's most famous wave, The Pass, a 500-metre righthander dotted with every type of surfer and surf craft know to man. On small to medium swells it's a

fun, mellow wave suitable for all abilities, although it's always crowded. On bigger swells it grinds off with a lot more grunt and it's even more crowded! Further inside the bay, The Wreck is another quality spot which offers hollow waves (mainly rights) peeling off a sandbar stabilised by the remains of a sunken ship. It's a favourite with locals like Garrett Parkes: "When it's on, it's super hollow with horseshoe bowls. So fun. It breaks in front of an old shipwreck which kinda adds to the thrill ... makes it a bit scary as well."

On the southern side of the Cape, Tallows Beach stretches from Cosy Corner (under the lighthouse) through Dolphins and down for several kilometres to Broken Head. This stretch of coastline captures any south swell going and the predominant summer northeasterly winds blow straight offshore. It's the playground for Byron's multitude of hot young surfers and the place where such luminaries as Danny Wills, Brendan Margieson and Kieren Perrow (to name just a few) cut their teeth.

Heading south, 15 kilometres down the road you reach the small town of Lennox Head and its famous pointbreak. Often touted as one of the world's great waves, Lennox can produce 500-metre rights that spit and spin down a boulder-lined point. It starts to break at about three feet and can handle anything up to 15. When it's good, one wave out here can change your life. Be warned though, the only thing more scary than negotiating the green slime-covered boulders on the way out, is trying to do it on the way in. The next point round, imaginatively called Boulders, offers waves of about a quarter the length of Lennox, but far fewer crowds.

That just leaves Ballina, another coastal town which offers a selection of world-class beach breaks either side of its rivermouth breakwall, plus a few slabby reefs for those in the know.

And all this in a stretch of coast less than 50 kilometres long! Choose between empty beach breaks with just dolphins for company, or world-class point breaks being shredded by legends, past and present. Quite simply no other surfing destination can offer what the Byron-Lennox-Ballina stretch does. The shortboard revolution was 40 years ago, but in Byron the good times just keep rolling on. **– Ben Mondy**

ABOVE LENNOX HEAD FIRING.
LEFT BYRON BAY LOCAL DANNY WILLS HACKS A TURN AT TALLOWS.

SIMON WILLIAMS

WHEN TO GO: January to April is the season for pumping cyclone swells.

AIRPORT: Brisbane (BNE).

ACCOMMODATION: Anything and everything from five-star hotels to hippy yurts.

WATCH OUT FOR: Crowded lineups are the main hazard, although sharks are occasionally sighted.

BOARDS: Take a couple of shortboards, and maybe a semi-gun if you plan to charge the points at size.

RUBBER: Most of the time you'll be in boardshorts or a shortie.

AFTER DARK: In Byron Bay, head for The Beach Hotel on the waterfront for drinks and live music. Grab something at Mac's Milkbar & Café if you want a bite to eat.

ALTERNATIVE EXCITEMENT: Byron Bay has a thriving arts and crafts scene, and an annual music and film festival in October.

AUSTRALIA

BELLS BEACH AREA

TAKE A DRIVE DOWN THE GREAT OCEAN ROAD

While Bells Beach itself is only a couple of hundred metres long, this stretch of untouched coast (it was Australia's first 'surfing reserve') holds a special place in the hearts and minds of surfers around the world. In fact it can make a pretty good claim to being the spiritual home of surfing in Australia. No other Aussie break possesses as much folklore and history as the big, cold, lumbering walls of Bells. It was the venue for the world's first pro surfing contest

... with a first prize of one pound! It was where Simon Anderson unveiled his thruster to the world in 1981, in awesome 15-foot waves. It was where Occy battled Tom Curren in the semi's of the '86 Rip Curl Pro, a heat still rated as one of the best in pro surfing history. For God's sake, even Patrick Swayze came here to face his demons and a '50-year swell' in the movie *Point Break*! As if all that wasn't enough, it was in this sleepy part of the world that Quiksilver and Rip Curl started making shirts and crude wetsuits back in the '60s, and where the head offices of those mega-companies remain to this day.

The righthand point at Bells has two distinct sections – Rincon and the Bells Bowl. Rincon is a racy wave that runs for 150 metres under the shadows of the iconic Bells headland. Best around high tide, it's a super fun wave but will only handle swells up to about four foot; any bigger and the waves start breaking on a wider section of the reef. The Bells Bowl, however, is the real Bells Beach. Breaking in the middle of the bay between the headlands of Bells and Winkipop, it starts showing itself at four feet, but can handle anything up to 15 feet.

Crowds are usually a factor at Bells. Since it's only an hour's drive from the sprawling metropolis of Melbourne, the lineup is nearly always busy. Weekday lunch hours in particular are worth avoiding, as that's when all the staff of the local surf companies bolt over for a quick fix. On the plus side, the big take-off area and consistent clean-up sets mean that you can often

be in position, on your own, when a set stacks up in the Bowl.

There are heaps of other good waves in the area too. Winkipop, another righthand point, is just a stone's throw from Bells and many consider it to be faster, hollower, longer ... just better all round really. The J-Bay comparisons are well deserved. Just north of Bells is the small town of Jan Juc, where Bird Rock offers zippy tubes around low tide. Keep driving and you'll come to 13th Beach, a Hossegor-style beach break. To the south of Bells there are points and bays with waves in every nook and cranny, if you know the right people to ask. If there's no swell on this stretch of the coast, then head around Cape Otway to Johanna, a punchy southwest-facing beach break which picks up anything going.

This is an area with surfing at its very heart. Cold water, big waves, hardcore locals and stunning scenery make it a must see, must surf. What are you waiting for? **– Ben Mondy**

OPPOSITE BELLS FROM THE AIR, WITH WINKIPOP IN THE FOREGROUND.

WHEN TO GO: Late summer or autumn, March to June.
AIRPORT: Melbourne (MEL).
ACCOMMODATION: There are campsites, backpackers and guest houses in the Bells vicinity.
WATCH OUT FOR: Crowded lineups and shallow inside sections.

BOARDS: The paddle out at Bells is gruelling so it's a good idea to have a little extra volume. For waves up to six feet ride a board an inch or two longer than your standard shortboard; if it's over six feet ride something between 6'4" and 6'10".
RUBBER: Pack a 3/2 for summer and

autumn, a 4/3 for winter.
AFTER DARK: The Torquay Hotel is a favourite watering hole for surfers, while the Bird Rock Café in Jan Juc rocks, especially on weekends.
ALTERNATIVE EXCITEMENT: Visit Surf World Surfing Museum in Torquay.

AUSTRALIA

MARGARET RIVER AREA

THE WONDERS OF WEST OZ

Western Australia is a serious part of the world for serious surfers, as was shown by the 2011 Margaret River Pro contest, when the pro's had to deal with a roaring 15-foot swell. Huge swells, generated by distant storms in the Roaring Forties, march their way across the southern Indian Ocean before slamming straight into the coastline of the Margaret River area, on the southwest tip of Australia. Many of these swells are well-organised long period groundswells, packing huge power. In fact, such is the power of this place it is regularly, and correctly, compared to Hawaii's North Shore.

The best-known wave, and the one where the pro contests are held, is officially known as Surfer's Point, but it's known to the locals as either Main Break or Margie's. Somewhat confusingly, it's actually located 12 kilometres west of the town of Margaret River. Not that it makes much difference; even from that distance, the roar of a fresh swell will rattle the hoardings of this classic Australian town, which lies in the heart of a famous wine region.

As you pull up to the Main Break car park, the level of activity and number of cars will tell you how good the waves are. An elevated view gives you a great vista of the Main Break peak, and also the several other world-class waves within a radius of a few kilometres.

It is the Main Break, however, that tends to be the focus of everyone's attention, as it picks up every ounce of swell available. It starts to break at about three feet, and up to ten feet the lefts are generally as good as the rights (although the lefts break into a deep channel, which provides slightly more safety from the regular clean-up sets). As the swell pushes past ten feet, the rights tend to close out, leaving the lefts to break further and further out... bigger, scarier and heavier. Waves with 40-foot faces have been surfed here, usually by bearded locals riding 10-foot Hawaiian rhinochasers.

On smaller swells, the peak 300 metres to the south, known inventively as Southsides, provides a less crowded option. Other waves in the area include big-wave spots The Bommie and Boat Ramps, while The Box and Grunters fall nicely into the mutant slabs category. Boodjiup offers the only beach break action in the immediate area, again, of world-class quality.

Gracetown, 15 kilometres up the road, is another hotspot for surfers' with quality point breaks on opposite sides of Cowaramup Bay. North Point is a world-class spot offering long barrelling rights up to 10-foot-plus. South Point's lefts are just as long but allow a few turns. At size, both are heavy and demanding waves for experts only. Less experienced surfers should head for Huzza's, inside the bay, which serves up fun waves breaking over a sand-covered reef. Other spots for intermediates include The Farm, Rocky Point and Windmills, all located further north around Cape Naturaliste.

Apart from the windy and rainy winter months, the Margaret River area is a true surfer's haven. Incredible waves, beautiful Australian bush scenery, relatively warm water and a sense that you're dealing with Mother Nature at her most powerful. Just pack some big boards... and a bigger heart. **– Ben Mondy**

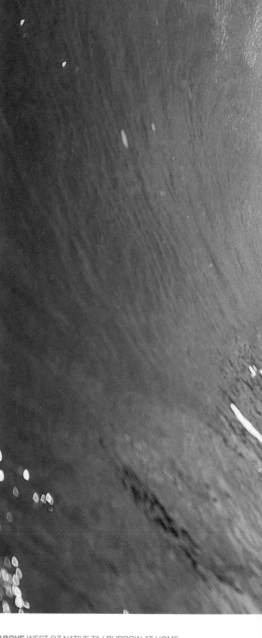

ABOVE WEST OZ NATIVE TAJ BURROW AT HOME.
LEFT MARGIES MAIN BREAK ALL LINED UP.

ANDREW SHIELD

WHEN TO GO: March through to May, when six- to eight-foot southwest swells, offshores and sunny skies are commonplace.

AIRPORT: Perth (PTH).

ACCOMMODATION: There are plenty of options in the town of Margaret River, and a few in Prevelly too.

WATCH OUT FOR: Heavy waves, shallow reefs and the odd shark are the main ocean hazards. On land, it's snakes and spiders.

BOARDS: Pack a shortboard for the fun three-foot days, a couple of semi-guns (you'll break at least one), and a seven-foot-plus gun if you want a piece of the action on the big days.

AFTER DARK: Margaret River has several good pubs; Settlers Tavern often has live music.

RUBBER: A 3/2 will do the job.

ALTERNATIVE EXCITEMENT: A wine tour, of course.

BARBADOS

BATHSHEBA TO SOUTH POINT

THE CLASSIC CARIBBEAN MISSION

When the publishers of Kelly Slater's autobiography *For The Love* **were looking for a covershot,** it was pretty much a no-brainer that they'd choose a sick action photo of The Great One standing tall in some mental, grinding world-class barrel. They did... but the wave wasn't Backdoor, Teahupo'o or Cloudbreak. Nope, the shot in question was actually taken at Soup Bowl, one of several gems on the small Caribbean island of Barbados.

Yes, Soup Bowl can be absolutely epic on its day – a wedgy, powerful righthand barrel, as intense as any other wave in the Caribbean. Trouble is, those epic days occur about as often as the West Indies cricket team trouncing England by 500 runs. Soup Bowl – situated at Bathsheba, halfway along the island's east coast – faces straight into the prevailing northeasterly trades, so a lot of the time it's howling onshore and blown to smithereens. If you catch a couple of calm mornings during the course of a week, you're doing pretty well. If you score proper offshores plus a chunky groundswell, then you've hit the jackpot. Give the locals some rrr-respect, they're a cool bunch and they rip. Getting in and out of the water across the ledgy reef can be quite interesting, with abundant urchins adding to the fun.

Fortunately, you still have plenty of options on days when the trades are trashing the east coast. Since the island is only 14 miles (22 kilometres) wide, it's a doddle to drive around and scope out the other coasts.

Up towards the northern tip of the island you'll find Duppies, a righthand point which offers long rippable walls when there's a moderate north or northwest swell running. Although it may look inviting to intermediates, it's best left to experienced surfers due to the long paddle out and currents. Avoid high tide as the waves get messed up by backwash from the cliffs.

Maycock's, a few miles down the west coast, is a mellow righthand reef popular with longboarders and intermediates. Its beautiful setting could almost be

described as idyllic... if it wasn't for the clatter of the cement factory nearby.

Further down the west coast are some really good reefs, among them Tropicana, Sandy Lane and Batt's Rock. Most days the west coast is mirror flat and you wouldn't even know those spots were there. But every now and then during the winter months a beefy north swell wraps down the coast and lights them up. They all get hollow, and Tropicana is so shallow you can only ride it at high tide. Advanced surfers only.

Past Bridgetown, Brandon's is a south coast spot which doesn't show unless there's a decent swell running. Its fun lefts break over a flat, urchin-infested reef just down from the Hilton.

Continuing along the south coast, Freights is a sand-bottom left point tucked in behind the headland at the eastern end of Oistin's Bay. It's so sheltered you rarely see anything but anklesnappers here. But very occasionally, when a southwest hurricane swell slams into the island, Freights transforms itself into a dreamy lefthander with aquamarine barrels for the lucky souls who happen to be on the island at the time. Around the headland, South Point is a far more consistent spot that always seems to have a wave of some description (even if it's only a disorganised windswell) thanks to the relentless easterly trades. When a lined-up groundswell hits, South Point shapes up to provide fun racy lefts which break over a flat coral reef. Hit it at lower stages of the tide as it gets messed up by backwash towards high.

There are many other spots on the island, including one or two classic secret spots. Happy hunting!
– Chris Power

RIGHT LUKE DILLON ENJOYING THE NORTH POINT WEDGES.
LEFT OLD SCHOOL BAJAN CHATTEL HOUSE, PROPPED ON ROCKS SO IT COULD BE MOVED.

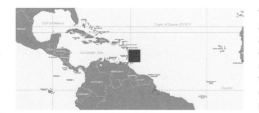

WHEN TO GO: September to March.
AIRPORT: Barbados (BGI).
ACCOMMODATION: Take your pick from glitzy mega-buck hotels to affordable self-catering apartments.
WATCH OUT FOR: Urchins and sharp coral at many of the reefs.
BOARDS: Bring a fish or floaty shortboard for the small days, a shortboard for decent swells, and maybe a step-up if a hurricane swell is due.
RUBBER: You'll ony need boardshorts.
AFTER DARK: There are clubs galore – try The Boatyard or Harbour Lights. You never know, you might bump into Rihanna.
ALTERNATIVE ENTERTAINMENT: Time your visit right and watch a test match at the Kensington Oval with the Barmy Army. Howzat!

BRAZIL

FLORIANÓPOLIS AND SANTA CATARINA ISLAND

SURF BY DAY, SAMBA BY NIGHT

Fun waves, warm water, beautiful Latino girls in G-strings, white-sand beaches and tons of nightlife. Any of that sound good to you? If it does, you should think about taking a trip to Santa Catarina Island. Situated way down in southern Brazil, the island is about 50 kilometres (30 miles) long and lies parallel to the mainland. On the ocean side is a string of beaches which pick up Atlantic swells from all directions, and on the landward side — linked to the mainland by a set of bridges — is Florianópolis, one of Brazil's coolest cities.

Santa Catarina Island is one of the best areas in Brazil to find waves, thanks to the consistent south swells it receives throughout the autumn and winter (April to August); these are generated by low pressure systems off Cape Horn. Spring (September to October) is also a good time to visit as east swells add to the fun, generated by tropical storms and hurricanes tracking across from Africa. Since nearly all the spots on the island are beach breaks, the area is well suited to intermediate level surfers as well as more experienced riders. Santa Catarina has produced many of Brazil's top pro's over the years including Adriano de Souza, Alejo Muniz, and brothers Flavio

MARCIO DAVID

and Neco Padaratz. Crowds and localism can be an issue at one or two spots but the vibe at the majority of beaches is friendly.

Towards the north end of the island is Santinho, a good beachie which works best on a southeast swell with northwesterly winds to clean things up. The lefts at the north end can be classic but it does get pretty crowded. Further down the coast, amid beautiful surroundings, is Mocambique, a six-mile stretch of beach with numerous peaks that can get hollow on good days. The beauty of Mocambique is you're virtually guaranteed a peak to yourself, even on weekends, such is the space. Praia Mole, about halfway down the island, is another pristine beach which has something for everyone; on a good day (with winds from the northwest) you'll find hollow lefts and rights all along the beach. Just around the corner is Joaquina, another quality beachie which has hosted numerous ASP events over the years. Expect to find crowds here if the waves are good. Campeche, a couple of kilometres south, can offer good rights on a solid south swell; it's a favourite haunt of top Brazilian pro Adriano de Souza. Next up is the rivermouth at Matadeiro, a fickle spot which occasionally serves up some nice sucky lefthanders. Towards the southern end of the island sits the little bay of Lagoinha do Leste, quite a tricky spot to find. Its seclusion keeps the numbers down so most days you'll only find a few other surfers indulging themselves in the perfect peaks, which are well protected fom the wind. The barrels will be just that bit sweeter as you've

trekked a while to find them.

The city of Florianópolis (or Floripa, as the locals call it) lies on the sheltered side of the island, just five kilometres from the surfing beaches. It's a well-organised, clean and cosmopolitan city with a low crime rate. There are some super cool bars and nightclubs here, and many more in the resort towns scattered along the ocean side of the island.

If you want to venture further down Brazil's southern coast you'll find several great surf spots within 90 kilometres (55 miles), notably Praia da Vila, Guarda do Embau (now recognised as a World Surfing Reserve), Silveira and Ferrugem. Praia da Vila (located near the town of Imbituba) hosts an annual ASP Prime surf contest, the Super Surf International, with a $250,000 purse. One of Brazil's best spots, it'll hold waves up to 15 feet and has drawn comparisons to Sunset Beach. Thanks to a great setup, the paddle out is never too bad and it breaks both ways offering huge walls for carves and snaps. **– Owen Pye**

OPPOSITE TOP PRAIA JOAQUINA, ONE OF SANTA CATARINA'S MOST CONSISTENT SPOTS.
OPPOSITE BOTTOM THE RIVERMOUTH AT MATADEIRO IS PRETTY FICKLE BUT OFFERS SUCKY BARRELS WHEN IT'S ON.

WHEN TO GO: April to October.
AIRPORT: Fly into Florianópolis (FLN) via Sao Paulo (GRU).
ACCOMMODATION: There are plenty of cool hotels in downtown Florianópolis, or you can rent an apartment near one of the beaches.
WATCH OUT FOR: Brazilian surfers are,

let's say, very competitive, so expect to get snaked now and then, and stay cool.
BOARDS: Bring a fish and a couple shortboards.
RUBBER: You'll want a 3/2 for winter and early spring, a shortie for the warmer months.

AFTER DARK: The nightlife here is all-time and there some amazing bars and clubs: Pacha, Posh, Taiko... the list goes on and on.
ALTERNATIVE EXCITEMENT: Drive around the Lagoa da Conceicao for some of the finest scenery imaginable.

CANADA

NOVA SCOTIA

FICKLE BUT FROSTY FUN

The vastness of Canada's interior is bookended by islands. In contrast to the western wilderness of Vancouver Island, the east side has Nova Scotia – New Scotland, in English.

You'd not know it but it is Canada's second most densely populated province. Outside of the capital, Halifax, it's as sparse and spacious as the rest of Canada. The beautiful isle of rolling granite bluffs, icy lakes and pine forests as far as the eye can see, has a turbulent history much like most of North America. The Cajun culture of New Orleans, that distinct French influence, comes from Acadian settlers forcibly expelled from Nova Scotia when the British warred the French for the island.

The island is also home to the world's largest tidal range on it's mainland-facing side in the Bay of Fundy has, according to the Guinness Book of Records, the greatest mean spring range with 14.5 metres (47.5 feet), and an extreme is of 16.3 metres (53.5 feet).

Surf wise the entire south coast has potential, and much like the other cold frontiers, access can be tricky. Especially in winter when you're hiking through waist deep snow to reach the shore. But it can be so worth it. The main swell season comes from hurricanes, so the prime season is similar to Europe, and swells don't last too long as the lows move away from the Eastern Seaboard. The cunning traveller would visit in deep winter as it's like surfing in a Christmas card scene. And if you do luck into a clean swell with offshore winds and no fog or blizzards, then you're in for a treat.

Trestles style boulder reefs are the main type of spot and there are some real classy ones. You don't need to stray too far from Halifax on the coast roads to see the potential. Like in Vancouver, the locals can suffer long droughts between decent surf, so be aware that your travelling self is welcome but tolerated on the condition of respect being given. As it should be everywhere. US photo trippers doing media strike missions peeve the locals; real travellers checking the place out and getting to know folk don't. If you're exploring really deep, be aware that cameras can be frowned upon. Even local pros aren't allowed to shoot some of the more treasured secret spots.

ABOVE OLI ADAMS TAKES FLIGHT ON A RARE SUNNY DAY.
LEFT YES IT IS AS FUN AS IT LOOKS. JUST WATCH OUT FOR ICE COVERED BOULDERS.

WHEN TO GO: September to April.
AIRPORT: Halifax (YHZ).
ACCOMMODATION: Limited in winter, motels are cheap, when warmer there are holiday rentals.
WATCH OUT FOR: The cold. It's seriously cold, even if you are used to European style winters it's a whole other world. Watch out on the roads for ice, and when deep in remote areas bear in mind getting stuck is really likely in a non 4x4 rental car.
BOARDS: A slightly bigger board to make up for all the rubber, normal shortboard style.
RUBBER: Hooded 6mm unless you're lucky enough to score a hurricane swell early season.
AFTER DARK: Halifax has enough bars to entertain you. Try the poutine and explore the craft ales.
ALTERNATIVE EXCITEMENT: Snowball fights. Ice skating. Hiking.

BOULDER POINTS AND REEFS ABOUND IN NOVA SCOTIA.

CANADA

VANCOUVER ISLAND

TREES, TREES, TREES, A BAY, THE VAST PACIFIC OCEAN AND THEN A FEW MORE TREES.

Vancouver Island's west coast is a wild place where boreal rainforest dips down from the coastal mountain ranges straight into the Pacific Ocean. This dense wilderness makes going surfing an absolute mission in all but a handful of areas.

The south coast is where most surfers live. Victoria, the capital of Vancouver Island, is a bit of a tech hub, and thus has spawned a fashionable army of surfers. However, closest surf is inconsistent and being situated up the Juan de Fuca straits, you need some special combinations of swell, tide and wind all coming together for the waves to turn on. When they do Jordan River is the best known break to head for, and is a super fun cobblestone point/ rivermouth, with a reputation for localism. Yet this is more down to inconsistency and the locals demanding respect for the weeks they wait for a decent wave. Turn up with a crowd and you won't be popular; show up alone or with a mate and show respect and you'll find more friendly faces than fierce ones.

The coast north of Jordan River turns into wilderness. There are waves for sure, but you need more than a few scout badges to head out here – this is Into The Wild style territory and demands a lot more than a fun hike to score some waves. Bears and mountain lions are common, and that's before you factor in heavy paddle-outs and solid Pacific swell.

Tofino is the self-proclaimed capital of Canadian surfing and with good reason, having produced a roll call of pro surfers brought up on a combination of punchy beach breaks and heavy reefs and slabs. Getting there is no mean feat; it's a solid drive over the central and coastal mountain ranges to the isolated port. Originally a logging and fishing town, it has morphed into a hub for the outdoors, an access point for boat and seaplane travel to the wilderness coast to the north, a starting point for fishing and whale watching trips, and the most popular place to go surfing in Canada. The town is cool and a great place to stay, with a mixture of health food eateries and frontier feeling bars, all set on the edge of the biosphere reserve Clayoquot Sound.

It's the surfing that has really captured the attention for the area, with pros like the Bruhwiler brothers, Pete Devries and Noah Cohen all hailing from the area, and all having made an impact globally. Cox Bay is the prime spot – the crescent beach has shifting sandbars but the best spot is a slurpy right-hander at the northern end. It's consistent but easily blown out, and in the winter often maxed out by solid Pacific swell. Just north is a series of sandy beaches that are more sheltered from wind and swell; none are amazing, all have their moments, but most of the time have fleets of beginners on foamies. Down the coast is Longbeach, which, when you emerge out of the trees looks almost idyllic, but its shifting sandbars are rarely epic, and more suited to learning to surf in the summer.

So where are all the good waves? Well this is why Vancouver Island is a genuine frontier when it comes to surfing; only about five percent of swell-facing coastline is accessible by car, a little more can be reached down logging tracks by 4x4, but most is genuine wilderness. This is both the beauty and frustration of Vancouver island. It's relatively mild water temps – warmed by the Kuroshio Current it's warmer than northern California – and exposure to consistent swell year round, make it an epic place to surf. The problem is that most of the good stuff is impossible to get to unless you are a local, know a local very well, or are a Bear Grylls sort of person with a lot of time on your hands. Epic slabs, points, beaches and reefs are all out there, all set amongst an incredible backdrop of temperate rainforest and mountains, it's just close to impossible to get there. And when you do you get there, you'd better be ready to live side by side with some big hairy critters. – **Tim Nunn**

LEFT PETE DEVRIES HAS CARVED A COLDWATER PRO NICHE AT HOME.
RIGHT YEP BEARS ARE AN ISSUE ESPECIALLY WHEN YOU'RE MAKING THE FRESHEST SUSHI.

WHEN TO GO: All year.
AIRPORT: Victoria (YYJ).
ACCOMMODATION: Rental cabins, or wild camping if you're going deep.
WATCH OUT FOR: Bears, bears, bears and mountain lions. Take advice before going remote.
BOARDS: Standard shortboards.

RUBBER: Hooded 5mm.
AFTER DARK: Fun bars in Tofino. Or listening for bears if camping.
ALTERNATIVE EXCITEMENT: Natural playground to enjoy most outdoor activities. That and running from bears. Or do you duck and cover?

CANARY ISLANDS

LANZAROTE AND FUERTEVENTURA

ATLANTIC ISLES WHERE THE WAVES PACK A PUNCH

Ninety kilometres off the coast of Morocco lie a group of Spanish islands which have become synonymous with heavy waves – the Canary Islands. Entirely volcanic in origin, they're blessed with year-round sunshine and epic waves. Dubbed the 'Atlantic Hawaii', some of the Canaries' urchin-infested slabs hold incredibly heavy waves with barrels as thick as hydrodynamic theory allows. The islands are surrounded by deep water, so incoming swells slam in with full Atlantic power producing thick, heavy waves which require 100 percent commitment from the second you think about getting to your feet. What comes next depends on your ability to control your rail and line up the section; if you don't, you'll suffer the consequences. From playful four-foot peelers to top-to-bottom quadruple-overhead monsters, Canarian reefs tick all the boxes. There's also a selection of less intense beach breaks which can be fun, although the reefs are what the crowds froth over.

The islands hoover up swell from all directions, but most of the big winter swells come from slow-moving North Atlantic lows which churn out a steady supply of northwest groundswell throughout the winter months. Hurricane swells from the east coast of the US can also reach the islands if the storms peel away from the continent early and don't dissipate too soon. Trade winds blow almost all year round, predominantly from the north east; the winds tend to be lightest in October and November.

There are seven main islands in the Canaries, and each offers a selection of surf spots ranging from good to world-class. Lanzarote and Fuerteventura are the furthest east of the islands and they're also the least mountainous; consequently they offer the best access to the coastline and they have the highest concentration of breaks.

Lanzarote's heaviest and best known spots lie in a cluster around the fishing village of La Santa on the north coast. El Quemao, a crunching left next to the village's tiny harbour, bears more than a passing resemblance to its Pacific cousin Pipeline. Offshore on a southeast Sirocco wind, El Quemao will tear you a new orifice if you don't treat it with the utmost respect. The takeoff is always steep, and you'll need to nail a heavy bottom turn to line up the second section which can sometimes suck almost dry. El Quemao is shallow, fast, heavy and will give you a shot of adrenaline you won't

forget. The locals are a tight-knit bunch who aren't too wild about visitors, whether you rip or not. Show respect and it'll improve your chances, but even then they won't welcome you with open arms.

A kilometre along the coast is La Santa Right (known locally as Morro Negro), a long, powerful righthander which breaks along a boulder-strewn point. It'll hold waves up to 15 feet and can be world-class on its day, with big open walls begging to be carved to bits. The inside can sometimes get bowly, with the odd barrel to be had. The current down the point is quite strong and the paddle outs are wearing, but catch it on a perfect six-foot day and you'll be hooting your head off. Get there early to beat the crowds.

Other quality spots on Lanza's north shore include the heavily localised La Santa Left ('The Slab') and San Juan, a long smashable left.

OPPOSITE JOSH BRADDOCK AND CHUNKY QUEMAO.
ABOVE LEFT LOOKS DECEPTIVELY FRIENDLY, IT'S NOT.
ABOVE RIGHT THE VOLCANIC LANDSCAPES ARE INCREDIBLE.

WHEN TO GO: November to March.
AIRPORT: Arrecife (ACE) for Lanza', Puerto del Rosario (FUE) for Fuerte'.
ACCOMMODATION: Rent one of the numerous self-catering apartments. Check out Surf School Lanzarote.
WATCH OUT FOR: Sharp lava reefs, urchins, car crime and localism.

BOARDS: Take a couple of shortboards for the small days, plus one or two bigger boards if you plan to surf sizable waves.
RUBBER: You'll want a 3/2 for the winter months; a shortie is fine the rest of the year. Bring boots to protect your feet.
AFTER DARK: Arrecife and Puerto

del Carmen are the best towns for nightlife on Lanza'. Over on Fuerte', Corralejo has plenty of cool nightclubs and restaurants.
ALTERNATIVE EXCITEMENT: Drive around Lanzarote's Timanfaya National Park and marvel at the perfectly-preserved volcanoes.

On straight north swells a cluster of reefs on the east side of the island turn on. Jameos del Agua, Punta de Mujeres and Arrieta offer softer waves which will appeal to intermediate surfers more than the bone-crunchers around La Santa.

The long arc of sand at Famara provides a beach break option for beginners, although wave quality is dependent on the state of the banks. If the swell is from the north or northeast, another beachie to check out is Orzola on the far northern tip of the island.

Most of Fuerteventura's best waves can be found at the northern end of the island, around the resort town of Corralejo. The Bubble, a few kilometres west of the town, is a sick A-frame which offers hollow lefts and rights breaking over a sharp, shallow reef. It works best on a northwest swell with a southeasterly wind. Deep-water waves jack up quickly and morph into good-length pits for those lucky enough to snag one off the locals. The Bubble is one of the busiest spots on the island and the locals aren't too willing to abide by general etiquette, so expect drop-ins when it's on, even

if you have priority and have been quietly minding your own business for a while. Hang around, be nice and let your surfing do the talking, then you'll have a better chance of taking one of the well-protected set waves. And get in early to avoid the crowds.

Other challenging spots for experienced surfers include Las Lagunas ('Spew Pits'), a gnarly righthand barrel near Cotillo; and Lobos, a long right point that peels down the side of a volcano, a short ferry hop from Corralejo. Intermediate level surfers can find fun waves at some of the less demanding reefs like Rocky Point, as well as a selection of beach breaks like Glass Beach, Cotillo and Playa de Esquinzo. **– Rob Barber**

RIGHT LEWIS LEADBETTER DEEP IN LANZAROTE.

CAPE VERDE ISLANDS

SAL AND BOA VISTA

DESERT ISLANDS WITH A FEW JEWELS

The Cape Verde islands are situated on the east side of the Atlantic, 570 kilometres (350 miles) off the coast of Senegal. There are ten main islands, arranged in a crescent-shaped archipelago. Sal and Boa Vista are the farthest east and also the most low-lying. The climate is distinctly arid with hot dusty tradewinds blowing from the northeast all year round and 10 to 12 hours of sunshine per day (except in the humid season, from July to September).

Sal and Boa Vista have big swell windows and pick up swells from both the North and South Atlantic. The biggest swells come from the northwest, generated by low pressure systems tracking across the North Atlantic between November and April. (It's worth noting that Cape Verde receives significantly less swell than the Canary Islands, since the latter are better located

to pick up west swells.) The east coasts of both islands tend to be onshore and messy most of the time, due to the consistent gusty tradewinds. But the west coasts are usually offshore, and Sal in particular offers a number of good surf spots. Directly offshore easterly winds tend to be more common at the start of the winter season (October to December), gradually swinging around to a more northerly direction by April. The ever-present trades make Cape Verde a paradise for windsurfers, and it was actually our sail-waving brethren who discovered its surf potential in the late '80s.

Ponta Preta is the jewel in the crown on Sal. It's located down a dirt track halfway between Murdeira and Santa Maria on the southwest coast. It's best at low tide on a solid northwest swell, when it produces epic

right-handers which peel down a boulder-strewn point. It can dish out some memorable barrels, but be warned, it gets pretty shallow on the inside. Aim to hit it early or late in the day to take advantage of the lightest winds.

The island has a handful of other good spots. Halfway up the west coast is Monte Leao, which occasionally delivers excellent rights that peel off into the bay. A relatively sheltered spot, it needs a big northwest swell to work. Towards the north end of the island you'll find Palmeira, a good spot to check if the ocean isn't playing ball. It's a fun little left-hander which breaks towards the harbour; although short, it offers a whackable shoulder.

The local fishermen occasionally catch sharks and our toothy foe are definitely out there, although they seem to keep to the deeper water away from shore. Only one attack has ever been recorded, in 2001. All the same, be vigilant.

Few surfers take time to travel to the other islands in Cape Verde, so there's definitely scope for exploration. Boa Vista, the nearest island to Sal, offers punchy beach break waves at Santa Monica on the west coast. Best on big northwest groundswell, it's almost guaranteed to be empty and can get nice and hollow. – **Rob Barber**

ALEX WILLIAMS

ALEX WILLIAMS

OPPOSITE CAPE VERDE GETS LESS SURF THAN THE CANARIES, BUT A SOLID NORTHWEST SWELL WILL GET THE POINTS AND REEFS FIRING.

WHEN TO GO: October to December.
AIRPORT: Sal (SID).
ACCOMMODATION: There's a good selection of apartments and hotels in Santa Maria.
WATCH OUT FOR: The main everyday hazards are the sharp lava reefs and urchins, so tread carefully. Sharks are

present but rarely seen. Petty crime can be an issue.
BOARDS: Pack a fish, a shortboard and maybe a semi-gun in case you score a chunky day.
RUBBER: Apart from the winter months, December to April, it's warm enough for boardies.

AFTER DARK: Santa Maria is the main tourist hotspot, with several good bars and a small but fun nightclub. The best place to eat is Zum Fischermann, which serves excellent fish.
ALTERNATIVE EXCITEMENT: Diving and windsurfing are all top class.

CHILE

VIÑA DEL MAR TO PICHILEMU

PARADISE FOR GOOFYFOOTERS

The coast of central Chile, from Viña del Mar to Pichilemu, holds some of the most consistent surf in the world and has welcomed a steady stream of travelling surfers since the '80s. It's a goofyfooter's heaven: long left points, lefthand rivermouths and heavy reef setups, many of which are genuinely world class.

With such a long coastline exposed to the Roaring Forties, Chile's endless kiss with the Pacific means an abundance of top quality waves. The surf can be extremely powerful, due to the country's exposure to open-ocean swells and its narrow continental shelf. On huge swells, wave heights at some of the most exposed spots quickly enter the tow-in only zone. The more sheltered north-facing bays can be a lifesaver when solid south swells march up the coast, with the added bonus of being offshore on the prevailing winds.

The chilly Humboldt Current cools the water all year round, and this can result in lingering fog and clouds. The cold ocean temperatures have an effect on the prevailing winds, often southerlies or southwesterlies, so its best to take of advantage of the mornings to plunder the dark green glass. With a broadly Mediterranean climate, the area can get cold in winter but remain dry for long periods in the other seasons.

Starting in the north, around the town of Quintero, you'll find some fun beach break peaks at Cachagua and Maitencillo. A few kilometres south are the inviting yet sometimes crowded left points of El Claron and El Papagayo, which can both hold solid swells. The local crew won't be too keen to see a whole gang of visitors all paddling out together, so take a low-key approach and be patient, then you'll be sure to get your fair share.

Continue south and you'll soon reach the beaches north of Viña del Mar — the swell magnets of Ritoque, Punta del Piedra and Renaca. The latter is a popular tourist beach but provides some excellent and powerful peaks with boostable sections. Although consistent it can suffer from crowds; avoid the weekend if you can. If the surf is too big for the Renaca beach breaks, head down to Las Salinas at the headland; the left point here should be on form.

Just north of El Quisco you'll find a punchy reef called El Mejoral at Algarrobo; it unloads just beyond the rocks and can get very good if the wind behaves.

Between Cartagena and Navidad you may find more quality lefts if you look hard enough; one in particular can get absolutely sick if you hang around for the Andes offshores to hold up its feathering lips. Further down the coast the left point at Punta Topocalma can get all-time – look for a clean groundswell and easterly winds.

The Pichilemu area offers a great variety of spots, including some which will handle genuinely massive swells. La Puntilla is one of the longest lefts in the country when the banks are good and the swell and wind are correctly aligned. Breaking into the bay just north of the town of Pichilemu, it can be a world-class point, best on a southwest swell with east winds. When everything comes together it's capable of supplying Mundaka-style barrels and sections that peel for hundreds of metres.

Around the corner to the south is a short left point called Infernillo, which can serve up sick barrels although it's susceptible to the wind. Watch out for strong currents off the rocks, especially when it gets big and the paddle becomes a marathon.

Five kilometres south of the town sits the infamous Punta de Lobos, one of the region's best big-wave spots. Offering huge carveable walls and the odd hollow section inside, Punta de Lobos is relatively protected from southwesterly winds and can supply jelly-leg rides over half a click long. There's a lot of water moving around when a fresh swell is marching around the headland, so watch for currents before you commit.

– Owen Pye

OPPOSITE TOP PUNTA DE LOBOS IS NOW THANKFULLY PROTECTED AS A WORLD SURFING RESERVE.
OPPOSITE BOTTOM CHILEAN LEGEND RAMON NAVARRO WAS INSTRUMENTAL IN THE PROCESS OF SAVING THE SPOT.

WHEN TO GO: October to February.
AIRPORT: Santiago (SCL).
ACCOMMODATION: Pichilemu has numerous hotels and hostels, or rent a cabana on the coast.
WATCH OUT FOR: Localism at a few of the prime spots, and the usual petty crime.

BOARDS: Take a whole quiver: shortboards, semi-guns for the points, and something longer if big drops at Punta de Lobos are more your style.
RUBBER: Take a 3/2 fullsuit for summer, a 5/4mm with booties for winter.

AFTER DARK: Pichilemu gets pretty busy in summer and there are several clubs. For dinner, try La Pica del Negro.
ALTERNATIVE EXCITEMENT: Head for the Andes and check out the amazing scenery of La Reserva Nacional Rio Los Cipreses.

COSTA RICA

GUANCASTE

SMALL WAVES, BIG FUN

Costa Rica is one of the few Central American nations that hasn't got a blood soaked history of civil wars, guerrilla fighting, CIA-inspired coups and crazed despot dictators. There are no commie insurgencies or private armies here. Which in layman's terms means it's safe. The flip side of this is the number of tourists who head here to do the Centro thing without putting their necks on the line, and consequently (as tourism is the biggest industry) the cost. Dirt cheap Costa ain't. If you're stopping off here as part of longer Centro trip then you'll definitely feel the financial pain when compared to neighbouring countries. That said, prices aren't crazy and if you do your research you can stay somewhere for a couple of weeks without completely blowing your travel fund.

CR has been on surfers' maps since the '60s and it's a chilled and easy trip. The waves are consistent and fun, suitable for pretty much everyone, from those just starting out to the numerous pro's who spend a few months here on winter escapes knowing that they'll score good surf, day in, day out.

Guanacaste is Costa Rica's northernmost province and it's home to loads of good spots which break pretty much all year round. Size wise, well, you can leave the rhinochaser at home. The surf is rarely bigger than head high, but equally it's rarely less than shoulder high. Now that's consistency. With a Pacific-facing coastline is all exposed to the same swell and has the same thermal conditions, it's also not the kind of place where you spend hours each day checking spot after spot: if it's

on then it's on. Hiring a car is worth it if there are a few of you, otherwise just get a transfer from the airport to one of the main towns and spend what you save on Imperial, the local beer of choice.

Tamarindo is one of the most popular options for an 'everything you need within a 10-minute walk' trip. It's a beautiful spot with the town itself lying between two national parks. The main road through the town is lined with places to stay and places to eat, and you'll meet plenty of people on their twentieth trip here; if it ain't broke and all that. Within walking distance of the town you've got Rivermouth (a hollow right), Pico Pequeño (a reef which can barrel with the right swell direction), and Playa Langosta (a selection of hollow beach break peaks—some better than others, and some more crowded than others, so take your pick). Aside from all this good shizzle right on your doorstep, the other big pull to Tamarindo is access to the classic spots of Witches Rock and Ollie's Point (of *Endless Summer 2* fame). As both these spots are situated in a national park, there's no accommodation close by and access is only really by boat (or a sketchy and not-really-worth-it 4x4 mission). This fact keeps crowds to a minimum, and you can

expect to score some classic surf with only a handful of other guys in a properly stunning locale. Boats leave Tamarindo at first light and return at dusk. It's not cheap though – you're looking at around $100 for a day trip.

Ten kilometres (six miles) south of Tamarindo is Playa Avellanes and its neighbour Playa Negra. If you're after the quiet life then this is a good place to stay...and you can be in the water before the Tamarindo dwellers have even finished their breakfast. Playa Avellanas has a rivermouth and a beach with plenty of quality peaks, while Playa Negra has a perfect righthand reef break.

When you're travelling around a new country, it's often the towns that you hear about first; your knowledge of the surrounding breaks then complete the picture once you've spent some time there. Nosara is a prime example of this – it's the next well-known town →

MIKE SEARLE

OPPOSITE ALAN STOKES COVERED IN COSTA.

WHEN TO GO: The prime months are May to September.
AIRPORT: San José (SJO). If you're flying from Europe, make sure that your stopover in the US is at least two hours so you have time to clear customs and make your connection.
ACCOMMODATION: CR Surf can help

you plan your trip anywhere in Costa Rica.
WATCH OUT FOR: Sunburn and the odd jellyfish.
BOARDS: It's all about hotdoggin' so pack accordingly...
RUBBER: You'll only need boardies.
AFTER DARK: Think 'a few quiet beers'

after a long day's surfing. There aren't too many places to party, but some towns have livelier bars and clubs.
ALTERNATIVE EXCITEMENT: Visit one of the National Parks; go zip-wiring; or just grab a beer and watch all the hotties on the beach.

down the coast from Tamarindo, and the destination
of choice for many CR veterans. More chilled out
than Tamarindo, there are just as many decent breaks
around but fewer surfers vying for a piece of the action.
Junquillal, Playa Marbella and Playa Pelada will keep
you plenty busy for starters.

Continuing south along the Nicoya Peninsula, Playa
Coyote is a long beach with fairly average waves but a
fun righthand point at its southern end.

The next gathering point for surfers is the area

around Santa
Teresa and Mal
Pais, a beachside
community which
sprawls along the
coast for several
kilometres.
(Technically,
it's situated in
neighbouring
Puntarenas
province, but
it completes
the stretch
of coastline already described so it makes sense to
include it here.) There are loads of groovy little haunts
here, from backpackers through to swish rental houses
with pools. The Funky Monkey and The Green Rooms
are both popular with surfers. Surfwise, there are
dozens of fun beach break spots straight out the front,
which keep the multitude of visitors happy. And if you
happen to be here when a bigger pulse of swell rolls
in, then you're in luck – there are several reefs close by
which can get pretty fruity. **– Roger Sharp**

EL SALVADOR

LA LIBERTAD TO LAS FLORES

TROPICAL RIGHT POINTS BY THE DOZEN

Directly translated from Spanish, El Salvador means 'the saviour.' And whether atheist or religious, you'll find salvation when you tuck into the mechanical right points here in the smallest country in Central America.

The south-facing coastline around the port town of La Libertad offers a handful of stellar setups. Just 30 minutes' drive from the international airport, La Libertad is home to El Salvador's best and busiest break, Punta Roca. On its day this is a world-class right point serving up fast-breaking barrels that spin along the shallow rock bottom. When it's on, a fierce local contingent vies with a pack of wave-hungry gringos for the best barrels. For

CHRIS STRALEY / A-FRAME

those who can't handle the steep take offs or the tricky paddle out at the point, the inside section (known as La Paz) offers a slower, mellower ride. La Libertad itself once had a reputation for being rather a sketchy town where thieves sometimes preyed on unwary surfers and tourists; however, the local police are apparently making efforts to step up patrols and stamp out robberies. Keep your wits about you and maintain a low profile.

To the west, about 20 minutes away by bus, El Tunco is a haven for backpackers, where the call of the beach bars can easily shift a well-intentioned dawn patrol back a few hours. Finding somewhere to stay here is easy, with a selection of cheap hotels and eateries right on the beachfront. At the northwest end of the beach, El Sunzal is a soft-breaking righthander with some fat cutback sections. Be sure to keep clear of the learner surfers on the inside.

Next to the rivermouth, La Bocana is a peaky beach break that can get hollow around low tide. It's one of the few quality lefthanders in El Salvador. The best section breaks right in front of a wall that has ONLY LOCALS painted on it in big white letters. It's written in English, not Spanish, just to be sure that everyone understands. Manners are essential out here; don't expect to snag the set waves. The local

kids shred and the older locals have the place wired. The atmosphere can get quite competitive when it's crowded, so it's best to take a backseat and hope for a lucky one. If the vibe gets too heated, sit down at the nearby bar, La Guitarra, have a cold Pilsener and watch the evening session go down.

Down in the southeast of the country there are yet more quality right points to be savoured. Las Flores is the best known of these, a classic sand-bottom point break that peels for up to 300 metres around a palm-fringed rocky headland. Racy at low tide, the waves get mellower and fatter at higher stages of the tide, although they're still fun for intermediates. Nearby Punta Mango is a fast, hollow righthander which peels down a boulder-strewn shoreline. Accessible by boat from Las Flores, it's a demanding spot for experienced surfers only.

There's plenty of accommodation in and around Las Flores and the beachfront has a mellower, less touristy vibe than El Tunco. As with any surf locale doing business the right way is to be encouraged as much as possible and the crew at Las Flores Surf Resort are all about sustainable development, offering class accommodation making a positive impact in the local economy with minimal environmental impact. There are other options of course for all budgets but being a good traveller means doing as little harm as possible. – **Brendon Bosworth**

OPPOSITE FEW TROPICAL DESTINATIONS HAVE SUCH A HIGH CONCENTRATION OF QUALITY RIGHTHAND POINTS AS EL SALVADOR. **LEFT** HAWAIIAN VISITOR DYLAN GOODALE GETS AIRBORNE.

WHEN TO GO: March to November.
AIRPORT: San Salvador International Airport (SAL).
ACCOMMODATION: Plenty of options of all budgets. Try Las Flores Resort right on the point for a classy experience.
WATCH OUT FOR: The spring high tide

at Las Flores – full tides murder this wave, especially when it's small.
BOARDS: Bring regular shortboards, maybe a fish for the smaller days.
RUBBER: You'll only need boardies.
AFTER DARK: Head to El Tunco at the weekends, where locals and foreigners mix it up on the dance

floors of the beach bars. Girls get free drinks on 'ladies nights'.
ALTERNATIVE EXCITEMENT: Close to La Libertad you can hire motorbikes and go riding through the forest. Or go on a canopy tour, way up in the tree tops, suspended by ropes.

ENGLAND

CORNWALL

The county of Cornwall occupies the far southwest of England, its north coast stretching for 90 miles (145 kilometres) as the crow flies from Land's End up to Bude. Back in the 18th and 19th centuries tin mining was the county's biggest industry, but gradually the abundant mineral-bearing seams were chipped out and depleted. Today, virtually the only reminders of this once great industry are the tall stone chimneys of the engine houses, scattered randomly across the undulating landscape of green patchwork fields.

Surfing in Cornwall began in earnest in the early '60s when Australian and American surfers arrived in the seaside town of Newquay, looking for summer lifeguard jobs. Today, surfing is big business in the town, with surf shops, surf schools and surf lodges everywhere you look. Fistral Beach, a five-minute walk from the town centre, is Newquay's best break. One of the most consistent spots in Cornwall, it picks up any west or northwest swell and works on all tides (although it's hollowest at low tide). Like the dozens of other west-facing beaches in Cornwall, Fistral is best on a clean, lined-up swell with southeasterly winds. Score a six-foot day with those kind of conditions and you'll be hooting – along with all the locals, who are a competitive but friendly bunch. Fistral has good facilities including shops, cafés and hot showers. You might want to avoid parking at North Fistral though, unless you possess the timekeeping of a Swiss watchmaker; stay one millisecond over the time limit and you'll be issued with an eye-wateringly hefty fine by the money-grabbing private company that operates the car park.

Just north of Newquay, Watergate and Constantine are two great beach breaks which can be super fun on a clean swell. Both spots tend to be best at higher stages of the tide.

South from Newquay, the coast road meanders this way and that (the Romans never made it this far) and you can take your pick from dozens of beach breaks which work on a variety of swell and wind conditions. Crantock, Holywell, Perran Sands, St Agnes, Porthtowan, Godrevy, Gwithian... all can be really good on

their day, it's just a matter of finding a good sandbank.

The landscape becomes hilly past the picturesque town of St Ives as the underlying geology changes from slate to granite. At Land's End, England's most westerly point, the full force of the Atlantic pounds the dramatic cliffs, to little avail. Nearby, Sennen Cove offers a long stretch of west-facing beach break where you'll find fun peaks on a clean swell, and plenty of space.

Cornwall's south coast provides surfers with a useful Plan B on a southwest swell with northerly winds. Praa Sands and Perranunthnoe offer fun shorebreak waves under such conditions, best from mid-tide to three-quarters up.

Last but definitely not least on this whistlestop tour of Cornwall is the county's premier reef, Porthleven. This short, righthand barrel breaks into the harbour entrance channel and it'll hold waves up to 12 feet. Frustratingly, it only gets classic a few times a year, and on those rare occasions the lineup will be hectic. Still, if you do manage to snag a set wave, the barrel will be big, green and spectacular. Porthleven works best around mid tide; low tide is stupidly shallow, and high is too backwashy.

You need a fair bit of patience to score really good waves in Cornwall. But if you are lucky enough to experience a week of decent offshore waves you'll understand how Cornwall has produced world class surfers of the calibre of Ben Skinner, Reubyn Ash and Ellie Turner. Yes, good things come to those who wait. And fortunately in this Land of Saints, patience is a common virtue. **– Chris Power**

ABOVE SEB SMART SOMEWHERE IN ST IVES BAY.
LEFT ALAN STOKES IS IN THIS BARREL, YES, IT'S SOLID.

SAM BREEZE

WHEN TO GO: September to October for beefy autumn swells.
AIRPORT: Fly from London's Gatwick airport (LGW), to Newquay (NQY).
ACCOMMODATION: Plenty of Air BnB options and the hotels are very reasonable outside of the summer months.

BOARDS: Bring a couple of shortboards, one with some volume.
RUBBER: Bring a 3/2 for the summer, a 4/3 for autumn.
WATCH OUT FOR: Summer flat spells and busy lineups.
AFTER DARK: In Newquay Tom Thumbs for craft beer and cocktails, the Stable

overlooking Fistral does fine pies, pizza and cider. You're never short of pubs in Cornwall. St Ives and Padstow have strong restaurant scenes.
ALTERNATIVE EXCITEMENT: Zip-wiring, coasteering, quad-biking, jet-skiing... there are tons of options if you want a shot of adrenaline.

FIJI

TAVARUA, NAMOTU AND BEYOND

A-GRADE WAVES FOR EVERYONE!

You might not know it, but in July 2010 the surfing world became bigger and better. This was the date that the Fijian government's new 'Regulation of Surfing Decree' allowed anyone to surf anywhere in Fijian waters. Prior to the decree, several of Fiji's best waves (including Cloudbreak, Restaurants and Namotu) could only be surfed by the guests staying at the respective resorts. This state of affairs had existed since the mid-'80s, after American Dave Clark had discovered Tavarua Island and its two world-class waves, Cloudbreak and Restaurants. Clark leased the tiny island off the local villagers and set up a luxury resort, a deal which gave him exclusive rights to the waves. The only way to surf the waves was to stay at the resort. As surfing in Fiji took off, neighbouring resorts set up similar exclusive zones to compete, meaning the quality of waves you could score ultimately came down to the amount of money you were prepared to spend.

The new decree changed all that. In a world where money talks, it was a rare win for ordinary surfers who just wanted to surf the best waves on the planet, and not have to sell their grandmother's left leg to do it. Mind you, a granny's limb might be a small price to pay for waves of this quality.

Cloudbreak is unquestionably one of the best lefts in the world. Breaking from four to 20 feet, it's a 500-yard freight train ride made up of long barrel sections interspersed by huge blue walls on which you can carve snowboard-like turns. There are three main sections: the point ('The Top'), the middle, and the inside ('Shishkebabs'). On a big clean swell all three sections will link up, but when that happens you'll probably spend most of your time at Middles while desperately trying to avoid getting shishkababbed. Recently, an outer ledge that stands up when it's 15 feet or more has become one of the 'new' big-wave paddle spots. An epic freesurf session took place here in June 2012, during the Volcom Fiji Pro, which featured some of the biggest, bluest and meanest tubes ever witnessed. Nathan Fletcher, Mark Healey, Reef McIntosh, Ian Walsh, Greg Long, Joel Parkinson, Damien Hobgood and John John Florence were among the names charging the 15-foot Cloudbreak mackers. "It was the single best day of big waves I think I've ever seen," frothed Hawaiian charger Ian Walsh. "It was like a video game."

When Cloudbreak is breaking at six feet, Restaurants will be just starting to show at two to three-feet. As a rule it's usually half the size of Cloudbreak, the reason being that it's tucked further inside the fringing reef, where it's situated right in front of Tavarua's restaurant. Kelly Slater describes this long, spiralling left as, "the most perfectly formed wave in the world", and he knows a thing or two about the subject. When it's good, Restaurants is so hollow and so perfect that it defies description. It's also super shallow (dangerously so at lower stages of the tide) and only suitable for advanced surfers. That these two waves exist so close to each other is one of the geographical miracles of the surfing world.

The neighbouring island of Namotu offers a range of great waves, which are not quite as demanding as those around Tavarua. On small to medium size swells, Namotu Left offers fun walls for carving; on bigger swells it gets chunky with some heavy barrels. Nearby, Swimming Pools is a fun, cruisy righthander; on a small to medium swell it's great for guys who like to ride fish or longboards. Finally, Wilkes Pass is a righthander opposite Namotu Island that, while somewhat shifty, throws up rippable walls and good barrel sections.

Tavarua and Namotu are part of the Mamanucas group of islands situated just west of Fiji's main island Viti Levu. Many more good spots can be found along the barrier reefs that fringe the south coast of Viti Levu, the best of these being Frigates, a bowly left situated about 12 kilometres (7 miles) offshore. Frigates can be ridden from four feet right up to 12 feet, when it becomes a serious spot for experts only. It's accessible by boat from resorts like Waidroka Bay on Viti Levu; alternatively there's a surf camp on the tiny island of Yanuca, closer to the waves.

To the southeast of Viti Levu are hundreds of smaller islands which have only recently been explored by surfers. These offer considerable potential for new discoveries, both in the winter and summer seasons.

Prior to July 2010, a trip to Fiji meant checking your bank balance, and then choosing between the resorts of Tavarua and Namotu. These days you can stay wherever you like, jump in a speedboat, and surf any wave that blows your hair back. Simply fix your budget, and pack boardshorts, suncream, fishing rods and a full quiver of boards. Then all there is to do is soak up the Fijian people's famous generosity of spirit and enjoy the surf trip of a lifetime. **– Ben Mondy**

RIGHT HARRY BRYANT AND CLOUDBREAK PERFECTION.

WHEN TO GO: April to October, the dry season, offers more consistent swell and offshore trade winds.
AIRPORT: Nadi International Airport (NAN).
ACCOMMODATION: Decide which waves you want to surf then choose between the numerous superb resorts in the area.
WATCH OUT FOR: Thick lips and heavy beatings on big days. Shallow reefs on small days.
BOARDS: Take a full quiver if you plan to tackle chunky Cloudbreak or Frigates.
RUBBER: It's boardshorts all year.

AFTER DARK: The resorts offer thunderous cocktails and shimmering pools, while the healthy backpacker scene keeps Fiji fresh and fruity.
ALTERNATIVE EXCITEMENT: Fishing, diving, snorkelling, sightseeing, Kava ceremonies, sailing... there's tons to see and do.

LANDES

ALL HAIL HOSSEGOR'S THUMPING BEACH BREAKS

The small town of Hossegor in southwest France is the centre of surfing in Europe, both geographically and commercially. The west-facing coastline of the surrounding Landes region offers some of the best beach break waves in the world, and it's produced many of the country's best surfers. Each year Hossegor hosts the Quiksilver Pro, an annual World Tour contest which is a favourite with pro surfers. There's something magical about the place. The endless beach break peaks, the pine forests, the bars and the relaxed continental vibe make this a classic place to visit, especially in the late summer and early autumn. Travelling surfers have been coming here for decades, many of them staying in vans or on campsites. Warm water, punchy waves, fresh baguettes and cheap wine... what's not to like?

If the swell is three to four feet and clean, the surfing possibilities here are endless. Some 240 kilometres (150 miles) of ever-changing beach breaks stretch from Bayonne all the way to Bordeaux. Known as the Côte d'Argent, this phenomenal stretch of sand is intersected only by a handful of rivers and estuaries. One of these doubles as the port of Capbreton, a haven for surfers and mariners alike. Just offshore from the narrow marina entrance, a deep-water ocean trench drops away into the Bay of Biscay. This trench is the reason why the waves here are world class. The full power of each Atlantic swell is focussed on this stretch of coast, targeting Labenne, Capbreton, Hossegor and Seignosse. The swell hits these beaches harder than anywhere else on the west coast of France so it's no surprise that the best surfers are attracted to this very same zone.

Since the late '80s Hossegor has also been the hub of the continent's thriving surf industry. The European headquarters of nearly all the major surf brands are located on the trading estates behind Hossegor and Capbreton. The surf media also congregate here to cover the contest scene. The focus is justified. Every year we see world-class conditions and performances at the Quiksilver Pro. Surf fans from across Europe – literally thousands of them – arrive by plane, train and van to enjoy the show. Hossegor is the surf town where something exciting always happens.

Even with all the hype, there's plenty of space to escape the mayhem and the summer crowds. The whole stretch of coastline is open to the same swell and conditions. Head further north and you may lose a foot in wave size, but the chance of finding an epic sandbank when you walk over the dunes remains just the same. Follow the coast road then hike along a sandy track through the pine forests – it's likely to be just you, your friends, and a small crew of locals looking for some peace and quiet.

Popular escapes away from the main scene include Vieux Boucau, Messanges, Moliets and St Girons. Each of these small towns is charming in its own way. All are nestled between the pine forests and the sand dunes, and they provide holiday destinations for folk who prefer things slightly off the beaten track. Saying that, summertime in these small resorts will still be quite hectic, though less so than in the bigger towns like Hossegor and Biarritz. July and August are the busiest months and accommodation prices can be exorbitant. Spring or autumn are a much better bet, for value and for waves.

Surfing here is all about the sandbanks. First you have to find a good one. They're usually marked by a crew sitting on the peak, but remember you can always find your own with a little adventurous spirit. Then you must learn the characteristics of your chosen bank; the way the rip pulls you up or down the coast, the way the tide affects the sections of the wave. Once you've got your spot figured out, hopefully the swell and wind will co-operate and you'll enjoy session after session. You just have to pray that the next big swell doesn't haul the →

RIGHT TOP MICAH LESTER CAPBRETON CAVERN.
RIGHT BOTTOM THIS IS WHY YOU NEED TO GO TO FRANCE.

sand away and trash your bank. Fear not though – if that happens, the same swell will create a new and even better bank somewhere else... you just have to find it! Even though there are no reef breaks here, the waves break and barrel with the same intensity. They just shift around a lot more, which I guess is why the promise of scoring the perfect wave here is so alluring.

You can end up driving around a lot searching for perfection, but in my opinion if you can't find good waves between the beaches of Labenne and Les Cazernes (just north of Seignosse), then there isn't a better wave anywhere on the French coast.

The heaviest waves in the area are La Graviere and La Nord, located just north of Plage Centrale, Hossegor's main beach. La Grav' offers bone-crunching barrels breaking right on the sand, while La Nord holds waves up to 12-foot plus. Add to them two other prime spots, VVF and La Piste (located just south of Capbreton), and you'll pretty much see where all the best action shots in France come from. These waves can be world class, and they also have the crowds to match. A selection of Europe's hottest grommets, best pro's and legendary veterans will always on the best peaks any time they're firing.

To watch the pro's in action at La Graviere or the tow surfers out at La Nord are great sights to behold, but the Landes coast offers something for everyone. If you find your own perfect peak somewhere with just you and your friends out, you'll soon fall in love with France. The fine wine, superb food and great nightlife will all just be a bonus! **– Gabe Davies**

ABOVE TOM CLOAREC, LA GRAVIERE .

WHEN TO GO: Late August to October.
AIRPORT: Biarritz (BIQ) or Bordeaux (BOD).
ACCOMMODATION: Apartments, villas, campsites, hotels take your pick. Wave Sisters offer surf and yoga courses and camps for women and girls. Boardingmania Surf Camp offer beachfront apartments and private lessons.
WATCH OUT FOR: Strong rips and heavy shorebreaks.
BOARDS: Take a couple of shortboards, plus a fish for summer fun or a semi-gun for late autumn juice.
RUBBER: Boardshorts in the summer; take a 3/2 for spring or late autumn.
AFTER DARK: The Centrale in Hossegor always has something going on.
ALTERNATIVE EXCITEMENT: The Pyrenees Mountains are incredible for hill walking, mountain biking and climbing and the River Dordogne is great for a bit of scenic kayaking.

waveSisters
SURFING & YOGA

ALL LEVELS

KIDS CLASSES

CHILD CARE

★ PORTUGAL ★ LANZAROTE ★ FRANCE

www.wavesisters.com   info@wavesisters.com   #wavesisters_surfcamps

FRANCE

BIARRITZ

The birthplace of surfing in France

The majestic city of Biarritz overlooks a series of spectacular beaches, small coves and picturesque rocky outcrops. It's the grandest surf city in Europe, and many would say the best. Watching the waves break from a beachside café after a day of warm-water surfing, you soon realise you're in an idyllic place.

Located beneath the Pyrenean mountains where the rolling Basque hills meet the coast, Biarritz has always been a city of grandeur.

Originally a summer escape for royals, the city may have faded a little from the days when Empress Eugenie (wife of Napoleon III) built her palace on the beach, but it still attracts the rich and famous. Ferraris and Porsches growl along the streets of the city centre, which are dotted with haute couture fashion shops. Surfing has played a big part in Biarritz's recent cultural revival and the city is proud of the fact. Alongside the popular sports of rugby and pelote, the annual surf events draw massive crowds and have a well-earned international reputation.

Biarritz has a very seasonal feel to it. High summer brings crowds, restricted surfing zones and long waits for tables in restaurants, while in the winter months it feels as if half the city has packed up and shipped out. Yet the city has enough character, attractions and waves for a visit at any time of the year. There's something for everyone here.

Surfing in Biarritz is split between three main beaches. **Cote des Basques (1)** is the most sheltered and mellowest of the town's breaks. It's a popular longboard spot and the best place for a surf lesson. It was here in 1957 that surfing was introduced to France by American screenwriter

GRANDE PLAGE

MASUREL / AQUASHOT

Peter Viertel, before being quickly adopted by the locals.

Grande Plage (2) is Biarritz's central beach, surrounded by all the glitz and glamour the city has to offer. It's busy, fun and a great

LEE-ANN CURREN DRIVES OFF THE BOTTOM AT GRANDE PLAGE.

LAURENT MASUREL / AQUASHOT

spot to watch from the promenade. It can offer decent waves, and the

rocky headlands provide shelter from crosshore winds.

The serious surfing around Biarritz takes place in **Anglet**, to the north of the lighthouse. The beaches here get more swell and the sandbanks are better too. A series of rock groins divide the beaches so you can often find a bit of space. Be aware that the standard in the water will be competitive. There are several surf shops and surf schools around **Chambre D'Amour (3)**. By far the best beach in the area is **Les Cavaliers (4)** at the north end of Anglet, which offers punchy, hollow waves breaking on coarse sand.

During the summer it's always best to surf early; when the weather is hot, onshore sea breezes often spring up by late morning.

Biarritz has no shortage of restaurants, bars and clubs. For *aperos* (early evening drinks) try **Les Cent Marches (5)**, a fantastic outdoor hangout above the winding footpath from Cote Des Basques; it serves tapas-style snacks and has a buzzing atmosphere. **Le Newquay (6)**, behind Grande Plage, is a busy bar with live music and Wi-Fi. For the best hot chocolate in town and a great escape on a stormy day, call in at **Miramont (7)**, a famous café and chocolate shop; it also has panoramic views of Grand Plage. The old port is a great place to grab a tasty seafood meal, while the **Hotel du Palais (8)** is worth a visit for afternoon tea to enjoy the decadent surroundings of one of France's grandest hotels.

LES CAVALIERS GETS HOLLOW.

If the surf's flat, the city offers many other attractions. **Le Musée de la Mer (9)**, overlooking to the old port, is a decent-sized aquarium with some decent-sized sharks. And just south of the city, at Ilbiarritz, is the futuristic **Cité de l'Océan et du Surf (10)**, a brand new multi-million-Euro arts complex with exhibition halls, a café and a surf museum. – **Gabe Davies**

LE MUSEE DE LA MER.

CITE DE L'OCEAN ET DU SURF.

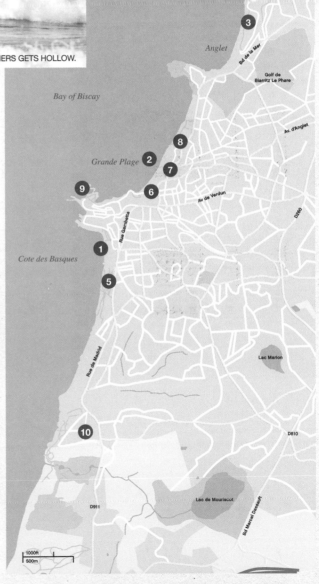

HAWAII

OAHU: THE NORTH SHORE

THE SEVEN MILE MIRACLE

There are no three words in the surfing lexicon that pack more punch than The North Shore. This is a stretch of coast that, if not the beating heart of surfing, is at least a main artery, pumping death and glory, myth and legend to the outer extremities of the surfing world.

First, the bare facts. The North Shore refers to the seven mile northwest-facing coast of the Hawaiian island of Oahu. Its assortment of reefs and consistent trade winds magically transform huge lumbering North Pacific winter swells into just about rideable waves. There's a whole assortment of waves on offer, from rippable peelers to widow-making death slab crunchers. The North Shore only breaks with any consistency from October to March, with the months of January and February often cited as the primo time to visit.

Of course, Hawaii's link with surfing is legendary –

it was born here as The Sport of Kings, first practiced by the Hawaiian chiefs, and then by the mere mortals who came under surfing's spell. Christian missionaries almost managed to wipe surfing from the islands in the 19th century, until the famous beach boys of Waikiki reintroduced the sport at the turn of the last century. One of them was Duke Kahanamoku, a gold medal Olympic swimmer, who was personally responsible for taking surfing to the wider world, introducing the sport to mainland USA and Australia. By the '50s, the North Shore's incredible waves had caught the eye of surfers from California, and by the '60s, surfers like Greg Noll, Buzzy Trent and Pat Curren were pushing the boundaries of big-wave surfing at spots like Waimea and Pipeline. Ever since then Hawaii has been known as the place to test yourself, a Mecca for all types of

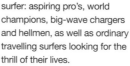

surfer: aspiring pro's, world champions, big-wave chargers and hellmen, as well as ordinary travelling surfers looking for the thrill of their lives.

And what a ridiculous number of thrills lie in wait along 'the seven mile miracle', between Haleiwa and Velzyland. Haleiwa (at the southwest end of the North Shore) is a pretty good place to start. A small yet bustling and historic town, it's home

to the world famous righthander of the same name, situated just next to the harbour. It starts breaking at three feet and will hold anything up to 15 feet; watch out for the shallow inside section. To the west is Avalanche, a hefty lefthander, while across the harbour is Puena Point, a rippable right. If you survive any, or all of these waves at 10 feet, there are plenty of bars and restaurants for a celebratory beer, or a thank-the-Lord coffee afterwards.

Heading northeast along the Kam Highway (the road which runs parallel to the North Shore) you come to the next cluster of spots: Laniakea, Jocko's and Marijuanas. These three spots tend to be criminally underrated, which has the benefit of reducing the crowds. They also tend to offer deep channels and a bit more water over the reef, resulting in, dare we say it, a fun option.

Trundle further along the Kam Highway, and the next break you come to is Waimea Bay. There's no need to write anything more about one of surfing's most legendary breaks, except to say that if you want to surf it, you'll need a 10-foot board and the balls and hide of a rhinoceros. If you lack those (like 99 percent of the population) you'll still find yourself drawn here when a massive swell hits, since the Bay provides one of the all-time spectator experiences.

Around the corner and past Foodland, the next mile or two of coast is known as the Pipe stretch. First up is Log Cabins, a demanding spot which throws up slabbing righthanders breaking over treacherous spikes →

OPPOSITE TOP: FREDDIE P, PIPE POISE.
OPPOSITE BOTTOM: WITH THIS AT THE BOTTOM OF HIS GARDEN IT'S NO SURPRISE THAT JAMIE O'BRIEN RULES PIPELINE.

WHEN TO GO: November to February.
AIRPORT: Honolulu (HNL).
ACCOMMODATION: Hotels are few and far between apart from the Turtle Bay Hilton. There are hostels or rooms to rent.
WATCH OUT FOR: Heavy waves, shallow reefs, localism at some of the prime

spots (especially Pipe), theft from unattended vehicles.
BOARDS: Bring a full quiver, or buy a couple of guns when you arrive.
RUBBER: You'll only need boardshorts, or maybe a short john for dawn patrols.
AFTER DARK: Not a lot goes on the

North Shore proper apart from the food vans, head to Haleiwa for bars and restaurants.
ALTERNATIVE EXCITEMENT: If it's rainy or onshore, a jaunt to Honolulu is your best bet.

of coral – sounds like fun, huh? A few hundred yards further is Rockpile, a left that breaks further out and often remains relatively uncrowded, probably because it only starts working at eight feet.

Next comes the most photographed 200 yards of beach in surfing. Off The Wall, Backdoor and Pipeline all lie within a stone's throw of each other, and break on slabs of shallow coral reef only yards from the shore. Off The Wall probably provides the best hope of a wave for the non-local or uneducated, being a shifty semi-closeout type of wave. It's often teeming with bodyboarders, however. Pipe and Backdoor are well documented as offering the heaviest barrels, and crowds, in the known universe. One wave out here though, and you'll be bragging about it in the pub for the rest of your life.

The Pipe stretch continues past yet more spots (Pupukea and Gas Chambers) to the small rocky headland of Rocky Point, where the much less intimidating Rocky Lefts and Rights have provided the North Shore's high-performance stage for decades.

Finally, our whistle-stop tour of the North Shore ends at Sunset, a wave with a takeoff zone as large as three football fields. Here, with the right board and the right commitment, you can take some epic drops, carve the biggest arcs imaginable, and try your luck charging the inside bowl section. Sunset should always be approached with respect, however. Even at a modest six- to eight-feet it's a heavy, unpredictable wave with the power to break boards like matchsticks; the hold-downs are often horrendous and if your leash snaps it's a long swim back to the beach.

The North Shore itself is a surprisingly low key place, being almost entirely residential, but it's steadily changing from small farms and beach houses to being a bit bling. It is still remarkably undeveloped compared to the rest of the island. In fact it's comforting that The North Shore is set up and designed for one thing and one thing only – surfing. And if you have a connection with the sport, on any level, there is no option – you simply have to go there. **– Ben Mondy**

RIGHT KELLY SLATER PULLING IN AT WAIMEA … AS YOU DO.

HONOLULU

South swell?
Head for town.

Honolulu sits on the south side of Oahu, nestled up against the flanks of an extinct volcanic crater. First settled in 1100AD, its name means 'sheltered harbour'. Its location led to it becoming an important shipping and whaling port in the 19th century, and it was proclaimed the capital of Hawaii by King Kamehameha III in 1850. When Hawaii became the 50th US state in 1959, Honolulu remained the capital. Today it has a population of more than 390,000.

Surfing has been part of Hawaiian culture for hundreds of years. British explorer Captain James Cook and his crew aboard HMS Discovery were the first Westerners to witness surfing in 1778. Wearing nothing but a few beads, Hawaiian men and women rode the waves on rudimentary surfboards carved from koa wood. But in the decades that followed, the Christian missionaries and settlers who arrived in Hawaii repressed surfing due to its nudity and perceived frivolity; work, not play, was the stern Calvinist philosophy, and surfing was 'against the laws of God'. At the start of the 20th century, however, Honolulu saw a resurgence in the popularity of surfing. In 1908 the Hawaiian Outrigger Canoe Club was formed at Waikiki Beach, joining the already established native Hui Nalu club, and beginning many friendly competitions. By 1911 surfing was in vogue once again, and over the following decades – helped by the legendary Duke Kahanamoku and 'hot dog' pioneer Rabbit Kekai – the stage was set for surfing in Hawaii to take off.

Today, the Waikiki breaks cruised by those pioneer surfers are enjoyed by hundreds of visitors any time there's a ripple of swell. **Queen's (1)** and **Canoes (2)** both offer mellow, fun waves for beginners and longboarders, and the former morphs into a decent right-hander on bigger swells. **Tonggs (3)**, and **Old Man's (4)** offer some fun lefts for intermediates. Boards can be hired on the beach and surf lessons are available for beginners. If you don't mind joining the throng of tourists, take a ride in an outrigger canoe, it's a good laugh.

Honolulu also offers a wide selection of breaks for experienced surfers and on a decent south

FLYNN NOVAK SLIDES AN ALA MOANA LIP.

PETE HODGSON / A-FRAME

MASUREL

MASUREL

MASUREL

swell – usually during the summer months – several reefs will really light up. World famous **Ala Moana (5)** is a barrelling left that rifles along the edge of the reef next to the Ala Wai Harbour entrance; don't expect to get too many waves here though, it's heavily localised and guaranteed to be rammed whenever it's on. If the waves are pumping a better option would be to head for one of the many other 'town' reefs: **Three's (6), Four's, Kaiser's (7), Flies, Kewalo's (8)**... the list goes on. This area is a swell magnet, and it's protected from the trades by the imposing headland of Diamond Head.

Surfing is big business in Honolulu, so naturally the city has many 'surfy' bars and clubs. In Waikiki, check out **Duke's (9)** (named after the great man himself), the **Mai Tai Bar (10)** at the Royal Hawaiian Hotel, and **RumFire (11)**, where you can sample more than 100 different rums from around the world. **Aloha Towers (12)** has several noisy, popular bars; but if you'd rather escape the tourists,

head for the **Harbor Pub (13)** at the Ala Wai Marina, or the **Fisherman's Wharf (14)**. The legendary Club Femme Nu on Kapiolani Boulevard offers guys a somewhat more, er, invigorating experience.

Honolulu has no shortage of great restaurants – you can tuck into top-notch steaks, pizzas and burgers in dozens of places, but there are also some standout traditional joints where you'll find proper Hawaiian dishes. Try Roy's Hawaii Kai if you're after some class, or Sam Choy's Breakfast Lunch & Crab for a casual bite.

Honolulu is steeped in a strong surfing tradition, and you should definitely check out the **Honolulu Surf Museum (15)** at 2300 Kalakaua Avenue; it has a huge collection of historical surf paraphernalia, including vintage boards, clothing, and even a gold ring worn by Captain Cook. Admission is free. **– Owen Pye**

ROGER SHARP

LAURENT MASUREL / AQUASHOT

HAWAII

MAUI

SPECTACULAR SCENERY, INCREDIBLE WAVES

Mention 'surfing in Hawaii' and most people's minds will immediately cut to mental images of giant bombs at Pipe and the famous North Shore. But, of course, Oahu isn't the only Hawaiian island with gobsmackingly incredible waves. Despite its location in the middle of the chain (and thus suffering significant swell shadows), Maui boasts some of the islands' finest waves. Some of these are genuinely unparalleled, such as the speedline rights of Maalaea and the humongous peaks of Jaws.

Most of the action on the Valley Isle takes place during the winter months (November to March), when chunky swells generated by distant Aleutian lows light up the breaks on the island's north shore. During the summer months, northeast trade winds blow persistently, making the south and west coasts offshore and setting the scene perfectly for any pulse of

CHRIS POWER

southwest swell that makes it up from New Zealand.

Tucked away on the south shore is a spot that makes a strong claim to be the fastest right in the world – Maalaea. This beast only raises its head once in a blue moon, but when it does, you'll be hard pushed to find a wave which breaks as quickly. It's not so much a freight train, more of a bullet train. It needs a huge southwest swell to really turn on, and it only breaks a handful of times a year, if that. When it does though, you're in for the ride of your life; after negotiating the steep drop you merely have to drive down the line as fast as you possibly can. Many drop into the deep barrels at Maalaea, but few make it out.

Summer swells also get a string of other spots on the southwest coast firing, all of which are guaranteed to be groomed clean by the offshore trades. Lahaina Breakwall is the best of these, a quality left which peels off down a shallow coral reef. Watch out for urchins.

As the coast road takes you around the northwest tip of the island you arrive at another of Maui's jewels, Honolua Bay. This classic righthand point is best on a booming north swell, with southeast winds to keep it clean. On those rare days, the different sections link up to provide warping barrels and huge walls just begging to be carved. Beware of the rocks on the inside, and the frothing crowds that descend on the place when the swell lines stack up from the north.

Kahului Harbour is a shallow slab situated just west of the harbour entrance in Kahului, the island's economic capital. Here hot local surfers and hordes

of bodyboarders vie for the pick of the fast sucky lefts and rights. This spot needs a big northeast swell to get going but can be good when it's on. Beware of crowds and polluted water (due to the close proximity of the harbour).

Further east along Maui's north shore you'll find some good but wind-sensitive spots around Paia Bay, Kahana and Hookipa. This area is usually the domain of windsurfers, but there are a number of breaks which can provide good waves early in the morning before the trades start to howl.

If you happen to time your visit with the arrival of a truly massive north swell, you could be in for a treat. Drive past Hookipa to Peahi, listen for the sound of thunder, and keep going to the end of the road... you will have just found Jaws, home to the biggest waves ever surfed. Unless your surname is Hamilton or Dorian you probably won't be out in the lineup; instead you'll be staring intently at the distant figures skipping down the faces of the 50-foot monsters out to sea, which unload like avalanches, shaking the clifftops. Enjoy the show. **– Owen Pye**

OPPOSITE: KAI BARGER , NICE 'N CASUAL AT HONOLUA BAY.

WHEN TO GO: November to March.
AIRPORT: Kahului (OGG).
ACCOMMODATION: Take your pick from backpacker hostels, apartments, condos and plush hotels.
WATCH OUT FOR: Heavy waves, shallow reefs, localism at some of the prime spots, theft from vehicles.

BOARDS: Bring a full quiver if you're coming in wintertime.
RUBBER: Boardshorts are fine most of the time but you might want a short john for dawn patrols or breezy days.
AFTER DARK: Kihei (on Maui's southwest shore) has loads of bars, it's ideal for a pub crawl. While you're

there, try Sansei Seafood for some excellent sushi.
ALTERNATIVE EXCITEMENT: Go outrigger canoeing at Kanaha Beach. Or drive up to the 10,023ft summit of Haleakala, Maui's huge dormant volcano (wear warm clothing – it's freezing up there!).

ICELAND

THE ICEBERG COAST

Iceland has become a darling of the surfing world; with the growth in pushing the cold frontiers of surfing further and further, this volcanic island has become the photo studio for brands, adventurers, left field pros and filmmakers alike.

It's position in the north Atlantic makes for consistent swell year round on every coast, but that same position puts it in line for some of the most vicious and changeable weather on the planet. So the swell may be relentless, but conditions can change quickly; perfect offshores can turn into storm force onshores can turn in minutes, so you have to make the most of what's in front you at all times. Likewise, being in the middle of the Atlantic, swells often sweep past, so they literally brush along the island as oppose to hitting it full on, so peaks in swell can last for just hours. It makes

it a frustrating place, but Iceland is about so much more than just the surf; the fact that the culture and environment are so spectacular, means that when the waves are rubbish, there are a million other things to do.

Roughly speaking Iceland has five areas to surf. As you descend from the clouds into Keflavik international airport, you get a bird's eye view of the main one, The Reykjanes Peninsula. This is home to consistent beach breaks at Sandvik, as well as heavy slabs at Grindavik and Iceland's most ridden wave Thorli at the the harbour town of Porláckshöfn.

Sandvik is where a lot of Icelanders learn to surf, and with the south coast warmed by the Gulf Stream, it is not as cold in the water as you may expect, which is more than can be said for the air temperature. The beach occasionally gets good, but on the whole is a

fun back up-break. Grindavik is home to Iceland's most ridden slab – out beyond the fishing harbour is a wave that catches every drop of swell, but it is fickle and shifty. When it's on it offers a long right barrel, when it is less than perfect a frustrating close out. Porláckshöfn has a great beach for learning on and a cobblestone reef that collects all swell, and is the most rippable wave in Iceland, but mellow enough to allow intermediate surfers to get in the water. The peninsula has other waves, but they are inconsistent, hard to get to and generally break over brutal lava reefs.

The south coast is all beaches, punctuated by rare ridges of rock like at the southern town of Vik. Here there is a fun beach break, and in the summer you'll share the lineup with puffins, and a myriad of other sea life. The banks change year on year, and it can get pretty hollow and have a wave when the rest of the coast is flat. A couple of hours further east is the glacial river mouth at Jökulsárlón – it's that spot where you see the icebergs on the beach. The waves are actually rarely good, and getting hit by ice whilst surfing is actually rather painful.

The east coast is a series of fjords, beaches and skerries blocking swell. It is probably the least explored stretch of Icelandic coastline due to it's distance from the capital Reykjavik and the fact it gets least swell. It does however hide a few gems, and it's always worth a closer look from the ring road around the island.

The north coast is full of waves, and the likelihood is that most of the good sessions you've seen on surf

RIGHT TOP IAN BATTRICK HAS SPENT MORE TIME THAN MOST EXPLORING THE COLD CORNERS.
RIGHT BOTTOM EXPLORING THE SOUTH COAST YOU'LL FIND SPOTS LIKE THIS.

WHEN TO GO: Any time of year if there's swell. Winter is obviously very hardcore with minus temps and blizzards.
AIRPORT: Reykjavík-Keflavík (KEF).
ACCOMMODATION: Hotels and hostels around Reykjavík, cabins and hostels further out in the sticks.

WATCH OUT FOR: Icebergs, hypothermia, snow and ice while driving, volcanoes.
BOARDS: A bit more girth to cope with the rubber. Never gets massive surf wise.
RUBBER: 6mm and all the accessories.
AFTER DARK: Expensive bar hopping

in Reykjavík, outside of towns try staring at the Northern Lights.
ALTERNATIVE EXCITEMENT: Hot pools, waterfalls, glaciers, pretending you're in an episode of Top Gear. Iceland is a stunning place to explore.

movies like Sipping Jetstreams and Under an Arctic Sky originate from here. It's actually quite tricky to predict swell up here as many forecasts chart simply fails to show the intensity of low pressure systems coming off Greenland to the north. Most spots up here are kept pretty quiet, but the coast road offers vistas over lineups which are almost always empty. It's a great place to strike out and search, and you may just find something a little special over a cliff or behind a harbour wall. One thing to mention up here though, the water is about six to as much as ten degrees colder than the south coast, so you'll need some serious rubber as the Gulf Stream fails to reach this coast.

The final frontier in Iceland is the Westfjords. While fairly easy to access thanks to Iceland's incredible road system, it is insanely fickle, but there are setups in the most incredible places.

An Icelandic surf trip is about so much more than waves though, if you come here expecting to surf perfect empty waves you'll be disappointed. But if you come wanting an adventure, in an otherworldly lineup, and don't mind putting some kilometres on your rental vehicle, you'll be rewarded in both memories and waves. **– Tim Nunn**

RIGHT EMPTY POINTBREAKS LIKE THIS TAKE A LOT OF DRIVING TO FIND…

INDIA

LAKSHADWEEP ISLANDS

INDIA'S HIDDEN TREASURE

The Lakshadweep Islands are situated 250 miles (400 kilometres) off the southwest coast of mainland India, and are part of the same undersea mountain range as the Maldives. Celebrated as India's only coral atoll islands, it's easy to see why they're such a popular underground tourist destination for Indians and in-the-know foreigners. The islands themselves are some of the most exotic and beautiful you'll ever see, with flawless white beaches, swaying palm trees and giant turtles wallowing just a few yards offshore. Being so far north in the Indian Ocean, you might not think there'd be quality surf here. But there most definitely is.

The Lakshadweeps have yet to be fully explored by surfers and many new discoveries are sure to be found. The best wave discovered so far is Rasta's, a hollow right-hander which hold waves up to six feet. It's named after Dave Rastovich, who stumbled across it with filmmaker Taylor Steele when they were bumping around India filming *Castles in the Sky* some years back. The set-up is pretty surreal, with a giant pier smack bang in the middle of the reef. The local elders tried in vain to prevent the pier being built and it has never seen a ship dock; it's simply too short and too close to the waves to be safe. Fortunately it doesn't spoil the machine-like right which peels down the point and over the reef. In fact the pier may have actually even improved the wave, as the swell has to squeeze itself through the piles as a set approaches, creating a wedging effect, which actually makes the

peak hollower on takeoff. On its day Rasta's can be every inch as hollow and ruler-edged as HT's in the Mentawais. The takeoff is steep and the only option is to pull in. Then, depending on the tide, you either get seriously shacked or you pop out onto a high-speed, rippable shoulder. South African surfer Craig Anderson scored flawless waves at Rasta's on a recent trip to the islands. "The set-up there is really good. Although we only got it four-foot, it was similar in power and style to Backdoor."

Aside from the surf, the vibe on the islands is something else. If ever there was a blueprint for a peaceful existence, it would be something like life on the Lakshadweeps. The people exude warmth and welcome visitors into their homes and places of work. Many of the local guys are fishermen; Lakshadweep seamen are famous throughout India for their skills and knowledge of the ocean. The women dress in bright saris, and can often be seen carrying trays of food on their heads.

Even on the larger islands, which have populations of several thousand, there are only two or three policeman, who apparently have very little to do besides processing the odd tourist visa. Crime, it seems, is of little concern to people here.

Although the Lakshadweep Islands are an expensive destination and you'll need to book your accommodation well in advance (as part of a 'sports' package tour), you won't ever forget your trip here if you score perfect empty waves. **– Alan van Gysen**

ABOVE: CALIFORNIAN TREVOR GORDON RACES A LOW-TIDE BARREL AT RASTA'S.

WHEN TO GO: April or May.

AIRPORT: Cochin (COK).

ACCOMMODATION: You'll need to book a 'Sports' accommodation package, well in advance (this is the only type of accommodation available for tourists).

WATCH OUT FOR: The reefs are shallow and coral is sharp. Also be prepared for intense airport and travel security. Alcohol consumption is prohibited on some islands.

BOARDS: Take a couple of standard shortboards and a step-up that goes in four- to six-foot barrels.

RUBBER: You'll only need boardies.

AFTER DARK: The locals serve the best food. The seafood is delicious, spicy and coconut flavoured.

ALTERNATIVE EXCITEMENT: Snorkel with giant turtles, play beach cricket with local teenagers, ride around the island on motorcycles, experience the people and culture.

INDONESIA

NIAS AND NEIGHBOURING ISLANDS

INCREDIBLE WAVES FOR THOSE WILLING TO GO THE DISTANCE

It takes a pretty special wave for its very name to become a synonym for perfection. Lagundri Bay, on the island of Nias, is one such wave. The setup is stunning – a large bay backed by coconut palms, with perfect, emerald-green righthand tubes peeling off the southern point. Add the keyhole, a narrow channel that enables dry-haired access, and you see why the very word Nias is held up as a benchmark for what a single wave can do to your soul.

First surfed in 1975 by travelling Australian surfers Kevin Lovett, John Geisel and Peter Troy, it didn't take long for word to spread about this incredible wave. When jaw-dropping images began appearing in surf magazines, Lagundri Bay and the village of Soraoke became a must-do pilgrimage for any hardcore surfer. Its location on the southern tip of the island of Nias,

itself 100 kilometres (60 miles) from the Sumatran mainland, meant there were no easy smash-and-grab trips to Lagundri. It was, and still is, an arduous mission to travel there. As a result, surfers tended to come for the long haul, staying with local families for months while waiting for the solid swells needed to light up a wave that was often called 'the best seven seconds in surfing'.

In 2005 a massive earthquake shook the region, causing widespread destruction and loss of life. Thankfully, aid flooded in and the resolute locals have been able to rebuild their villages and their lives as best they can. The earthquake also affected the area's waves, as the reefs were raised violently upwards, some by more than a metre. Lagundri Bay, by some miracle, was one of the few waves that actually improved. Pre-earthquake, the wave needed a solid six-foot swell to break and the barrels were perfect but almond shaped. Post-quake, it started breaking and barrelling at three feet... and on solid swells it turned into a throaty beast that had few rivals (in terms of hollowness) in all of Indo. Jamie O'Brien scored two 10-foot swells here in 2010 and 2011, and the epic footage from those sessions were among the highlights of

his subsequent movie *Who Is JOB?* That footage put Nias firmly back where it had been in the late '70s – one of the world's most iconic locations with one of the world's best waves.

Unfortunately, other waves in the area didn't fare so well. A quality left across the bay called The Machine (a saviour for goofyfoots) disappeared, while the previously challenging Indicators became pretty much impossible. However, Rockstars – a hotdog right, about 25 kilometres up the coast – remains a fun respite from the grinding barrels and crowds of Lagundri.

Elsewhere, in the nearby Hinako Islands, two previously world-class spots, Asu and Bawa, were detrimentally affected by the quake. Bawa, formerly the best big-wave spot in Indo, was made famous in the early '90s when Tom Curren tackled it at 10 to 12 feet on a 5'6" fish; these days it's nowhere near as good as it used to be, a sad loss. Asu, a long lefthand barrel, still has quality, but those who surfed its famous Napalm section pre-2005 say it's a shadow of its former self.

To the north of Nias, the Banyak Islands offer quality without the crowds. The Bay of Plenty, on the island off Tuangku, features a mirror image left and right at the bay's extremities, with a smaller left deeper in the bay. However it is the island of Bangkaru, and its mythical Treasure Island, that drags intrepid surfers this far north. This righthand reef can run for 500 metres, with several hollow sections and a relatively forgiving reef. Get this on, and all the hard yards travelled will be forgotten. **– Ben Mondy**

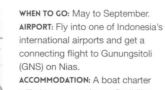

WHEN TO GO: May to September.
AIRPORT: Fly into one of Indonesia's international airports and get a connecting flight to Gunungsitoli (GNS) on Nias.
ACCOMMODATION: A boat charter will give you maximum flexibility. Alternatively, stay in a losman at

Soraoke village in Lagundri Bay, or at one of the land camps in the Hinako or Banyak Islands.
WATCH OUT FOR: Powerful waves, sharp coral, malaria, earthquakes... Nias is no easy option.
BOARDS: Bring a couple of short boards, a semi-gun, and maybe a

step-up and a gun.
RUBBER: Boardshorts.
AFTER DARK: Read a book, drink a beer and save your energy for the next morning's epic barrels.
ALTERNATIVE EXCITEMENT: Visit the ancestral king's house at Bawomataluo.

INDONESIA

MENTAWAI ISLANDS

PERFECTION, AT A PRICE

CLASSIC WAVES AT LANCE'S LEFT.

There is simply no place on the planet that boasts the consistency, variety and perfection of the Mentawai Islands. From grinding barrels to playful peelers, 'the Ments' offer more than 50 recognised spots (many of them world class), and heaps more yet to be discovered.

"When we first found this place it was like heaven," recalls Australian Matt Cruden, whose boat the Mangalui has been scouring these the waters since the early '90s. "Back then, we'd actually be stoked when we saw another boat, just so we could have a beer and boast about the waves we'd been getting."

Twenty years down the track, seeing another boat doesn't quite elicit the same reaction (especially when it's carrying 15 Brazilian pro's), but in recent years numerous land camps have sprung up, offering an alternative to the boat charter option.

Starting in the northern archipelago, the area known as Playgrounds offers around 20 world-class waves, all within a three-hour sail of each other. The pick of the bunch are the perfect but ultra heavy lefts of Kandui and the turbo rights of Rifles, which wrap around the opposite sides of Karangmadjat, a beautiful palm-covered island. On their day these two breaks offer some of the longest, heaviest, most perfect waves in the world. The shallow reefs (and especially their end sections) must be respected, doubly so considering how far you are from any type of proper medical care. Elsewhere in this area, waves such as Burger World, E-Bay, Pitstops and Bank Vaults offer much more

playful versions of perfection.

A number of land camps have now set up in the Playgrounds area, which means crowds are pretty much a given, boat or no boats. However, the sheer number and quality of the waves still make this a true surfing paradise.

Heading south from Playgrounds, you reach a cluster of lefthanders at the northern end of Sipora Island, the largest in the Mentawai archipelago. Telescopes is a world-class left which can peel for 200 metres; while it offers some great barrels, it's more user-friendly and predictable than many of the other waves in the Mentawais. Nearby are two other consistently good lefts, Iceland and Scarecrows, which are both swell magnets. This is a less travelled and often happy hunting ground, as many surfers will be drawn to the more famous waves further south...

At the the southern tip of Sipora you'll find Lance's Right, also known as HTs (Hollow Trees), perhaps the most recognised wave in all the Mentawais. Its greeny-blue, perfect righthand barrels have featured in countless magazines and surf vids for well over a decade, and for good reason. An easy A-frame takeoff gives way to a 100-yard stretch of reef that produces cartoon-like perfect barrels. As Indies Trader captain Martin Daly once commented; "If you can't get barrelled at HTs, you can't get barrelled anywhere."

Continuing south you reach Pagai Utara and Pagai Selatan islands. Among the multitude of breaks in this southern part of the chain, Macaronis stands out as

ANDREW SHIELD

the wave with the greatest all-round appeal, being one of the most rippable and perfect waves in the world. Drawing off a shallow ledge and then spinning down the reef, it's a wave that offers real power and real performance. It also handles a slight onshore better than any other wave, anywhere. Not far from here is a more recent discovery named Greenbush. This is a ferocious left designed for pro's, hellmen and protective outerwear.

That just leaves Thunders (a long left that sucks in all available swell and handles real size), Roxy's (a whackable right), Nago Left and Nago Right (gnarly, mirror-image barrels), and about 50 other waves that you'd protect with your life if they were at the end of your street.

It's now more than 20 years since the Mentawai Islands were discovered by surfers, and despite all the media attention and the number of boats operating in the area, no other part of the surfing world can rival this chain in terms of quality and consistency. The land camp and charter boat options are definitely not cheap, but with access getting quicker and easier, and new waves being found all the time, very few surfers come back from this part of the world wishing they'd saved their money. **– Ben Mondy**

SHARPY

LEFT THIS IS WHY WE GO TO INDONESIA.

WHEN TO GO: May to September.
AIRPORT: Fly to Kuala Lumpur, Singapore or Jakarta, get a connecting flight to Padang (PDG), then hop on a boat.
ACCOMMODATION: Most charter boats do 10-day trips. Boats vary from 'economy' standard to 'super deluxe', with prices to match. Do a 10-day boat charter leaving from Padang or land camps like Bilou Beach Villas are the more comfortable option.
BOARDS: A good quiver is essential.
AFTER DARK: If you're on a boat, it's all about mates and beers and talking story. If you're on land, it's not much different, just with a pool table.
RUBBER: Boardies.
WATCH OUT FOR: Mossies, sharp and shallow reefs.
ALTERNATIVE EXCITEMENT: Visit a couple of the local villages, or go trekking.

INDONESIA

SUMATRA: KRUI AREA

INDO PERFECTION FOR LANDLUBBERS

Sumatra is the largest island in Indonesia, its vast elongated landmass stretching for some 1,800 kilometres (1,100 miles). The island is a zoologist's paradise and its extensive rainforest is home to numerous endangered species including tigers, elephants, orang-utans and rhinos. Sumatra is a dream destination for geologists too, with no less than 35 active volcanoes, one of which blew its top as recently as 2010. Oh, and it's also one of the most wave-rich environments on earth!

The small fishing town of Krui is situated towards the southeast end of the island. The ocean floor drops away steeply along this stretch of coast so the area receives the full brunt of south and southwest swells marching up from the Roaring Forties. Sumatra straddles the equator, and consequently the climate is hot and humid all year round, with water temperatures ranging from 26-29°C (80-83°F). So we're talking boardies, rash vests and lots of sunscreen.

ALEX WILLIAMS

The Krui area has been referred to as the poor man's Mentawais, a cheaper land-based option for those who can't afford a $2,500 boat charter around the islands. But the area is now becoming popular for other reasons, namely that it has a great selection of breaks and way fewer crowds. On the downside, the long journey can put some people off. You usually have to stay overnight in Jakarta, then take an early morning flight to Bandar Lampung, where you'll clamber into the back of a Jeep to begin a six-hour drive through the mountains. But it all becomes worthwhile when you reach the coast – the place just oozes excitement and adventure, with water buffalo on the beach and dense jungle just metres from the shore.

The collection of high quality waves in the area start with the easiest to find, Krui Left, which is situated straight out in front of the town of Krui. It needs a big swell to work, but when it does it offers a lefthander similar to Bingin on Bali. There's also a super-shreddable right just a stone's throw away.

Just around the headland, in front of the Secret Sumatra camp, is an A-frame reef called The Peak which offers short, super-hollow lefts and rights. It's one of the funnest waves you'll ever surf; it's almost impossible not to get barrelled here.

Continuing south, the next spot along the coast road is Mandiri, a super-fun beach break which never seems to go flat. Punchy and hollow, Mandiri has to be right up there as one of the best beachies in the world.

A few kilometres further south you reach a pair of outstanding lefthanders. Ujung Bocor is a long left point which offers fun waves on small to medium swells, and some decent barrels on bigger swells. Just around the next bay, Way Jambu (the 'Sumatran Pipeline') is a much more serious prospect, for experts only. The swell needs to be perfectly lined up in order for the sections to link up, but when it's on Way Jambu can provide some mind-boggling barrels. It's best on the push from mid tide up – even then, beware of the numerous shallow sections. If everything comes together, you may just get the barrel of your life here.

North of Krui there are yet more breaks, of all types and orientations. Honey Smacks is a lefthand slab which offers an intense drop and a quick barrel at low stages of the tide, thus making it popular with bodyboarders. On the right swell, the first section looks a bit like small Pipe. It fills up with the tide and then offers a nice drop, a barrel section and some fun walls.

Further north is Jimmy's Reef, a great option when the wind is sideshore or onshore at Krui. There's a long left and a short right, both of which serve up some great barrels.

The Krui area is just one short stretch of the perfectly orientated coastline of southern Sumatra. Surfers with the time and inclination to investigate other stretches of the coast will doubtless discover many more epic breaks. **– Rob Barber**

OPPOSITE BRIT TRAVELLER MITCH CORBETT GETS HIS FILL AT JIMMY'S RIGHT.

WHEN TO GO: June to September.
AIRPORT: Fly into Jakarta (JAK), then get an internal flight to Bandar Lampung (TKG).
ACCOMMODATION: There are some good surf camps in the area, but if you're on a tight budget cheaper local losmens are also available.

WATCH OUT FOR: The jungle creatures are worth avoiding (mosquitos, spiders, scorpions, and so on). Also, be aware of the risk of earthquakes and tsunamis.
BOARDS: Bring a good selection of boards – a couple of shortboards for the smaller days, a semi-gun for the

good days when the reefs get big.
RUBBER: Boardies.
AFTER DARK: Play cards or just relax after another eight-hour surfing day.
ALTERNATIVE EXCITEMENT: Snorkelling, fishing, spear-fishing, hiking...you won't be bored.

INDONESIA

JAVA: GRAJAGAN

WELCOME TO THE JUNGLE

There is perhaps no purer surfing experience than two weeks in G-Land. This is surfing stripped back to its elemental basics. A kilometre of precisely angled coral reef sweeps the consistent Indian Ocean swells into a variety of perfect waves, ranging from open-face peelers to roaring tubes. Nowhere in Indo picks up more swell, and from June to September a perfect offshore kicks in mid-morning, every morning, providing a basic rhythm to the daily existence.

For accommodation there's a choice of three surf camps nestled between the shore and the dense impenetrable jungle. There are no bars, restaurants, nightclubs or shops to provide any distraction from the natural arts of surfing, eating and sleeping. Basically this is the most primitive, unique and goddamn near perfect surf experience that exists anywhere on the planet.

The actual wave is located on the eastern side of the Bay of Grajagan, on the very eastern tip of Java. Indian Ocean swells travel unmolested from the Roaring Forties and then refract around the 1,500-metre fringing reef; waves spiral through several different sections, the last of which – Speedies – is one of the best tubes on the planet.

It was Grajagan's geographical prominence that first led to its discovery back in 1972. While on a flight to Bali, American Bob Laverty spotted the reeling lefts from his airplane window, thousands of feet below. Instantly recognising the potential, he made a vow to find this incredible-looking place. With the aid of his good friend Bill Boyum and a couple of 70cc

motorbikes, he did just that, scoring an epic three-day swell. Bill and his brother Mike became regular visitors to G-Land, and Mike later set up a primitive camp there. Among its first guests were two of the best surfers in the world at the time, Gerry Lopez and Terry Fitzgerald. "Those first trips to G-Land were absolutely incredible," remembers Terry. "We'd arrive with just enough rice and water to last five days. We'd surf our brains out and then just pray that the boat would return before our food and water ran out. We'd be sunburnt and starving, but it didn't matter because we had this amazing wave all to ourselves."

Mike Boyum's original camp of tents and rickety huts was taken over by Balinese entrepreneur Bobby Radiasa in the late '70s, and over the course of a few years he built it up to become the world's first proper surf camp. His camp, Bobby's, is still operating to this day. Of course these days the chances of having the waves to yourself are fairly limited – with another two camps just along the bay, the average number of guests at G-Land is around 40-60 people. However, with such a huge area of reef, a variety of different sections, and plenty of hours in the day, the crowds are manageable. If you really want it, you will find a wave that will stay in your memory forever at G-Land.

G-Land has four main sections. Kongs, the furthest break out, gets the most swell but it can be pretty shifty and disorganised; it's good fun on a small, clean south swell, however, offering some rippable walls. Money Trees is the most consistent and longest section of the

reef, where the majority of G-Land sessions go down. If you're good, you can ride perfect peeling barrels here for 200 metres or more. On big swells the corduroy lines wrapping down the reef will peak up once again at Launching Pads, and suddenly you're into Speedies, the fastest, hollowest, and shallowest section of the reef. Ridiculously long tubes are the reward for those with the skill and nerve to take on Speedies at its best.

Further inside the bay there are a few less hectic waves including Tiger Tracks, a fun righthander which serves up some rippable walls around high tide. Getting there involves a sweaty, hour-long walk, however.

These days travelling to G-Land is an altogether easier proposition than it used to be, back in the day. You can still do the traditional all-night white knuckle bemo ride (and ferry crossing) from Bali, but now a two-hour speedboat ride from Bali is available for those with a bit more cash and a determination not to die in a horrible road accident. Or, if you really want to travel in style, follow Kelly Slater and Shane Dorian's example and drop into a 10-foot swell via helicopter. –
Ben Mondy

STU NORTON

OPPOSITE SPEEDIES WILL TEST YOUR TUBE-RIDING SKILLS TO THE LIMIT. **RIGHT** TRADITIONAL BOATS IN GRAJAGAN VILLAGE.

WHEN TO GO: June to September.
AIRPORT: Fly into Denpasar (DPS), then get a speedboat across to G-Land (a bumpy two-hour ride).
ACCOMMODATION: Bobby's G-Land Camp is probably the best.
WATCH OUT FOR: Packs of Brazilians, rogue sets and the generator turning

off at 10pm.
BOARDS: Take at least three: a shortboard and two semi-guns, ideally pintails.
RUBBER: Boardshorts are all you'll need.
AFTER DARK: The camp kitchen, DVD screen and pool table is the sum

of all the after dark excitement in G-Land.
ALTERNATIVE EXCITEMENT: Jungle treks, fishing, books, backgammon and beers will get you through a rare flat spell.

INDONESIA

BALI

THE GATEWAY TO INDO

Bali is internationally revered as the home of the perfect warm-water barrel. Distant storms in the Roaring Forties provide an almost non-stop supply of swell from April through to October, which quietly travel for thousands of miles before striking the pristine reefs around the coast of the island. These two elements, combined with consistent offshores during the dry season, produce some of the finest waves on the planet.

Bali has naturally become a popular destination for travelling surfers and at times it can get pretty hectic in the water, but with a little adventurous spirit uncrowded perfection is still very much attainable. Some of the better known breaks that advanced surfers will want to experience include Uluwatu, Padang Padang, Bingin, Canguu, Nusa Dua and Keramas. For intermediate level surfers there are several more forgiving breaks, among

them Balangan (on a small swell), Dreamland and Kuta Beach.

Bali is the gateway to Indonesia for scores of travelling surfers, and many pro's also base themselves here as it's a prime place to score sick action shots for the magazines. As a result it's become the surfing hub of this part of the world.

Kuta – Bali's party town – is a fun place to hang out for a while, but be sure to escape before it sucks all your money away. And unless you step out of the craziness you won't experience the real Bali, which is culturally quite different from Indonesia's other islands, being home to the vast majority of the nation's Hindu population.

Bali's nightlife is the mainstay of its economy, and since the awful terror attack in 2002 it has recovered well. There are now more bars, clubs and ladyboys than ever to tickle your fancy!

Indonesia is generally cheap but western style prices are on the rise in Bali as it loses its charm to badly thought out development.

The Balinese swell magnet of Uluwatu sits at the western tip of the oval-shaped Bukit Peninsula, south of Kuta. It works on very small swells all the way up to 12-foot-plus and consists of a series of lefthand peaks spread out along the reef. The furthest out is Temples, which has a greater

susceptibility to the wind but tends to be less crowded due to the length of the paddle to reach it. Then there's The Bommie, a chunky section out the back that can (on a big swell) link through to the next section, The Peak, which breaks in front of the cave; this gets very hollow and very crowded. Finally, the inside section is Racetracks, which offers dredging pits over a very shallow reef. Access to Ulu's is via the famous cave; at high tide it can be pretty sketchy getting in the water, and there's always a strong current, so figure that into your paddle out plan.

The emerald green waves of Uluwatu are some of the fastest and most playful to be found anywhere in the world, but these days you need to really hustle with the crowd (or get lucky) to get your share. On the plus side, at any one time there'll be six or seven photographers shooting the action from the cliff and they'll offer you the chance to buy shots of yourself after your session. Haggle and expect to pay 40,000 Rupiah (about $4 - $6) per shot – the more shots you buy, the cheaper they become. The Edge bar at the top of the cliff is owned by top local surfer Made Lana, and it's a great place to enjoy a cool Bintang after your session. If you really want to live it up, spend some time in the infinity pool at Blue Point Bay which overlooks Ulu's – it's an awesome place to watch the incredible sunset and also a great treat to appease non-surfing girlfriends!
– Rob Barber

RIGHT THIS IS WHY THE BUKIT PENINSULA DRAWS SURFERS.
LEFT RACETRACKS.

WHEN TO GO: May to September.
AIRPORT: Denpasar (DPS).
ACCOMMODATION: From cheap losmen to five star opulence, it's all here. Mind, Body and Soul Surf Bali offers women's surf and yoga retreats.
WATCH OUT FOR: In the water, the crowds and shallow reefs are the main hazards. On land, beware of all manner of crazy drivers and the local police force's bogus fining system.
BOARDS: You'll need a minimum of three boards: a normal shortboard and a couple of pintails, say a 6'6" and a 6'8".
RUBBER: Boardshorts are all you'll need... but don't wear green ones. Seriously.
AFTER DARK: Head to Seminyak for the best bars and restaurants.
ALTERNATIVE EXCITEMENT: Whitewater rafting, volcano hikes, natural hot springs, jet skiing, parasailing and diving.

INDONESIA

LOMBOK

DESERT POINT'S WORLD-CLASS BARRELS, AND MORE...

JASON REPOSAR

"I've had a few tubes in my time, but the one I had at Desert Point this year was by the far the longest. Longer than I've had at Kirra, longer than I've had... well, anywhere!" That's how Dingo Morrison recalls a recent wave at Desert Point, where he managed a continuous 20 seconds behind the curtain. So, are you interested yet?

Luckily for us mere mortals, you don't have to have the skills of a pro to rack up tube time like this. Twenty-second tubes can happen to anyone, anytime Deserts turns on. Whenever the old, 'What's the best wave in the world?' debate kicks into life, in a surf magazine or a beach bar, it's not long before Deserts muscles into the argument, and usually right to the top of the list.

Situated on the far southwest tip of Lombok, Deserts is pure mechanical perfection when it's on – the waves refract textbook-style around a geometric arc of coral reef, airbrushed by offshore trades that blow all winter long. And if it all sounds too good to be true, well, that's because it kinda is. This is by no means a consistent wave; a number of often elusive factors all have to come together at the same time for it to turn on. Ideally you need a massive swell from a precise southwest direction, and certain tides that happen only a few days each month.

To complicate matters, Desert Point's proximity to the Lombok Strait – Indonesia's deepest and most dangerous stretch of water – often means you'll have to deal with one of the strongest sweeps on earth, which will whisk you out past the takeoff zone and into the pirate-riddled strait without hesitation.

But all is forgotten as soon as, like magic, Deserts switches on. An easy takeoff launches you into an ever-growing, perfectly pitching wave. The razor-sharp coral gets closer and closer to your fins as you streak along the wave, leading to a point where you are either locked in for one of the most orgasmic tubes of your life, or alternatively, you cop a strafing across a live, bacteria-filled cheese grater.

If you're looking for waves which are more forgiving, and more consistent, then head for the village of Kuta (not to be confused with its namesake on Bali) on the south coast of the island. This area offers a whole range of waves, and while they may not be world class like Desert Point, many are still super fun (and a lot less fickle). Mawi is a consistent left, while Grupek is a huge sweeping bay which is home to five different spots, both left and rights. **– Ben Mondy**

PETE FRIEDEN

LEFT DESERT POINT ISN'T OFTEN LIKE THIS – BUT WHEN IT IS, IT'S FLAWLESS.
RIGHT THE VIEW FROM THE BARREL AT DESERTS.

WHEN TO GO: May to September, when the southeast trade winds blow offshore almost every day.
AIRPORT: Fly into Denpasar (DPS) on Bali, then hop on a domestic flight to Selaparang (AMI).
ACCOMMODATION: You can find losmen-style accommodation near Desert Point at Bangko Bangko, but these days most surfers arrive by charter boat. In and around Kuta there's a good range of accommodation.
BOARDS: You'll just be racing tubes, not doing turns; so as well as your usual shortboard, bring a couple of boards that are a little narrower.
RUBBER: Boardies, all year round.
WATCH OUT FOR: Sharp coral at many of the reefs.
AFTER DARK: Bintang all round.
ALTERNATIVE EXCITEMENT: Head for Mount Rinjani, Indonesia's second highest volcano.

INDONESIA

SUMBAWA: LAKEY PEAK AREA

SUMBAWA'S HIGH-PERFORMANCE HOTSPOT

The island of Sumbawa is situated in southeast Indonesia, between Lombok and Sumba. Halfway along its southern coast is a cluster of stonking waves. The prime spot here is Lakey Peak, a ridiculously fun A-frame reef. There's a short hollow right (which can lengthen on the right swell direction), and a longer, more popular left. On a clean swell, the peak breaks so mechanically that it almost begs you to backdoor the left and pull in for an easy tube with all the trimmings. The left and the right are both best around mid tide; the left gets progressively hollower (and shallower) at lower stages of the tide, but the right becomes too sketchy. On a big swell you'll see some serious bowls here, and towards low tide the lefts get

thick and heavy. There are now more places to stay than ever in the area, and with swollen crowds the vibe in the lineup is sometimes pretty tense. Get in early to beat the rush and to make the most of the dawn glass before the onshores kick in.

Just across the channel is Lakey Pipe, a thick-lipped lefthand slab which serves up short but intense barrels. The take off is a fairly easy roll in, but be ready for the wave to jack up as it hits the slab... then it feels as though you're going below sea level, before you (hopefully) get belched out into the channel.

If the crowds at Lakey's frustrate you, there are several other excellent waves nearby. Walk north along the beach for 10 minutes and you'll reach Nunga's, a

long left which wraps enticingly into the next bay. There are a few hollow sections for brief cover-ups and some spankable walls. Walk another 40 minutes along the beach (or hop on the back of a moped) and you'll reach Periscopes, an excellent barrelling right. It needs a biggish swell to come to life, but when it does it offers a perfect barrel which will be loved by the naturalfooters after hours of backhand tube-riding at Lakey's. Best around high tide, it'll comfortably hold double overhead waves. Expect company when it's on.

Head south from Lakey's and you'll find a racy righthander called Cobblestones, about a 45-minute walk away. This spot picks up a bit more swell than the waves around Lakey Peak, and the open faces allow

plenty of room for turns. There's also a short hollow left just across the channel. Try to hit Cobblestones from mid to high tide to score the best conditions. Some say it has a sharky feel to it, but maybe that's just the price you pay for surfing without a crowd. **– Rob Barber**

WHEN TO GO: The prime times are April and October in the shoulder season but this part of Sumbawa can be worth a gamble in the wet season as there are some good spots further around the coast which will be offshore in the prevailing northwesterlies.
AIRPORT: Fly into Denpasar (DPS), then hop on internal flight to Bima Airport (BMU) on Sumbawa.
ACCOMMODATION: Try the Aman Gati.
WATCH OUT FOR: Crowds and moped scams are the main hazards. Also, beware of stonefish in the lagoon.
BOARDS: Take a shortboard, a step-up and a semi-gun.

RUBBER: You'll only need boardies.
AFTER DARK: The Aman Gati has a nice relaxed bar with a pool table and surf films on the big screen.
ALTERNATIVE EXCITEMENT: Go fishing, or visit one of the local villages like Dompu.

IRELAND

DONEGAL BAY

GREEN HILLS, EMERALD WAVES

The northwest coast of Ireland is a surf destination like no other. It has a vast combination of breaks providing rideable conditions almost every day of the year. If you time your sessions right, between the ever-changing Atlantic squalls, you may very well score the best waves of your life.

Any surf trip to this region involves driving around the stunning Donegal Bay. The area includes some of Ireland's major surfing hotspots: Easkey, Strandhill, Bundoran and Rossnowlagh. Handily the new 'Wild Atlantic Way' is a coastal tourist route connecting the whole coast with points of interest highlighted. Today these small towns or beach resorts rely more than ever on surfing for their survival. Ireland's 'Celtic tiger' boom years saw a massive amount of money poured into construction and regeneration projects along the west coast, but things are different now. Tourism has become

one of the main sources of income for the region and the year-round draw of surfing has never before been so important to these towns. A summer's day will see hundreds of people taking surfing lessons at the most popular beaches. Towns like Bundoran are playing to their surfing strengths; surf hostels, surf schools and surf shops are flourishing, keeping the town buzzing with fresh faces and crisp Euro notes.

Don't be put off by the often harsh weather forecasts. When the sun shines here the green rolling mountains become spectacular backdrops, as dramatic as the North Atlantic waves you'll be riding. Ben Bulben, the best-known peak, is often snow-capped in the winter and overlooks the entire bay. Together with an assortment of lakes, castles and glacial valleys, there's enough dramatic scenery to fill your memory card in no time. It's the same scenery that inspired the classical Irish poet Yeats, and numerous artists and songwriters.

The waves here can match those found anywhere in the world. If size and girth matters then measure the mighty waves of Mullaghmore against any in the world and you won't come up short. It's firmly on the world's big wave radar and big sessions are a real show to witness.

Intermediate and advanced surfers can find perfect waves of all sorts at the numerous reefs around Easkey and Bundoran. You just need to be in the right spot at the right time to scoop the magic combination of optimal wave size, swell direction, tide and wind. If you're just sampling your first waves, or passing the time between pints, then Strandhill, Rossnowlagh and Tullan Strand all have fantastic beginner waves with skilled coaches on hand to help out the keen improver.

Surfing has taken over Donegal Bay as few could have imagined. It's strange to think that even as recently as the '80s, many of the prime spots like Bundoran Peak and Easkey Right rarely saw crowded lineups. The standout surfers of the early days, such as the Britton brothers and Grant Robinson, have been followed by crops of young pro surfers, some of whom have achieved international recognition like Conor Maguire and Gearoid McDaid. For many, the ethos of soul surfing has been replaced by the need to make a living from the sport they love.

The region also has no shortage of mysto breaks, secret spots and heaving slabs. In recent years the surf media has latched onto one dramatic discovery after another... and then forgotten about them just as quickly. Likewise, all sorts of big international contests have come and gone. But beneath all the hype Donegal Bay still offers the essential things all surfers need and love: perfect waves, pure and simple. Yes, Irish perfection still awaits the dawn patrolling local, hardy traveller or weekend warrior. **– Gabe Davies**

SHARPY

RIGHT OLI ADAMS AND A DONEGAL DAWN SESSION.
LEFT IRISH PERFECTION.

WHEN TO GO: The prime months are September to April.
AIRPORT: Dublin (DUB) for international flights, Sligo (SXL) for domestic flights.
ACCOMMODATION: There are plenty of options around Bundoran. Check out iSurf Ireland for lessons around Strandhill and while there hit Shell's

Café for awesome food.
WATCH OUT FOR: Some of the reefs are really heavy on a solid swell, so if you aren't sure of your ability, go and find an easier wave.
BOARDS: Take a couple of shortboards, plus a step-up.
RUBBER: You'll want a 3/2 for summer

and early autumn; a 4/3 or 5/3 for the colder months.
AFTER DARK: Find a bar with a traditional music session, order a Guinness and take it all in.
ALTERNATIVE EXCITEMENT: Mountain biking, kayaking, horse riding, golf... take your pick.

IRELAND

CO CLARE

THE WEST OF IRELAND IS HOME TO SOME LEGENDARY SURF SPOTS AND SPECTACULAR SCENERY

Like it's cousin to the north, Donegal, the Clare region is stuffed with an almost unfair amount of classy reefs.

Lahinch is the surf town for the region, home to shops, surf schools and some legendary nights out. It's also well situated as a base for exploring the regions salty delights like Crab Island and Spanish Point. There's beaches and reefs all over from the beginner friendly Lahinch beach to the world-class big wave madness of Aileens. The bulk of the spots were well known until just over a decade ago, when Mickey Smith and guys like Fergal Smith, Tom Lowe, Blounty and John Mac rewrote what we knew about Irish surfing when the Cliffs, Laurens and Rileys shocked the world. The mellow reefs of Clare were now joined by media friendly, world-class, mega barrels and a for a long time Clare got the lions share of Ireland's media attention. That's calmed down and it's back to the relaxed place it's always been. Fergal is now heading up the famous Moy Hill community farm and Mickey is off being in Ben Howard's band.

The beautiful coast featuring stunning spots like the Cliffs of Moher and the Burren carries on as ever, standing tough against the fierce Atlantic assault. It's somewhere you really need to visit, just bring a smile and a good attitude in the water and you'll have a blast.

TIM NUNN

ABOVE IRISH TOW SURF RESCUE LEGEND PETE CONROY AT RILEYS.
OVERLEAF LEADING THE IRISH CHARGE CURRENTLY IS CONOR MAGUIRE.

NORTH ATLANTIC OCEAN

WHEN TO GO: Any time of year if there's swell. Autumn/winter for the big wave spots.
AIRPORT: Dublin (DUB) or Shannon (SNN).
ACCOMMODATION: Air BnB are available and there's loads of options in and around Lahinch.

WATCH OUT FOR: Away from the fun beaches and reefs this is serious stuff with difficult access. Rockfalls from the cliffs, shallow reefs and the full force of the Atlantic make this one of the most dangerous surf areas in Europe.
BOARDS: Shortboards and a your gun

if you want to go large.
RUBBER: 3/2 in summer, hooded 5mm and all the bits for the winter.
AFTER DARK: Lahinch is a good place to let your hair down.
ALTERNATIVE EXCITEMENT: Go help Ferg work the farm, explore the Burren and the beautiful scenery.

MADAGASCAR

TULÉAR AREA

A PLACE LIKE NO OTHER

Situated in the southwest corner of the Indian Ocean, Madagascar is the fourth largest island on the planet, occupying an area roughly the size of France. Its coastline stretches for more than 4,800 kilometres (3,000 miles), and when you factor in its location – staring right down the barrel of the Roaring Forties – it's no surprise to hear that Madagascar gets some really good waves.

This apparent gift from the gods is tempered slightly by the fact that most of the breaks are well offshore, making access to a boat pretty much essential if you want to score waves. Furthermore, you need to bear in mind that Madagascar is a poor country and many of the amenities are basic to say the least.

Most surfers visiting Madagascar head for the town of Tuléar on the island's southwest coast, or to the smaller settlements of Ifaty and Anakao (to the north and south respectively). Tuléar has a decent sized harbour, which makes it the best spot from which to jump on a boat and get out to the waves. Alternatively, you can paddle out to a handful of breaks, such as Resorts; or you can hop on a pirogue (a small outrigger) to access some of the waves to the south. However, the best breaks are up to four kilometres (two miles) from the shore and they're all are susceptible to the wind and tide, so it makes sense to be on an organised trip with a knowledgeable guide.

The best known wave in the area is Flameballs, a fast Indo-style left with three barrel sections and solid carveable walls between. You can score rides of up to 300 metres here, but watch out for the shallow inside section. The wave is a fair distance out to sea (around 45 minutes by boat) so if you haven't booking a package with a travel company the daily cost of hiring your own pirogue can become expensive. Flameballs is best surfed on higher tides and it's only properly classic if the wind is from the southeast.

Other favourites in the area include Jelly Babies, a consistent A-frame peak which offers fun lefts and rights; and TT's, a quality left which can offer plenty of barrel time. If the swell is tiny then you need to head all the way south to Puss-Puss, a mellow right-hander; if it's flat here (and it rarely is) then go home.

Madagascar is famous for its incredible flora and fauna. It really is like nowhere else on earth, due to the fact that its plants and animals have evolved in isolation for some 80 million years. Lemurs, chameleons, 'spiny cactus' trees, huge bottle-shaped baobabs – the biodiversity here is mind-boggling. The Malagasy people are no less intriguing, with a culture steeped in taboo and magic.

Climatically, Madagascar is pretty varied – a central range of mountains keeps the east of the island relatively moist, while the west is arid. So you'll find tropical rainforests in the east, and areas of semi-desert scrubland in the southwest. Tuléar sits in this hot, dry region, so bring plenty of sunscreen.

As a surfing destination Madagascar isn't an easy option. It's a pretty hardcore trip and you need time, local knowledge, a good boat and a nice place to stay to make it worthwhile. South African surfer Greg Bertish, who's been here every year since 1999, sums it up like this: "Great surf, great beer, no crowds, and a harsh but beautiful landscape." **– Alan van Gysen**

ALAN VAN GYSEN

OPPOSITE, TOP SOUTH AFRICAN SURFER KYLE LAIN SQUEEZES INTO A BARREL ON A SMALL DAY AT FLAMEBALLS. OPPOSITE, BOTTOM JELLY BABIES – CONSISTENT AND FUN.

WHEN TO GO: During the Southern Hemi winter, May to September.
AIRPORT: Tuléar (TLE) via Antananarivo (TNR).
ACCOMMODATION: To reach the best reefs you need a boat and a guide, so stay at one of the surf resorts.
WATCH OUT FOR: Malaria is an issue so you need to take precautions. Sharks are present but they're rarely seen and seem to be well fed. The shallow coral reefs are the main everyday hazard for surfers.
BOARDS: Take a normal shortboard, and one which will handle six-foot down-the-line screamers.
RUBBER: Boardies.
AFTER DARK: Try the Zaza Club in Tuléar. The local rum is good.
ALTERNATIVE EXCITEMENT: Take a ride in a zebu cart, go to Pirate Island, or visit the Parc National d' Andohahela with its weird 'spiny cactus' trees.

MALDIVES

MALÉ ATOLLS

THE ORIGINAL MALDIVES EXPERIENCE

The Maldives are a chain of 26 coral atolls situated about 400 kilometres (250 miles) southwest of India. The atolls are made up of around 1,200 tiny islands scattered across a huge area covering some 90,000 square kilometres. As well as being incredibly spread out, the Maldives are also incredibly low-lying; the highest point in the islands is a mere 2.4 metres above sea level.

Each one of the 26 atolls is peppered with reef passes, and many of these offer the perfect bathymetry for peeling waves. The southeast-facing coast of North Malé Atoll is home to a dozen or so breaks, ranging from fun to world-class. Many of these need a fair amount of swell to get them going, but time it right and you stand to hit the jackpot.

Crowds have become something of an issue here in recent years due to the number of resorts, the numerous

charter boats that operate in the area, and the proximity to the capital, Malé. Fortunately the vibe is still mellow and the locals are friendly.

The best time to visit the islands is generally considered to be April to June, as the winds are light and there's a good supply of swell. September and October can also be good.

There are about a dozen spots to namecheck on North Malé Atoll. Starting on the eastern side of the atoll (and going around in a clockwise direction towards the southern tip), the first decent spot is Chickens. This sick lefthander breaks off a small S-shaped island which is a bit of mouthful – Viligilimathidhahuraa. Chickens is a goofyfooter's paradise, sometimes breaking for hundreds of metres; on good days (with northwesterly winds) it can offer long barrels.

Across the channel is Coke's, named after the Coca-Cola factory on the adjacent island. This righthander is one of the best waves in the region, offering some sweet barrels. It'll hold waves up to eight or even ten feet, and it's pretty heavy at that size with strong currents adding to the fun 'n games. The crowds here are often hectic, so get in early before the hordes descend.

Continuing south, Lohi's breaks in front of the new Huduranfushi Resort (previously Lohifushi Resort). It's a spitting left that grinds its way down a long reef, with a couple of hollow sections here and there. Lohi's has hosted numerous WQS events in the past, which says something about the quality of

the waves. That's the good news. The bad news (unless you're staying there!) is that access to Lohi's is restricted to resort guests only.

Another prime left with restricted access is Pasta Point, which breaks opposite the Chaaya Dhonveli Resort. Named in honour of the resort's original Italian owners, Pasta Point is a super-fun wave which serves up some tasty barrels on a clean, solid swell. It'll handle anything up to eight feet. The number of surfers staying at the resort is limited to 30, many of whom tend to be, let's say, 'recreational' surfers from countries like Germany and Switzerland. So if you've got deep pockets...

Sultan's is arguably the best wave on North Malé Atoll. It's a consistent, long, point-style righthander which breaks from three to eight feet. After a steep takeoff you hurtle along the mid section which walls up in front of you, allowing a few snaps; when you reach the end section things get pretty lively with a nice barrel if you're lucky. Sultan's can comfortably handle the bigger days and it also gets a bit of protection from southwesterly winds. Unfortunately, everyone knows how good it is, and it's consequently one of the most crowded spots on the atoll. Get in early to avoid the zoo, and head here first if the swell is small – it's the local magnet. Right next door is Honky's, essentially the left off Sultan's. It has two distinct sections and it grows and throws on the inside. The neighbouring island is owned by the army, so boat access is the go. Watch out for strong currents sweeping through the reef passes either →

RIGHT SULTANS AND HONKYS IN ALL THEIR GLORY.
LEFT THE VIEW WE ALL CRAVE.

SIMON WILLIAMS

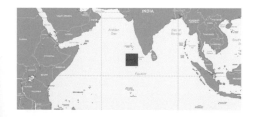

WHEN TO GO: Best months are April to June and September to October.
AIRPORT: Malé (MLE).
ACCOMMODATION: There are several land-based resorts, which offer daily boat trips out to the reefs. Or you can reach further into your pocket and go for a more flexible boat charter

check out The Perfect Wave online for package options.
WATCH OUT FOR: Sharp coral at some of the reefs, tidal rips, intense sun.
BOARDS: Take a shortboard, a fish, and a step-up in case you strike it lucky and score a solid swell.
RUBBER: Boardies all the way!

AFTER DARK: Boats or resorts will have their own booze supply. In male the new airport island is aiming to be a bit more of a party vibe. Good restaurants already.
ALTERNATIVE EXCITEMENT: Some of the best diving in the world, ridiculous fishing, windsurfing and kiteboarding.

ABOVE AUSSIE LOU HARRIS AT NATIVES ON SOUTH MALÉ ATOLL.
BELOW ANOTHER TOUGH DECISION.

ALEX WILLIAMS

side of the island.

Jailbreaks, a little further south, is a righthander which offers long rippable walls which sometimes get hollow. There are two takeoff zones and the waves peel off at a nice consistent speed, allowing plenty of manoeuvres. Years ago, there used to be a prison on the island; the view through the bars must have been enough to drive even the most hardened criminals crazy.

South Malé Atoll is about a third the size of its northern neighbour, but it also has a number of excellent spots on its southeast-facing coastline. These tend to be slightly smaller than the spots further north but they're always less crowded.

Guru's is a sick little lefthander that works best on a big south swell. It breaks quickly and can give some tasty cover-ups. Nearby is Quarters, a fun right which peels around a tiny island and works best on westerly winds.

Further south you pass the breaks of Kate's and Foxy's before reaching Natives, located near Kandooma Resort. This is a short but sweet righthander which works on any solid swell with a southwesterly wind.

Last but not least, Riptides is a fast-breaking right which reels off a small reef in the middle of the channel, down near the southern tip of the atoll. The currents can be treacherous here (like any of the spots that sit next to a narrow reef pass), so check the tidal situation with your boat captain before leaping overboard. On the perfect day, when everything comes together, it's one of the best waves in the region. **– Rob Barber**

the perfect wave
surf experience

The Perfect Wave are the world's largest surf travel network
and the biggest surf tour operator in the Maldives.

Kandooma is the best Family Surf Resort in The Maldives,
and we operate the biggest fleet of Charter boats.

[PH] +33 (0)5 58 47 65 01 [M / Whats App] +33 (0)6 33 383015 [W] www.perfectwavetravel.com

MALDIVES

HUVADHOO ATOLL

YET MORE DREAMY ATOLL SETUPS...

The southern atolls of the Maldives were first explored by surfers in the '70s, but remained a well-kept secret until the early '90s when surf charters began to visit the area. Addu Atoll is the furthest one south, but it's small, reputedly sharky and only has a couple of good spots. Huvadhoo Atoll is a better bet as it's about ten times the size and has many more spots.

Like the 25 other atolls in the Maldives, Huvadhoo was formed over the course of millions of years as coral reefs slowly built up around the rim of a now-sunken volcanic peak. The end product is a roughly circular ring of tiny islands resembling a string of pearls. Between each tiny island is a reef pass – and consequently there are waves almost everywhere you look!

Huvadhoo is well-placed to soak up the juice from southern hemisphere swells generated in the Roaring

Forties. The downside is that it's pretty remote, and until recently the only way to score its perfect lefts and rights was by chartering a boat – not a cheap option. However, a new surf camp at has recently opened on the island of Fiyoaree, close to one of the best spots, Beacons. Other camps are sure to spring up before too long.

The southeast coast of Huvadhoo is perfectly exposed to incoming swells and holds the majority of the atoll's treasure, but the west and far northeast also have some gems. There's a steady supply of swell from March right through to October; but annoyingly, the monsoon season (hulhangu) kicks in from May to August, bringing stormy conditions and southwesterly winds which blow out many of the prime spots. So try to schedule your trip sometime from March to April or September to October to maximise your chances of scoring decent swells and favourable winds.

Starting on the west side of the atoll (and going around in an anti-clockwise direction), the first spot you'll see if you fly into Kaadedhdhoo Airport is, wait for it, Airports. This is a fun right but it needs a sizey pulse from the southwest to get going. Northeasterly winds blow offshore.

From Airports it'll take your boat a couple of hours to cruise round to the south side of the atoll, but once there you'll find Beacons, arguably the best wave in the region. It's a heavy right which booms across a shallow coral shelf, and it'll hold waves up to solid eight feet. It's best on a southwest swell; any waves swinging in from

the southeast will pinch shut, so pick 'em carefully.

Continuing east, the next break along the atoll is Castaways (also known as Dhiraagu), a fairly predictable left which gets faster and steeper the further you let it run. On the right swell the sections will link up to give long rides.

Tucked inside the reef pass adjacent to the small island of Vaadhoo, Blue Bowls is a quality right which offers long point-break style walls, plus a few blue bowls to boost out of. It works on all swells and at any stage of the tide, so it's a useful spot.

Gani Point (also known as Five Islands) and Two Ways are a pair of breaks about half an hour's cruise to the east. The former is a fast and hollow righthander which can serve up some beefy barrels on a chunky swell. The latter is a less intense peak offering rights and lefts (hence the name); it's a popular spot for intermediates but needs quite a big swell to work.

Towards the eastern side of the atoll are a couple of racy lefts, so the goofyfooters can at last rejoice! Love Charms is a fun spot which works on easterly winds. It gets better as the swell gets bigger, with fast walls and a few barrels. Four or five kilometres further east, Tiger Stripes is a long left which wraps around the tip of the island of Gaddhoo, where there's a small town with a yacht marina. Something of a swell magnet, Tiger's features a nice speedy wall and a hollow inside section. It's best to avoid the latter at low tide, or else you'll find yourself paddling back to your boat with claw marks down your back. **– Rob Barber**

RIGHT EXPLORE AND YOU SHALL FIND … AND YES IT IS AS FUN AS IT LOOKS.
LEFT SOUTH AFRICAN SURFER DAVID VAN ZYL SNAGS A HOLLOW ONE AT BEACONS.

WHEN TO GO: March to April or September to October.
AIRPORT: Fly into Male (MLE), then get an internal flight to Kaadedhdhoo (KDM), or hop on a charter boat and cruise down (a 48-hour journey).
ACCOMMODATION: A boat trip will give you the most flexibility; The Surf Travel Co offers a number of yacht packages.
WATCH OUT FOR: Sharp reefs, strong tidal rips, and intense sun.
BOARDS: Take a couple of shortboards plus a step-up for the juicier spots.
RUBBER: It's super warm, you'll only need boardshorts. Reef shoes or booties are a good idea.
AFTER DARK: Avoid cabin fever by watching a movie, reading, playing cards...
ALTERNATIVE EXCITEMENT: Ever swum with a whale shark? Here's your chance.

MEXICO

OAXACA

THUNDERING BEACH BREAKS, REELING RIGHT POINTS. ANY TAKERS?

The state of Oaxaca (pronounced 'wah-ha-kah') in southern Mexico has a long south-facing coastline, which gets battered by Pacific swells throughout the prime surf season of May to October. Meaty swells generated in the South Pacific are welcomed in by an offshore deep water trench, and many of the region's thundering beach breaks and reeling sand-bottom points have become world famous destinations. If you can handle the mosquitoes and avoid the banditos, Oaxaca will serve up the goods for an epic surf trip.

Puerto Escondido is a laid-back beach town and fishing port 500 kilometres (300 miles) southeast of Mexico City. Its long beach – technically Playa Zicatela – is quite simply the heaviest and most consistent beach break on the planet. On big days the waves break with fearsome force and takes no prisoners. Detonating right

and left, with strong rips, Puerto holds massive swells and breaks with brutal power. More boards get snapped at Puerto than anywhere else on the planet. Since many of the waves close out, it's a given that at some point during your stay in Puerto you will get an absolute flogging. Furthermore, Puerto's openness to beefy south swells means that the waves can step-ladder in size during a session and easily catch you out. Despite the dangers, Puerto remains a perennial favourite with big-wave chargers from across the world. Evidently, claiming a quadruple-overhead keg makes all the pummellings worthwhile! Rise at dawn to score offshore winds, as it nearly always turns onshore by 11am; then it's time to find some shade from the incredibly hot sun. Occasionally the waves glass-off in the evening, especially if there's an approaching thunderstorm, so it's worth resisting the afternoon beers just in case. Puerto breaks throughout the tide and rarely goes completely flat (although flat spells are common in January). On small to medium size days it can get crowded, but when it starts to get big the crowds thin out pretty quickly. If you want to take it on at size, head to the harbour and paddle out from there. Beware of loose boards – some local surfers don't wear leashes on big days as they're said to increase the chances of snapping your board.

In the sheltered southern corner of Playa Zicatela is La Punta, a fun left point which offers a change from Puerto's relentless beach break slammers.

Further east along Highway 200 there are several good spots like Colotepec and Rio Cozula, and the

potential to find a pumping secluded break here is considerable. With a consistent supply of swell and so many breaks nestled around the headlands off the 200, the area is wide open to hardcore travellers who fancy an adventure. Don't travel at night though – bandits are sometimes encountered in this area.

Past the town of Cruceita the coast swings around to a southeast-facing direction, so swells from the south and southwest wrap in at an angle. The good news is that there are some cracking righthand points here. The not-so-good news is that they're often affected by gusty northeasterly winds, which blow cross-shore at many of the points.

One of the gems along this stretch of coast is Barra de la Cruz, an inconsistent but occasionally incredible spot. To be at its best it requires a big south swell, light northwesterly winds and perfectly aligned sandbanks... something of a tall order. But when everything comes together the waves here resembles Kirra in its heyday – long, mechanical, tubular rights which break for hundreds of metres. Barra was something of a secret until 2006 when Rip Curl held a CT event there →

RIGHT LUCHITO SANGACHI AND A MONSTER PUERTO CAVERN.

WHEN TO GO: May to October.
AIRPORT: Fly into Mexico City (MEX) then get a connecting flight to Puerto Escondido (PXM) or Huatulco (HUX).
ACCOMMODATION: In Puerto there are options to suit all budgets. Further south it's advisable to stay with one of the surf tour companies in Salina Cruz as they know all the best spots.
WATCH OUT FOR: In the water, sledgehammer lips and heavy hold-downs on big days are the main hazard. On land, beware of thefts and muggings (don't walk along the beach alone at night).
BOARDS: A four or five board quiver is essential if you want to charge the bigger days at Puerto.
RUBBER: Boardshorts, maybe a vest.
AFTER DARK: The nightlife in Puerto goes off – check out Bar Fly.
ALTERNATIVE EXCITEMENT: Hire a quad bike or try your hand at big game fishing.

ALAN VAN GYSEN

and the lucky pro's scored epic once-in a blue moon conditions. Since then, not surprisingly, it's become a lot busier, but get in early and you should still beat the masses.

Further along the coast, just east of Garrapateras, is Punta Bamba, a short sucky right which peels off next to an old rock jetty. Around the next headland you'll find Punta Chipehua, which can offer superb rights on a big south or southwest swell, although again it's susceptible to the pesky trades.

As you approach the town of Salina Cruz more options open themselves up. Punta Chivo is a less intense wave, suitable for intermediates and longboarders. The trades can make it messy, but it'll be fun if the winds are northwesterlies. Finally, just outside Salina Cruz, is Punta Conejo, a prized right point which can really deliver the goods when there's a decent south swell and the cross-onshore wind calms down a bit or swings around to the northwest. When it's good, Punta Conejo offers fast long rides and a whackable lip you can hit time after time. Hook up with one of the local surf tour companies and they'll drive you right to the water's edge in one of their 4x4s.

Oaxaca is an awesome region of Mexico and most of the local people you'll meet will be kind and courteous. However, Mexico is one of those countries where you need to keep your wits about you at all times. Muggings, pickpocketing and crime are all too common in poor built-up areas, so always keep your valuables and wallet well hidden.

Be sure to sample the local cuisine – traditional Mexican food is extremely cheap and will give you a new found respect for flavour. The nightlife is also great, particularly in Puerto Escondido, with a good mix of travelling surfers and backpackers all up for a good time. **– Rob Barber**

MICRONESIA

POHNPEI

INCREDIBE P-PASS, AND A FEW OTHER SPOTS TOO

The Federated States of Micronesia consist of 607 islands scattered over two million square kilometres of the western Pacific, situated roughly halfway between the Philippines and Hawaii. Politically they're a sovereign island state; geographically they're part of the larger Caroline Islands group. The largest island in the FSM is Pohnpei, and its main town, Palikir, is also the country's capital.

Pohnpei is encircled by a barrier reef roughly eight kilometres (five miles) from shore. There are about a dozen reef passes and these are the locations of the island's best surf spots, which conveniently face a range of different directions allowing plenty of options whatever the swell or wind direction. As a result, Pohnpei is a veritable surfing playground.

P-Pass (Palikir Pass) is the main attraction on Pohnpei, a righthander about as perfect as you could ever possibly want. At three to four feet P-Pass is a racy, super-fun barrel which peels along in a whirl of technicolor blue and distorted coral. At that size it's an easily manageable prospect for experienced surfers. The excitement level steps up when the waves hit five to six feet, and the barrels get rounder and heavier. When P-Pass hits eight feet or bigger (which doesn't happen often) things get serious, and the wave starts to resemble Backdoor. Prime conditions at P-Pass attract pro surfers from Hawaii and Australia, and it's these rare booming sessions that provide the epic photos you'll have seen in the magazines. "It's such an amazing wave at six- to eight-foot plus," froths Aussie legend Gary

Elhardey, "one of the best right handers I've ever seen. When it's glassy, the colours of the reef and the water are just insane... it's like surfing in a dream."

P-Pass can be surfed on all tides but gets a tad shallow at low. The ideal swell direction is a straight north, and the prevailing easterly trade winds will groom the waves nicely. Yup, breaks like P-Pass make the world a beautiful place.

A few kilometres to the east are two more reef passes, Easy Pass and Main Pass. Quality righthanders peel into both of these, but they tend to be overlooked by visiting surfers who descend on P-Pass en masse and can't be bothered to look elsewhere. Easy Pass is, guess what, the easier of the two, a fun spot on a three- to four-foot swell around high tide when there's enough water to cover the main part of the reef (beware the shallow inside section though). Main Pass picks up more swell than P-Pass and it's only ridden on medium to big swells, as the inside is too shallow to surf on small days. It'll hold waves up to 10 foot plus, and some who've surfed it at that size have compared it to Sunset Beach in Hawaii. In other words, it's really a spot for experienced chargers only. On a sizey swell it serves up long blue walls with plenty of space for big turns, followed by a heaving top-to-bottom barrel on the inside. Forget low tide.

Pohnpei gets a steady supply of swell from low pressure systems heading off across the North Pacific from Japan. Occasionally, a typhoon swinging past the Philippines will generate a beefy southwest swell, but

these are infrequent. The 'early season' from October to mid-December is generally considered to be the best time of year to visit, when the winds are light. P-Pass and the other passes on the north side of the island receive swell right through the winter to April, but the trade winds are often stronger in the second half of the season, from January to April.

The barrier reef continues around the east side of the island, again with reef passes here and there. There are some good spots along this stretch, which tend to work best in August and September on days when the trade winds die down or switch direction altogether. Freddo's can hold a chunky swell and will serve up rippable walls and the odd barrel. Further south, wrapping into the pass near Dehpehk Island, is a lefthander named Spaghetti's (a nod to Macaroni's in the Mentawais, which it does its best to imitate).

There's huge potential for discovery in other parts of Micronesia. With so many islands, there must surely be more world-class waves out there just waiting to be found – the only limitation is how much money and time you have to spend looking for them. –
Owen Pye

SIMON WILLIAMS

OPPOSITE P-PASS DOESN'T BREAK AT THIS SIZE TOO OFTEN, BUT WHEN IT DOES, THE PRO'S COME RUNNING. JAMIE O'BRIEN. RIGHT ALL SMILES IN THE BOAT.

WHEN TO GO: October to December.
AIRPORT: Fly to Pohnpei (PNI).
ACCOMMODATION: Try Palikir Marine Adventures, just across the lagoon from P-Pass.
BOARDS: Bring a full quiver with boards up to 7'0" if you're planning to tackle P-Pass or Main Pass at size.

RUBBER: Boardshorts are all you'll need.
WATCH OUT FOR: Shallow sections of the reefs, and sledgehammer lips when it's six foot plus. On land, expect a lot of rain – it really chucks it down here.
AFTER DARK: If you're in town and

you need a bite to eat, head for Sei Restaurant or The Village Hotel.
ALTERNATIVE EXCITEMENT: Visit Nan Madol, the intricate stone ruins of an ancient city that dates way back to 7th century. Diving, snorkelling, fishing, there's plenty to do.

MOROCCO

TAGHAZOUT AREA

MINT WAVES

Lying between the pulsing Atlantic and the orange sands of the Sahara Desert, Morocco is a sizable country which occupies an area the size of California and Nevada put together. Its 1,800-kilometre (1,100-mile) coastline stretches from the Strait of Gibraltar all the way south to Western Sahara, and dotted along it are some of the best point breaks in the world. A long-time favourite with travelling surfers, Morocco offers affordable accommodation and a variety of waves, which sees those in the know coming back year after year.

The climate is similar to that of Southern California – baking hot in the summer, comfortably warm from November through to February. During those winter months Morocco becomes a getaway for Euro surfers who are glad to leave their 5mm wetties and hoods at home and slip back into their summer suits.

Morocco is a Muslim country and it's important to respect its laws and culture. Female visitors should dress modestly when walking around towns and villages. It's fine to take photos of the scenery, but don't take photos of local people, especially women, without asking first. And be aware that it's illegal for Westerners to smoke hashish.

Arabic is the mother-tongue, but most Moroccans speak French and a few also speak a little English.

Many of Morocco's best and most famous breaks are dotted along a 50-kilometre (30-mile) stretch of coast around the fishing village of Taghazout, just north of Agadir. Here the coastline is broadly southwest-facing, and big northwest swells marching down the coast wrap and peel around any headland they encounter. The geology of the area also helps, with gently dipping sedimentary strata creating point breaks and reefs here, there and everywhere.

The incredible waves around Taghazout were first ridden in the mid '60s, and the area became a Shangri-La for travelling surfers in the '70s and '80s. Back then, there was no running water or electricity in the village. These days there are plenty of home comforts and a good selection of places to stay; from cheap dives, through to smart apartments and surf camps (there are now upward of 15 surf camps in Taghazout and the neighbouring village of Tamraght). Taghazout is the perfect base from which to explore the numerous waves within walking distance of the town. Many apartments and surf camps have sea views, so at the end of another three-session day you can wind down with a beer and watch the waves reel down Anchor Point as the sun sinks behind the horizon.

Within walking distance of the village are half-a-dozen notable spots. Killer Point, the furthest north, is a long righthand point which will hold waves up to 15 feet, when it breaks miles out to sea. Steer clear of the rocks and caves at the base of the cliffs. The Source and Mysteries are a couple of less obvious peaks in the adjacent bay, but there's no way you'll miss Anchor Point, especially when it's firing at eight to ten feet and peeling for the best part of a kilometre! (More about Anchor's later.) On a booming swell, the incoming lines will peak up again and spin off down Hash Point, in front of the village, before finally petering out at Panorama's. The crowds get spread out between the various breaks, although Anchor Point always draws the biggest pack. To the north of Taghazout are yet more right points (Boilers, Dracula's and others), and seven kilometres further around Cap Ghir is Tamri, a punchy beach break which picks up any swell going; head here when all the points are flat.

The Taghazout area attracts surfers of all abilities from far and wide. There are always loads of Euro wave riders, who journey from as far afield as Norway, Sweden, Germany, the UK and Ireland to get their fill of the winter wave action. Joining them are locals like Ramzi Boukhiam, Othman Choufani, Abdel Harim and Yassine Ramdani, who are all WQS standard and a pleasure to watch. The lineups are competitive at all the main breaks and you may have to be assertive to snag →

BONNARME

your fair share of the waves – but it's worth the hassle.

On a big swell, Anchor Point is one of the best point breaks in the world. Situated just north of Taghazout, Anchor's got its name from the dozens of rusty anchors that used to surround the derelict fish tinning factory on the point. Nowadays the anchors are gone, but the ruins of the factory provide an atmospheric backdrop to the action in the water. Anchor's will hold any swell going, it's offshore on an easterly wind, and it works throughout the tide. From mid to high tide it can serve up some lovely long walls, which are great if you're looking for some big open faces to carve. At lower stages of the tide the inside section transforms itself into a down-the-line racetrack,

with the occasional barrel.

The jump off at Anchor's is not for the inexperienced. Get your timing right and you'll be rewarded with a dry hair paddle out. Get it wrong and you face a duck-diving extravaganza in the fast flowing sweep which will take you all the way back to Taghazout if you're not careful! The standard of surfing on the peak at Anchor's is always the highest in the area. The locals usually take most of the choice waves, but international surfers of a good standard should also get their fair share. If you're not getting much joy at the peak, then paddle (or drift) 75 metres down the point and pick off the waves that the hot rats either miss or blow. At low tide, the inside section gets pretty throaty and things are

spiced up nicely by the cross waves bouncing off the point which create some hollow wedges. It's possible to link ten turns and then pull in for a couple of barrels on a decent wave. The paddle back to the peak against the sweep is tiring but worth it. When you're done for the day, exit the water by riding a wave to the inside, waiting for a lull, and then scrambling up the slimy boulders (watching out for urchins). Alternatively, ride a wave as far as you can and then let the sweep take you to the sandy inlet between the point and the first building on the road to Taghazout. Dawn sessions are always a good idea to beat the locals and slackers to the first hour of the morning feast. Or try mid-morning when everyone goes in for breakfast. **– Rob Barber**

LEFT INLAND IS A TRIP AS WELL.
RIGHT MOROCCO RUNS FROM FUN ALL THE WAY TO
INSANE BARRELS.

WHEN TO GO: November to February.
AIRPORT: Agadir (AGA).
ACCOMMODATION: In Taghazout Mint Surf have school and accommodation options. Munga Guesthouse is a boutique operation offering yoga and coaching. In Agadir Paradis Plage is a luxury eco-resort offering yoga and a surf training program.
WATCH OUT FOR: Dodgy drivers, petty crime and iffy sanitation.
BOARDS: Take a couple of shortboards and something longer for the big days. You'll be doing a lot of paddling so a 6'4" or 6'6" would be a good bet.
RUBBER: A 3/2 will do the job.

AFTER DARK: Try a lamb or fish tagine (stew) at a local eatery.
ALTERNATIVE EXCITEMENT: The marketplaces are buzzing hives of colour, scent and flavour. Go haggle. For a complete change of scene, drive into the Atlas Mountains – in cold winters you can even snowboard.

OTHMANE CHOUFANI
Big wave pro surfer
Team Member Paradis Plage

Paradis Plage
Surf, Yoga & Spa Resort
Agadir **.** Morocco

00212 (0) 5 28 200 382
resa@paradisplage.com
www.paradisplage.com
KM 26, Route d'Essaouira, Imi Ouaddar
Agadir - Morocco -

Follow us on

Paradis Plage is the nearest year-round sunny oasis, away from the tourists hotspots of Agadir, literally a little piece of paradise - and the first luxurious Eco-Resort in Morocco to combine Surf, Yoga and a traditional SPA. An authentic experience, only 3 hours away from Europe, on a stunning 5 km beachfront, utterly dedicated to the wellness of your body and mind.

Located near the famous surf village of Taghazout and a dozen of world-class surf spots, Paradis Plage created a tailored surfing experience designed to help you learn and progress faster. Thanks to a personal surf training program in our new beachside fitness facility, a daily Yoga practice in our seaview Shala, and an exclusive partnership with Rip Curl including quality equipment and trained coaches, you will have the guarantee to surf better no matter your skills. Paradis Plage brings to you a unique opportunity to take care of your body and your mind as well as our natural heritage thanks to the resort's green policy including an international « Green Key » eco-label and a strong partnership with Surfrider Foundation.

Partners & labels

Green Key

MOZAMBIQUE

PRAIA DO TOFO AREA

BOARDSHORTS AND BARRELS ON AFRICA'S EAST COAST

Mozambique's Praia do Tofo is one of those rare places where life slows down just enough to put things into perspective. With a relaxed 'string the hammock to the nearest coconut tree' vibe, an abundance of fresh seafood, and the potential for heavy barrels at nearby Tofinho, this east African nook gives itinerant surfers a chance to revel in the good life without murdering the bank balance.

A brisk walk (or short drive) south of the main beach at Tofo, Tofinho is the premier, albeit fickle, wave in this area. Here, a slab of sandstone juts into the azure Indian Ocean and forms a quality inside point. However, this is really the prelude to the main event, the ledgy outside section. When it's solid, hefty righthanders peel off in front of the grassy cliff and, if the sand is stacked properly, shunt onto the inside where they beg to be torn apart by big carves and hacks. The takeoff zone gets heavy when it's big and a group of dedicated locals will show you just how deep you can sit if you've got the balls. No one will think less of you if you watch from the hillside, camera in hand, sipping on Tipo Tinto rum (the local speciality) with a bag of freshly roasted cashew nuts to keep you company.

Less experienced surfers can find an easier ride at Tofo, where a shifty right runs softly along the south side of the beach. When the swell is smaller, head for Back Beach, south of Tofinho, which kicks up some peaky sections. Watch out for random slabs of rock here and there. Dino's Left and Backdoor are a couple of other options in the area for advanced-level surfers.

On flat days, hook up with one of the many dive operators who can take you snorkelling with the large, but harmless, whale sharks whose filter-feeding mouths look like the bottom end of a vacuum cleaner when you're up close and personal. Fishing trips, dolphin diving, and scuba diving can also be arranged.

The locals in Mozam' are mellow and friendly, despite the fact that many of them live hard lives mired by poverty. The older generations endured a long and brutal civil war, which started in 1977 (just two years after the end of a decade-long war against the Portuguese for independence) and ended in 1992. Besides scarring the country's populace, the wars also left behind a sea of unexploded landmines, which have cruelly stolen limbs from many Mozambicans. But, thanks to the concerted efforts of various NGOs, Mozambique was declared landmine free by 2015. So , although the best advice is to stick to the well-travelled areas and don't go off solo into unmarked territory, the only explosions you'll experience these days will be those caused by waves detonating on reefs and sandbars. – **Brendon Bosworth**

ALAN VAN GYSEN

RIGHT JORDY SMITH HAS MADE THE MOZAM' MISSION A FEW TIMES TO TUNNEL IN TOFO.
LEFT THE POINT AT TOFINHO.

WHEN TO GO: April to October.

AIRPORT: Fly into Maputo International Airport (MPM) then get a connecting flight to Inhambane (INH).

ACCOMMODATION: Try Fatima's Nest or Bamboozi Beach Lodge at Tofo. Those looking to own the morning dawn patrols at Tofinho should head for Turtle Cove, situated on the hill above the point; owner Nic Tasioulas is really dialled into the waves and has some killer pics of classic days.

WATCH OUT FOR: Malaria – bring insect repellant and sleep under a proper net at night.

BOARDS: Bring regular shortboards and a mush-pig for the smaller days.

RUBBER: In summer just boardies.

AFTER DARK: Head to the beach bars and restaurants at Tofo.

ALTERNATIVE EXCITEMENT: Connect with one of the dive operators at Tofo and go snorkelling with whale sharks and manta rays.

NAMIBIA

WALVIS BAY AND SWAKOPMUND

SKELETONS AND DIAMONDS

South Africa's northwestern neighbour is no picture perfect surf destination. Not by a long shot. Namibia's 1,000-mile desert coastline is lonely, inhospitable and populated by some of the largest seal colonies in existence. The arid Namib Desert is so harsh that the country's original inhabitants, the San, called it, 'the land God made in anger'. In later years, early European mariners dubbed this notorious shoreline 'the Skeleton Coast', as it was strewn with the bones of seals and whales. Before long it was also home to innumerable shipwrecks and the ghosts of stricken seamen. Portuguese sailors called it, 'the gates of hell'. But with finely sculpted sand dunes and thumping left points, ridden by few surfers, Namibia and its otherworldly desert coastline maintains a rugged beauty that is definitely its own.

Diamonds are big business in Namibia. Namdeb, a joint operation between global diamond giant De Beers and the Namibian government, own parts of the southwestern coast in a region known as the Sperrgebiet, which means 'forbidden territory' in German. The diamond zones are fenced off and access is strictly prohibited, although there are some punchy reefs close to Luderitz that are not in the mining areas. If you bump into a surfing diamond diver in a bar you might hear tales of unridden gems peeling off quietly in the restricted zones. Unfortunately, no amount of begging will get you an all-access pass. Recently, the Namibian government designated the Sperrgebiet as a national park, but tourists can only visit a small segment of the park, accompanied by a guide holding a concession from the Ministry of Environment and Tourism.

A dedicated local crew surfs the reefs and beaches around Walvis Bay and Swakopmund. Walvis Bay is a harbour town where fishing and cargo handling are the main industries, while Swakopmund is a holiday town which is home to a large German community. One of the favourite spots in the

area is Guns, a fast-breaking left with a ledgy barrel section, located between the two towns. The locals also ride other spots that are only accessible by four-wheel drive and they regularly set off on exploratory missions when the conditions are right. A capable off-road vehicle and an accurate GPS system are a real bonus. As is getting up early, since the winds come up quickly.

In 2008 Namibia landed in the spotlight when the entire surfing world saw footage of Cory Lopez screaming through the eternally spinning tubes of Skeleton Bay, a spot whose location is still a closely guarded secret. This is one of Namibia's premier waves, offering insanely long barrels. It's heavy as hell though, especially at low tide when the sets will smash you into the sandbar if you happen to catch the rail inside one of the mud-sucking pits. The takeoff is tricky, as the bottom drops out immediately and sends you lurching into the clutches of the beast, leaving little time to think about anything except setting your rail and gunning straight for the exit hole – which seems to be continually running further away from you. The local seals, some of them brutes, and the great white population that snack on the blubbery critters, add to the rush, while early morning mists make dawn patrol sessions at the isolated venue particularly eerie. Definitely not a wave for beginners. **– Brendon Bosworth**

ALAN VAN GYSEN

WHEN TO GO: April to September.
AIRPORT: International flights land at Windhoek (WDH). From there fly to Walvis Bay (WVB).
ACCOMMODATION: Anything from backpackers to expensive hotels.
WATCH OUT FOR: Don't try to surf in the Cape Cross Seal Reserve. This

protected area is a no-go for surfers and is strictly policed, with fines if you get caught.
BOARDS: Bring a regular shortboard and a step-up. If you manage to find Skeleton Bay bring some spares, preferably boards you don't mind snapping!

RUBBER: 4/3 fullsuit. Boots and hood advisable since winds can be chilly.
AFTER DARK: Perched on stilts in the Walvis Bay lagoon, the Raft restaurant is the place for seafood.
ALTERNATIVE EXCITEMENT: Ride a quad bike on the massive dunes around Swakopmund.

New Zealand is not an especially big country – it occupies an area considerably smaller than California, for example – but it seems massive when you're driving around it. Vast mountain ranges, towering volcanoes, wide plains... the scenery is epic, both in scale and beauty. But it's the population, or lack of it, that gives the place such a sense of spaciousness. Towns and villages are spread well out, and you can count the number of big cities on one hand. Out in the countryside you'll see a farmhouse here and a whitewashed church there, but most of the terrain is farmland, forest, hills or mountains.

Taranaki – North Island's westernmost region – is arguably the best area in the country for waves, thanks to its unique geography. The coastline runs in an almost perfect semi-circular arc for 110 kilometres (70 miles), and bang in the middle is an awesome, often snow-capped, volcano – Mount Taranaki. Beaches, reefs and points are dotted along the coast, all facing slightly different directions. So whatever the wind direction, you can nearly always find somewhere that's offshore. Consequently the region is a nirvana for surfers – just as long as you don't mind the chilly water and have the patience to wait out the frequent windy days.

New Plymouth, the largest town in the region, grew up as a trading post in the 19th century and later became an important cargo port. It's a cool town with a thriving arts scene, some hip coffee bars and several decent surf shops.

Just east of the town, Waitara Bar and Waiwakaiho

Rivermouth are a couple of north-facing rivermouth spots which can occasional get really good, although they only work on massive swells. When it's on, Waiwhakaiho is a classic A-frame with fun lefts and rights, best at higher stages of the tide.

New Plymouth's town beaches – Fitzroy and East End – similarly require sizey swells to work, so they rarely break in the summer. During the cooler months, however, you'll find some hollow low-tide waves at Fitzroy, and some whackable (slightly smaller) mid-tide walls at East End.

A couple of clicks west of New Plymouth, Back Beach is a powerful beachie which picks up more swell than the town beaches; it's offshore on an easterly wind.

Follow the coast road – aptly called Surf Highway 45 – for 20 kilometres (12 miles) and you reach the small town of Okato, which is where things start to get really good from a surfing point of view. The low-lying coast here is made up of a series of small bays with a generous scattering of points and reefs. Access to many of these spots is through private farmland, and while the vast majority of the farmers are cool about surfers crossing their land, it's important for everyone's sake to keep on good terms. So stick to the tracks, and leave all farm gates as you find them.

Goofyfooters will love Kumara Patch (a long, racy left point) and Rocky Lefts (a low-tide lefthander which serves up a few nice barrels). Both spots involve a bit of a hike (no bad thing as it keeps the numbers down) and they're offshore on a southeasterly wind.

If wrapping right points are more your thing, find your way to Stent Road. That may be easier said than done since the road isn't signposted; every time the council puts up a new road sign it gets pinched by souvenir hunters! You'll find it in the end. A world-class right which holds waves up to 12 feet, Stent Road peels down a boulder-strewn point and serves up some juicy hollow sections when it's good. It works on any swell from the west, and on all tides. If the main peak is crowded, just surf one of the other sections. Light northeasterlies provide perfect offshore conditions.

About 40 kilometres (25 miles) further south you reach Opunake, a small town with a laid-back vibe and colourful murals on the buildings. The town's crescent-shaped beach gets some fun waves, and yet more good breaks can be found to the south, including Mangahume (a perfect A-frame peak which will hold big swells) and Green Meadows (a quality right point).

Taranaki's ever-changing swells and winds will have you scurrying up and down Surf Highway 45 on a daily basis, but you'll always find a wave somewhere. And one thing's for sure, you won't ever lose your bearings with a 2,500 metre volcano acting as a whopping great landmark wherever you go. – **Chris Power**

CHRIS POWER

OPPOSITE STENT ROAD, ONE OF TARANAKI'S MANY TASTY SETUPS.

WHEN TO GO: February to April for consistent autumn swells.
AIRPORT: Auckland (AKL).
ACCOMMODATION: Hotels, guest houses, backpacker hostels – take your pick. Alternatively hire a camper van and travel at your own pace.
BOARDS: Check out Quiver NZ – you

can hire longboards (they do hold a few shortboards) for your trip around NZ and save the air travel faff. For the rest of us shortboards are the go.
RUBBER: You'll want a 3/2 for autumn, a 5/3 for winter.
WATCH OUT FOR: Shallow rocks at some of the points and reefs.

AFTER DARK: For live music head for The Matinee or the Basement Bar in New Plymouth.
ALTERNATIVE EXCITEMENT: Get your hiking boots on and climb Mount Taranaki! It'll take you about eight hours and you'll need a guide; summertime only.

SHARPY

Nicaragua is a dream destination for any surfer looking for clean, fun, consistent waves without having to go to the ends of the earth. Its Pacific coastline is sub-divided into five departments, the southernmost of which is Rivas. This area is becoming recognised as one of the best smiles-per-mile trip destinations in Central America. Not only is this stretch wide open for the South Pacific swell machine to deliver the corduroy, it's also blessed with super-consistent offshore winds, grooming every peak and feathering lip after lip after lip. This surf-friendly phenomenon is due to the papagayos winds, which intensify over Lake Nicaragua just inland and blow offshore for 300 days of the year.

Late spring and early summer (from May to July) is the best time for swell, but that's not to say the rest of the year isn't worth a gamble – Nicaragua is one of the most consistent surf destinations you can fly to. Talking of flights, when you arrive in Nicaragua you'll land in Managua, but don't hang around in the city for long as it's rife with crime.

Rivas Department offers an assortment of good spots strung out along its southwest-facing coastline, which runs parallel to the elongated Lake Nicaragua. About ten kilometres (six miles) northwest of the town of Las Salinas is a fishing village called El Astillero. Here you'll find a decent reef near the rivermouth which serves up long lefthanders when it's on. Best at lower stages of the tide, it starts working at four feet and will hold any size swell.

Just south of Las Salinas you come to Playa Sardinas, where'll you'll find a quality A-frame roof called Popoyo (slightly confusingly located three kilometres from the village of the same name). The waves here are best at low tide, when the right serves up some good barrels and the left provides longer, whackable walls. On massive swells an outer reef called Bus Stops breaks over a shallow slab way outside; the currents here are strong and you'll need a big board to get into the waves, so this is a spot for advanced surfers only. Nearby are some fun beach break wedges; explore a little and you'll be pleasantly surprised.

Further south are yet more excellent waves, but you'll need a boat to access many of these as they break off private property. Near El Gigante you'll find the punchy beach breaks of Playa Amarillo and Playa Colorado, and a reef called Panga Drops, which will dish up some hefty waves on a solid swell. A long headland juts out at the southern end of the bay, →

OPPOSITE BRIT TRAVELLER STU CAMPBELL, PITTED IN NICARAGUA.

WHEN TO GO: Nicaragua gets swell all year round but the prime months are from May to July.
AIRPORT: Managua (MGA).
ACCOMMODATION: Surfing Turtle Lodge at Islas Los Brasiles is a lively beachfront hostel and Rancho Santana at Playa Santana is your spot for laidback luxury with a hint of rugged elegance. Other camps are dotted around the better spots.
WATCH OUT FOR: Tropical diseases, mozzies, reef cuts and banditos.
BOARDS: A couple of shortboards (one with a bit of float) should do it.
RUBBER: Boardshorts and maybe a vest are all you'll need.
AFTER DARK: Expect standard surf camp activities such as table tennis, surf films and early nights.
ALTERNATIVE EXCITEMENT: The old colonial city of Granada is worth a visit, or you could climb a volcano or go fishing.

and tucked inside it is Manzanillo, an inconsistent but occasionally epic left point which can serve up long, hollow waves on a big south swell. Manzanillo is only accessible by boat – the surrounding land is private property and the Italian owner apparently employs armed guards who have chased trespassers off the beach at gunpoint!

Keep heading down the coast and you'll find plenty of fun waves around the town of San Juan del Sur, which is a good place to be based if you're not going for the surf camp option. Just north of the town is Punta Quilla; to the south are Playa Remonso, Playa Tamarindo and Playa el Yanqui. But watch out for banditos in this region as attacks and robberies have been reported. – **Rob Barber**

RIGHT: MACHADO CARVES A PLAYFUL WALL AT MANZANILLO.

NORWAY

LOFOTEN ISLANDS

SPECTACULAR MOUNTAINS DROPPING INTO THE ARCTIC OCEAN

Norway was summed up well by the Hitchhiker's Guide to the Galaxy author Douglas Adams:

Slartibartfast: Did you ever go to a place - I think it was called Norway?

Arthur Dent: No. No, I didn't.

Slartibartfast: Pity. That was one of mine. Won an award, you know. Lovely crinkly edges.

Those crinkly edges of the wild coastline are Europe's longest west-facing coast. 83,000 kilometres of fjords, skerries, islands and adventure await. The main surfing area is around the oil industry rich town of Stavanger in the south. Lush beaches and a few points have been sessioned since the late sixties, with US oil workers bringing in boards for the fledging local crew. These days there's a strong scene and the winter sports savvy locals have taken to sliding on fluid water as well as they have the frozen stuff. There's potential on the whole coast, where you can access it, but geography and the lack of roads are a real issue in some places – and check with locals on the deal as there used to be bans on certain Jæren spots in winter to allow birds to nest.

At the other end of the country from the populous south is the poster child for coldwater surfing: the Lofoten Islands. The word 'spectacular' doesn't do the place justice. Mountains drop into the sea in a wild landscape that looks like it was dreamt up by Tolkien. It's a magical place to visit whether you score waves or not, and it's one of the few places you can claim to have surfed in the Arctic Circle, as Iceland, apart from one small island offshore, isn't.

Unstad is the famous bay home to a fickle but world, class right and a super fun left. You can stay here and hit the spots that have been all over the magazines the last decade. It's busier than it was, but it's such a pain to get to that it will never be mobbed. Driving from the south would take forever so most folk fly up to Bodo then rent a car. Just beware it's dark as hell in winter, so most surfers visit in Autumn when it's actually reasonably warm, for the Arctic, or in spring when you're guaranteed to be surfing in snow. An added bonus is that it's one of the best places in the world to see the Northern Lights, as evidenced by Mick Fanning's stunning shoot in 2017. **– Roger Sharp**

ABOVE MICAH LESTER ENJOYING THE ARCTIC.
ABOVE LEFT THE FAMOUS BAY AT UNSTAD, FICKLE
BUT IF YOU SCORE IT YOU'LL BE STOKED.

WHEN TO GO: September to May.
AIRPORT: Fly into Oslo (OSL) and get a local flight up to Bodø (BOO), then it's an expensive rental car drive. You can fly to Lofoten if you're minted.
ACCOMMODATION: Arctic Surf in Unstad have cosy cabins.
WATCH OUT FOR: The cold. It's no joke up inside the Arctic Circle. Inquisitive orcas might join you in the lineup.
BOARDS: Standard shortboards, it never gets that big.
RUBBER: Hooded 6mm and all the bits.
AFTER DARK: Booze is expensive in Norway so bring duty free. There is some bar action in Leknes.

ALTERNATIVE EXCITEMENT: If you're here in snow season there are some lifts for a little bit of snowboarding. Hiking, exploring, marvelling at the mind-blowing scenery.

PANAMA

THE WESTERN PROVINCES

TWO COASTS, DOUBLE THE POSSIBILITIES

The dual coastlines of Panama boast a large number of classy surf spots. Serviced by consistent southwest swells which pound the Pacific coast, and seasonal yet punchy east swells which hit the Caribbean coast, the thin isthmus between North and South America is a veritable grotto of world-class waves.

Panama's three westernmost provinces – Chiriqui, Veraguas and Bocas del Toro – offer all the variety you could possibly want on a surf trip. Much of the south-facing coast of Chiriqui is unremarkable beach break, but near the town of Remedios the topography becomes more varied with rivermouths and a scattering of small islands. There are a cluster of breaks in this area, all within easy reach of the local surf camp, Morro Negrito. The Point (a racy low-tide left) and Rio Tabasara (a fun rivermouth sandbar) are just south of the camp; meanwhile P-Land (a hollow, wrapping lefthander) and Nestles (a short, hefty right) break either side of a tiny island called Isla Silva de Afuera, a short boat ride away.

Continuing southwest into Veraguas province, the terrain becomes much hillier. Near the tip of the peninsula lies one of Panama's best waves. Santa Catalina is a classic righthand reef situated close to a small fishing village which shares the same name. It's a super-consistent spot (despite appearing to have a narrow swell window due to the islands nearby) which rarely goes flat between May and September. On a solid six- to eight-foot swell the rides will be as long as a soccer pitch, and by the end of the session your legs will feel like you've just played 90 minutes against Man

United. The tides are big here and Santa Catalina is only good from mid to high, so it's vital to check out the tide times. It'll hold waves up to 12 foot plus – bring a big board if you fancy tackling it at size. With several surf camps in the area, plus a keen local crew, crowds are unfortunately a factor; but the length of the wave tends to spread people out.

Punta Brava, around the corner to the south, is a gnarly lefthander which is always a good couple of feet bigger than Santa Catalina. From low to mid tide this rocky spot offers short intense barrels for expert surfers.

If the Pacific coast isn't doing it, or you've opted for a winter trip, Panama's Caribbean coast also has some great spots that are worth checking out. The Bocas del Toro Islands lie close to the border with Costa Rica and during the winter months (December to February) the area gets tons of waves. Easterly trade winds generate a consistent supply of windswell, and juicier groundswells periodically pump through from localised storms rumbling off northern Colombia and Venezuela. Although surfing is gaining popularity in Bocas del Toro, the lineups remain relatively uncrowded and the mellow vibe is more Caribbean than Central American. The town of Bocas del Toro is another draw for travellers, with its colourful wooden houses and funky waterfront bars. On the downside, it rains almost daily in this part of Panama and the roads often become quagmires.

The nearest spots to the town are a couple of lefthand reefs, Paunch and Careñeros. Most days these breaks are small and crumbly, but when a solid swell

hits they shape up to provide fast, hollow waves.

A short boat ride away is Silverback, a beefy righthander which breaks over a sharp reef offering short but intense rides for advanced surfers. It needs a big swell to break but will hold anything the Caribbean wishes to throw at it.

To the north of the town is a beach known as Bluff which has to be one of the heaviest beach breaks in the Caribbean. The waves jack up quickly out of deep water and throw square kegs which slam onto the sand. Advanced-level surfers will be able to snag a few quick barrels here, but you're guaranteed to hit the bottom. Hard. Most days it's probably best left to the boogers.

Bocas del Toro is one of those hit or miss destinations where you can get nothing one week, and score an insane session the next – as British pro Alan Stokes found out. "After a week of mushy surf and downpours, the clouds parted and we chanced upon a super-sucky lefthand wedge. You could take off behind the peak, pull in, and get shacked really deep for a few seconds. We didn't know if anyone had surfed it before, or even if it had a name. We surfed it for two days, absolutely firing. Six foot, really hollow and nobody else out there except us."

So give Panama a try. Spin the bottle, head north or south, and see what you find.

– Owen Pye

STU NORTON

OPPOSITE BLUFF, POSSIBLY THE HEAVIEST BEACH BREAK IN THE CARIBBEAN. BRIT GLOBETROTTER JAYCE ROBINSON PREPARES FOR A SAND-BLASTING.

WHEN TO GO: April to October for the Pacific coast; December to February for the Caribbean coast.
AIRPORT: Panama City (PTY).
ACCOMMODATION: Bocas del Toro has plenty of accommodation to suit all budgets. On the Pacific Coast, your best bet is to stay at a surf camp.

WATCH OUT FOR: Malaria and other tropical diseases, reef cuts.
BOARDS: Bring a couple of shortboards, plus a longer board for chunky days at the reefs.
RUBBER: You'll only need boardies.
AFTER DARK: There are some cool bars and restaurants in Boca del Toros

(try El Pecado or El Ultimo Refugio). Entertainment at the surf camps will probably involve playing pool and sipping ice cold Balboa beer.
ALTERNATIVE EXCITEMENT: Visit Isla de Coiba National Park on the Pacific coast where you'll find amazing jungle scenery and waves.

PAPUA NEW GUINEA

BISMARCK ARCHIPELAGO

TROPICAL FUN, FEW OTHER SURFERS

The Bismarck Archipelago, situated off the northeastern coast of Papua New Guinea, is made up of a handful of large islands, and hundreds of smaller atolls and coral reefs. The most surf-rich area is an arc of islands which starts in the west at the Admiralty Islands, and extends to New Hanover and the multitude of small islands in the Kavieng area at the northeastern tip of New Ireland.

This part of PNG is renowned for its spectacular surfing and diving in crystal clear waters. The coast is littered with surf breaks, while below the waves are dozens of awesome dive spots, including planes and boats from World War II. Most of the natives in the coastal areas make a living from fishing or coconut farming, and they're friendly and welcoming. The archipelago offers loads of potential for adventurous surf travellers; it's also stunningly beautiful and largely untouched by western influences.

SIMON WILLIAMS

The Admiralty Islands, at the western end of the archipelago, are some of the few places on earth where you can go on a surf trip and not see hide nor hair of another wave rider (apart from the local fishermen who catch the odd line of whitewater in their canoes). The area offers total isolation from the rest of the world, plus some of the most perfect waves on the planet. Twiggy's, near Manus Island, is a perfect righthander, named in honour of the late Australian surf photographer Kevin 'Twiggy' Sharland. The wave holds a perfect shape and zips along a shallow coral reef, offering a flawless barrel from the take off to the channel. You can stall on takeoff, hang in the barrel, come out with a snap to lose your speed, then sit in the shade for a while longer. There are four other quality waves nearby, and elsewhere in the Admiralty Islands there must be loads of unridden breaks. British pro Spencer Hargraves, who spent a week in the area on a boat charter, rated it highly. "The waves were beyond perfect, and we were the only guys there. The whole place is amazing with this incredible backdrop of beautiful tropical islands. Huge butterflies would fly through the lineup between sets and there were all sorts of fish swimming underneath us. The water was the warmest I've ever surfed in, and the cherry on the cake was not seeing another surfer the whole trip."

New Hanover is the next large island in the archipelago, and its north coast is home to Clem's Place, a new surf camp which combines all the creature comforts of home with the beauty and freedom of living on a remote tropical island. The camp overlooks its own break, Clem's Right, a long and hollow righthander which is one of the best spots in the region. Other breaks like Malili (a racy, barreling left) and Vala Vala (a reliable righthand reef pass) are a short boat ride from the camp.

The 40 kilometre (25 mile) stretch of sea between New Hanover and New Ireland is crammed with some 35 small islands and atolls, and these offer a smorgasbord of waves to suit all abilities. Senta Pass (a long fast left), Ral (a swell magnet with lefts and rights breaking next to a small uninhabited island) and Edmago Island (a quality left adjacent to another tiny island) are among the best spots. They're all within easy reach of Lissenung Island Resort, a superb diving resort which also caters for surfers.

Finally, at Kavieng, on the northwest tip of New Ireland, you'll find yet more quality reefs. Pikinini (Mongol Point) is a heavy spot situated just north of the town; on a big northwest swell, beefy rights reel across a super shallow reef for 200 metres, offering thick-lipped barrels for the brave. A few hundred yards across the harbour channel is Nusa Left, a fast and hollow goofyfoot's dream, which breaks over a similarly shallow reef. Watch out for the sketchy end section here.

In short, the Bismarck Archipelago is a remote yet uncrowded tropical surf paradise. It gets less swell than Indo, but the trade-off is minimal crowds. Just keep your eye on the tide – when it's low, many of the spots get super shallow, super quickly. **– Rob Barber**

OPPOSITE TOP A TYPICAL PNG SETUP – TWIGGY'S IN THE ADMIRALTY ISLANDS. **OPPOSITE BOTTOM** GOLD COAST PRO DRU ADLER ENJOYS A BIT OF SOLITUDE IN PNG.

WHEN TO GO: November to April.
AIRPORT: Fly into Port Moresby (POM) then get a connecting flight to Kavieng (KVG).
ACCOMMODATION: Try Clem's Place on New Hanover, or Lissenung Island Resort near Kavieng (packages available from The Surf Travel Co).

Boat charters are also available.
WATCH OUT FOR: Malaria, stonefish, and cuts from the shallow reefs.
BOARDS: Take a couple of shortboards and a step-up in case you score a solid swell.
RUBBER: PNG is right on the equator so you'll only need boardies.

AFTER DARK: Enjoy incredible fish meals at your camp or aboard your boat charter.
ALTERNATIVE EXCITEMENT: The diving is incredible. You can swim with some 175 different species of fish at Lissenung Resort and explore sunken planes and boats.

PERU

CHICAMA AREA

LUDICROUSLY LONG LEFTS, ANYONE?

In a world of non-stop digital content where new spots are found and quickly blown open by Facebook check-ins or stray tweets, and where the number of travelling surfers multiplies by the day, one would be forgiven for thinking the game is up for the world's best spots. Take Pipe, or Padang Padang, or even Chopes on a chunky swell – if you want to surf epic waves at the best breaks, you know you're in for serious crowds, aggro lineups, and one wave every three hours. But not everywhere. On Peru's desolate northwest coast you can step back in time and find classic waves going unridden, which peel off for as far as the eye can see.

The name which everyone knows, but few have actually experienced, is Chicama. The longest left in the world, Chicama is an oceanic marvel; its textbook bathymetry capable of producing mind-bogglingly long rides. Chicama is not, however, the only reason to visit this stretch of coast, which lies 600 kilometres (375 miles) north of Peru's capital, Lima. There are several other point breaks here with equally mesmerising waves. Just make sure you're ready for the bleakness of the region – it's a huge, barren desert, often shrouded in fog. Be sure to bring a good book and a

crammed iPod for the downtime between sessions.

The 80-kilometre (50-mile) stretch of coastline from Pacasmayo to Trujillo (the region's main city) is dotted with a series of quality lefthand point breaks. These include (from north to south) Pacasmayo, Puemape, Chicama, Punta Prieta and finally Huanchaco. Swells from the south or southwest wrap around each headland to create the perfect point break setup. Tucked in behind these headlands, the points enjoy offshore conditions most of the time thanks to the prevailing southeasterly or southerly winds.

The chilly Humboldt Current cools the water all year round, and brings with it lingering sea fog and cold air. Although you can get away with a shortie in the summer, a 3/2mm fullsuit will be needed for the cooler months of May to December.

Despite its world famous reputation, Chicama remains refreshingly free of crowds. This is in part due to the desolate location, and also to the sheer length of ride – waves peel for up to four kilometres (two and a half miles), all the way from the outer headland to the pier. Although you can't surf the full length of the point in one ride (the sections don't quite link up) you can do it in three or four, if your legs hold out. The sweep running down the point is quite strong so it's pointless to paddle back towards the headland after a ride; most people catch a few waves then just get out and walk. Guests staying at the local surf lodge hitch rides in their Zodiac to save walking (a practice which has caused a little local resentment), but the vibe in the lineup is

generally still mellow and cool. At low tide the waves break over a sand bottom most of the way, with a few rocky patches here and there. Depending on the swell size and direction, some sections will occasionally offer brief cover-ups, but most just wall up for hundreds of yards, begging to be carved to pieces until you are spent.

North of Chicama, the next point you come to is Puemape, 20 kilometres (12 miles) up the coast as the crow flies. Puemape is a deserted fishing village with eerie abandoned buildings; these days its only attribute is the consistent lefthander which reels down the headland for an age. Breaking quickly in front of a rocky outcrop, the wave decelerates to become a long carvable wall as it wraps into the bay. Although it picks up more swell than Chicama, it doesn't have quite the same level of protection from the headland so it often gets ripped up by cross-shore southerly winds. You'll need a 4x4 to make it down the long dirt track from the highway.

Ten kilometres further north you reach Pacasmayo, another super-long lefthand point. It's a rockier spot than Chicama but picks up more swell and can often be a better shape. It'll happily hold 12 foot waves, although it only gets that big a few times a year.

To the south of Chicama you'll find two more left points at Punta Prieta and Punta Huanchaco. The latter is home to the caballitos de totora who've been cruising the waves on their reed watercraft for countless generations. **– Owen Pye**

OPPOSITE: ENDLESS LEFTHANDERS AT CHICAMA – AND THAT'S JUST THE INSIDE SECTION.

WHEN TO GO: May to September is the best time for swell, although the summer months are less foggy.
AIRPORT: Fly into Lima (LIM) then get a connecting flight to Trujillo (TRU).
ACCOMMODATION: There's a new(ish) surf lodge at Chicama. Cheaper accommodation is also available.

WATCH OUT FOR: Rocks and urchins at some of the points. Fog-induced depression.
BOARDS: Take a floaty shortboard for the typical small days, plus a longer board in case a macking swell hits.
RUBBER: Despite its latitude, close to the equator, you'll need a 3/2.

AFTER DARK: Head to Trujillo for some action at the weekends.
ALTERNATIVE EXCITEMENT: Visit Chan Chan (near Huanchaco), the ruins of an ancient mud-brick town built around 1300 AD. Or go hiking in the Cordillera Blanca mountain range, with glaciers and hot springs.

PHILIPPINES

SIARGAO ISLAND

WORLD-CLASS CLOUD 9, AND MORE...

There are more than 7,000 islands in the Philippines, and by definition countless surf breaks. However one small island, Siargao, attracts by far the biggest number of visiting surfers due to it being home to the jewel in the crown of the Philippines, Cloud 9. This perfect righthander is famous for its barrels, and also for its history. The break was discovered in 1988 by feral American surfer Mike Boyum, who was on the run from the authorities on drug charges. Travelling under the name 'Max Walker', Boyum was looking for a remote hideaway where he could lie low and surf perfect waves all alone. He found that place on Siargao. Fourteen years earlier Boyum had set up the world's first surf camp at Grajagan in Java, and he must have thought he'd found another surfing nirvana when he arrived on Siargao. But as things turned out, the eccentric traveller had little time to enjoy his discovery; a few weeks after arriving he embarked on a 50-day cleansing fast... and after 47 days he was found dead in his beachfront cabin. The epic waves Mike Boyum had stumbled upon remained empty for another four years. Then, in 1992, pro surfers Taylor Knox and Evan Slater rocked up on a Surfer Magazine shoot with photographer John Callahan. They scored epic waves at Boyum's reef, which they named Cloud 9 after a Filipino chocolate bar. The mag ran a cover story about the discovery, and surfers around the world began fantasising about riding the beautiful waves in Callahan's photos. In the 20 years since, many thousands of surfers have made the long trek to Siargao to sample the pure perfection of Cloud 9.

These days there are two surf camps at Cloud 9 and a viewing platform smack in front of the peak – yet the wave is still as perfect as it's ever been. The peak jacks up and throws quickly, but even your gran could get barrelled here. Southwesterly winds are offshore and, like most of the spots in the Philippines, Cloud 9 needs a typhoon groundswell from the northeast to really get going. No one knows the reef better than the pack of local groms, who rip on battered old boards left behind by travelling surfers. Be patient, show respect, and you'll be sure to reap the benefits.

If the crowd at Cloud 9 gets too much for you, the good news is that there are a number of other great breaks nearby. Many involve short boat rides but these are widely available and cheap. Tuason Point, just around the corner to the south, picks up any swell going (which is good considering there can be long periods of small swell in the Philippines). A powerful wave when over head-high, catch it early in the morning when it's glassy and pick your line carefully, it gets heavy. It works best at high tide with a westerly wind. Nearby, Rock Island (also known as Tuesday Rock) is a fun righthander that peels off a tiny island a short boat ride

from General Luna. It's quite exposed so best on windless days.

To the north of Cloud 9, near Pilar, yet more reefs can be found. Stimpy's is a heavy left which wraps around a small island and breaks onto a shallow reef; a fast and warpy barrel, it needs full commitment from takeoff on the bigger days. Nearby, Pancit is a mellower right, best at lower stages of the tide. Continue north to San Isidro and you'll find a fast lefthander called Pacifico just north of the rivermouth. Elsewhere there are yet more breaks, but Cloud 9 and its neighbouring reefs should certainly provide enough action to satisfy your initial cravings. – Owen Pye

OPPOSITE SPANISH TRAVELLER PABLO GUTIERREZ BAGS A CLOUD 9 BEAUTY. RIGHT CLOUD 9 AND ITS FAMOUSLY RICKETY VIEWING PLATFORM.

WHEN TO GO: The Philippines are prone to inconsistency as they rely on typhoons in the southwest Pacific to generate groundswells. These are most frequent from August to November.
AIRPORT: Fly into Cebu (CEB) then get a ferry across to Siargao Island.

ACCOMMODATION: Try the Sagana Resort at Cloud 9. Pilar and General Luna are other good places to base yourself.
WATCH OUT FOR: Reef cuts, going stir crazy off season.
BOARDS: Bring a couple of shortboards plus a step-up or semi-

gun for the heavier reefs.
RUBBER: Boardshorts or a shortie.
AFTER DARK: General Luna has a couple of bars and clubs.
ALTERNATIVE EXCITEMENT: Take some time out to snorkel, dive and explore the countless islands.

PORTUGAL

NAZARÉ TO SINTRA

PORTUGAL'S PREMIER COASTLINE

The west coast of Portugal is one of Europe's main swell magnets, able to vacuum the smallest bump from the North Atlantic and lay it out across the region's points, reefs, slabs and beaches with super consistency. From the biggest ridable waves in the world at Nazaré, via the freakish beach break of Supertubos, to the world-class points of Ribeira d'Ilhas and Coxos in the south, the whole area is loaded with quality waves.

While Portugal has a beautifully warm climate, the chilly Canaries Current keeps the water cool, meaning a 3/2mm wettie is standard uniform throughout the year. During the autumn months, low pressure systems tracking across the North Atlantic generate beefy northwest groundswells which light up the breaks along the entire coast. These months are always the busiest of the year, with scores of visitors joining the locals surfers in the lineups. Portuguese surfers are on the whole friendly, but a respectful attitude needs to shown at the tight takeoff zones of some of the gnarlier waves in the area.

Nazaré you'll know well; the freakshow happens deep winter but it's also fun when it's small as it'll still have a wave when further south is flat.

Peniche has a different feel to prettier Ericeira in the south. Once a town of industrial toil, it's developing nicely now the fish factory doesn't stink the town out. The old town sits on a low-lying rocky outcrop which was once an island; it's now joined to the mainland by a narrow sandy isthmus, with beaches on either

side. On the south side of the isthmus, and taking full advantage of the prevailing northerly nortada winds, sits Peniche's jewel in the crown, Supertubos. When it's on, the 'Portuguese Pipeline' breaks onto a punishingly shallow sandbank and can deliver fast, hollow barrels. It works best on fuller tides and can handle triple overhead waves. There's a fine line here between a deep makeable keg and a board-snapping closeout, especially when it's big. Offshore on a northeast wind, Supertubos works on any swell from the west quadrant. You'll always find a frothing crew of local surfers and bodyboarders in the lineup when it's on, but hit it early and you should score plenty of waves. Get a grinding barrel here and you'll never forget it. It's no surprise it's

become a popular stop on the World Tour.

Just north of the town there's a reef at Baleal, which offers fun lefts when the wind is from the south. And further up the coast, past Ferrel, are a number of punchy beach break spots which can be ace fun on a small to medium swell.

Just south of Peniche there's a right point break tucked in behind the fortress at Consolaçao. This spot can hold big swells but it's quite a fat wave and the rocky seabed is urchin city.

Further south are a string of good beach break spots which are often overlooked in favour of the better known waves in the area. The unimpeded nature of the west-facing coastline means that all these beaches →

ABOVE PEDRO BOONMAN ON A RED LETTER DAY AT SUPERTUBOS.
LEFT NAZARE LINES.

WHEN TO GO: September to April.
AIRPORT: Lisbon (LIS).
ACCOMMODATION: The Peniche area has plenty of options including great surf camps right on the beach like Baleal Surf Camp. Around Sintra, SaltyWay Travel is a surf camp also offering yoga and climbing. In classy Estoril head to Blue Boutique Hostel for surf and yoga.
WATCH OUT FOR: Car break-ins, clean-up sets on solid west swells.
BOARDS: Take a couple of shortboards plus a step-up if you plan to tackle the heavier spots on beefy swells.
AFTER DARK: Portuguese seafood is famous and there are many local restaurants worth seeking out to get a traditional experience. Parties start late in Portugal, so wait 'til midnight and follow your nose.
ALTERNATIVE EXCITEMENT: Hike up to the castle in Sintra or hit the skatepark at Tiago's shop in Ericeira.

can fire on their day, and they don't need big swells to get going. Ten kilometres south of Peniche is Praia de Areia Branca, a decent beachie located just off the N247 before it angles back inland to Lourinha. When the lineup is packed at Supertubos and an easterly wind is blowing, this spot can be a saviour.

Continuing south, decent peaks can also be found at Praia de Ribeiro, which is somewhat more sheltered than other beaches in the area. It never gets too crowded and has a peak in the middle giving both lefts and rights; avoid high tide though. Seven kilometres down the coast, south of Maceira, you'll find Praia de Porto Novo, which offers yet more beach break peaks and a rivermouth at the north end. The breaks here provide a good opportunity to escape the pack and get some juice to yourself.

Next up is Santa Cruz, a small seaside resort which bears little resemblance to its Californian namesake, although it does offer some fun beach break peaks when the wind is from the east.

Towards Ericeira the landscape changes, becoming more hilly. The scenery resembles that of the Great Ocean Road in Australia – the coastline is mostly steep cliffs, but here and there are bays and inlets where the gently dipping limestone strata provide all manner of points reefs and slabs.

Coxos, five kilometres north of Ericeira, is one of Europe's best points, a fast-breaking right which jacks up and rifles along a shallow ledge for a good 200 metres. Powerful chunks of North Atlantic swell unload here with a heavyweight punch, snapping leashes, boards and bodies without a second thought. Getting in and out can be tricky as the rocks are sharp, and the small takeoff zone can get a little tense if respect isn't shown; play by the rules and you shouldn't have too much to deal with... except maybe a punishing reef beat-down should you put a foot wrong! On solid days you'll need a step-up or semi-gun to race the speedy sections at Coxos. It's best from low to mid tide. Advanced surfers only.

The next break south, Ribeira d'Ilhas, is a mellower right point which has been an ASP contest venue for decades. From the top of the hill the setup is similar to Bells Beach in Australia, with stratified cliffs overlooking a wide, gently sloping rock platform. On a clean four- to six-foot swell, lovely long righthanders peel into the bay which you can carve apart for hundreds of metres. There's often quite a sweep running southwards down the point so select a board which paddles well.

Just before you reach the edge of the town are a couple of spots which are worth locating, if you're up for a challenge. Reef is a gnarly righthander which slams onto a shallow limestone slab, offering short intense

barrels for the very brave. It works from low to mid tide. A stone's throw away is Pedra Blanca (White Rock), a hollow lefthander which detonates over a shallow and uneven reef, best from mid to high tide. Both spots are pretty fussy and only work on a clean groundswell with glassy conditions or light offshores. If the waves are good, expect to encounter a crew of hot local surfers and bodyboarders at both spots.

Ericeira itself is a picturesque little town with narrow cobblestone streets and whitewashed houses. It makes a good base if you're staying in the area, and even if you're only passing though it's a cool place to spend an afternoon wandering around. Stop at a pastelaria (cake shop) for coffee and cakes.

Five kilometres south of the town is São Julião, a consistent beach break which serves up fun waves on small to medium swells. It's the best spot in the area for beginners and intermediates.

Continuing south you reach beautiful Sintra, crowned with an ancient hilltop fortress built by the Moors in the 9th century. From the top you get unbelievable views over the surrounding landscape. Back down at sea level, Praia Grande is another punchy beachie which can deliver Hossegor-like barrels on its day. **– Owen Pye**

Baleal Surfcamp

Peniche, Portugal   since 1993

The Original Portuguese Surfcamp

—

celebrating 25 amazing years!
1993–2018

www.balealsurfcamp.com

PORTUGAL

THE ALGARVE

BEACH BREAKS GALORE

"Sorry mate, everywhere's blown out in a westerly, best go to the pub..." It's the curse of many a surf trip. Your destination may be loaded with classic setups but unseasonable weather can shaft even the best-laid plans and leave you sobbing inconsolably into your continental lager for days. Enter The Algarve. With two coastlines facing in completely different directions (giving you options in pretty much every wind direction), the chances of finding decent waves in this region of Portugal are almost a dead cert.

Hot, dry and dusty (most of the time, anyway), The Algarve stretches right along Portugal's southern coast; head 250 kilometres southwest across the Gulf of Cadiz and you're in Morocco. But the water is cool, so you'll need a wettie, even in summer.

Unless you're hitting it in a van or camping then

you've got two main options in terms of where to stay: Lagos or Sagres. If you want to be in an authentic Portuguese town with plenty of things to do, then head for Lagos. The name literally means 'lakes' and the town has been around for a couple of millennia. It's got proper history and stuff. First settled by the Carthaginians, it (like most of Europe) got turned over by the Romans, and then over the centuries by various other mobs like the Moors. All of whom have left the odd building, which gives Lagos that proper old town feel. It was from here that Portuguese explorers set sail to explore the unknown world in the Middle Ages. Oh, and it's also a massive party town.

If you want to be closer to the surf (with two decent breaks within walking distance), then Sagres is the other option. Here you're on the southwesternmost tip of Europe – go out to the cape and you feel like you're halfway across the Atlantic. The town is much smaller than Lagos but it has embraced its geographic position for surf tourism and there are now bars, restaurants, surf shops and plenty of places to stay.

The west coast is a wild, unspoilt area protected from development because it's a national park. Here you'll find bay after bay of west-facing, punchy beach breaks. With stupendous cliffs and humbling beachies it feels a bit like Cornwall after a few too many protein shakes. There are some great spots (enough of them to spread the crowds), and there can't be a surf mag in Europe that doesn't draw a significant percentage of their 'sunny European sessions' shots from this stretch

of coastline. Some spots can be reached by tarmac roads, others only by dirt tracks. Be warned – the dirt tracks can be treacherous and there are few signs; if you want to go exploring it pays to have a 4x4, a GPS and a good map. Alternatively, hook up with a guide from one of the numerous surf camps. Castelejo, Cordoama, Amado, Odeceixe and Carrapateira are just some of the spots along this stretch of coast.

Further north, Arrifana is a rocky right-hand point which turns on when the swell hits six feet. Able to handle pretty much everything the Atlantic can chuck at it, and sheltered from the northwesterlies, it's a demanding spot for experienced surfers.

If the west coast is maxed out, or it's onshore, then it's time to alter your perspective and head for the south coast. Here you'll find shelter from the cursed *nortada* (a summer wind which can blow out the entire west coast of Portugal for weeks on end) as well as yet more good beach break spots. When there's a decent low pressure system in the mid or south Atlantic, breaks like Zavial and Beliche turn on, providing everything from playful shoulder-high peelers through to meaty overhead grinders. **– Roger Sharp**

OPPOSITE THE ALGARVE'S WEST COAST GETS SOLID.

WHEN TO GO: Autumn's the safest bet, but you can score it at any time.
AIRPORT: Faro (FAO) or Lisbon (LIS). You can hire a car pretty cheaply; Lagos is about an hour's drive from Faro, or around four hours' drive from Lisbon.
ACCOMMODATION: The legendary Surf Experience surf camp in Lagos

have 25 years experience in guiding, coaching and partying. There are also plenty of holiday rentals and villas dotted around.
WATCH OUT FOR: Submerged rocks (hidden at high tide) at beach breaks like Praia da Cordoama and Praia do Amado.
BOARDS: Two or three shortboards will

do it, from your groveller through to something you can use in six- to eight-foot goodness.
RUBBER: Bring a 3/2.
AFTER DARK: Sample some all-time seafood or top notch pizza, then hit the town and party.
ALTERNATIVE EXCITEMENT: Heard of golf? It's big down here.

PUERTO RICO

ISABELA TO RINCÓN

CARIBBEAN JUICE

Situated between the Dominican Republic and the Virgin Islands, Puerto Rico is to the Caribbean what O'ahu is to the Pacific: the go-to destination for big, powerful surf and all that accompanies it. The island is about 160 kilometres (100 miles) long by 50 kilometres (30 miles) wide, with a population of around three million. The northwest coast, from Isabela to Rincón, is generally considered the prime area for surfing – here you'll find a string of breaks which receive wrapping north swells while simultaneously being offshore on the prevailing easterly trade winds. Throughout the winter months, low pressure systems moving up the eastern seaboard of the US generate short-lived but sometimes juicy swells which light up the island's breaks. PR benefits from the fact that the second deepest oceanic trench in the world lies just off its northern coastline; this allows incoming swells to pound its shores with unfiltered power and size.

Near the town of Isabela are a cluster of north-facing breaks which receive a consistent supply of swell and are often good on calm days. Middles, Golondrina's, Jobo's and Shacks can all turn on to provide quality waves on calm days. Indeed Middles was the venue of the 2010 Rip Curl Pro Search event. Watch out for patches of shallow reef here and there.

Close to the airport you'll find Wilderness, an aptly named spot which can offer excellent bowly lefts and rights breaking over a ledgy, rocky reef. It'll hold sizey swells, but the bigger the waves the stronger the rips. Down the coast is the revered Gas Chambers, a world-class right which breaks with an absolutely sick barrel,

albeit rarely. Total commitment is required to paddle into a wave here, but those that do are in for something to remember. Watch out for aggro locals and backwash – both can get heavy. A stone's throw away is Crash Boat, a high-tide right which breaks off the breakwater next to the Aguadilla Country Club. It's a great wave on its day, but again the vibe can be heavy.

Further west, near the resort town of Aguada, is Table Rock, a hard-breaking righthand reef break with a sketchy inside section. It's another spot for experts only. Less experienced surfers should head to more user-friendly breaks like BC's (on the beachfront at Aguada), Sandy Beach, Antonio's or Pool's (a few kilometres to the west), which offer plenty of fun peaks, as long as the easterly trades aren't blowing too strongly.

Towards Rincón the orientation of the coast swings through 90 degrees; this area is home to a series of quality righthanders which peel off with mechanical regularity when a solid north swell wraps around the low cliff-lined headland. The first and most consistent spot is Domes, named after the incongruous nuclear plant nearby (which was decommissioned in the '70s). Domes was the main venue of the 1968 World Championships, the contest that put Puerto Rico on the surfing map. The waves, though fun, tend to be sectiony and they're often crowded if good. Just around the corner is Indicators, situated near the lighthouse. It's a faster-breaking but much sketchier prospect. A few hundred metres south you come to Maria's ('The Point'), another right point which serves up fun rippable waves which peel for a couple of hundred metres on a good day. The reef here is fairly flat and it's nearly always offshore, so the lineup often gets pretty crowded, with intermediates and longboarders adding to the throng. The waves are hollower at low tide.

Tres Palmas, two kilometres south, is PR's big-wave break, which lights up a few times a year on booming swells to provide PR's chargers with a Sunset-style drop. It'll comfortably hold waves up to 15 feet.

Finally, close to the boat ramp at Rincón, nestles Black Eagle (also known as Little Malibu). This sheltered spot doesn't break too often, but it's a quality wave offering fast, hollow barrels which spiral across a very shallow coral reef. **– Rob Barber**

ABOVE BREAKS LIKE WILDERNESS COME TO LIFE WHEN A SOLID NORTH SWELL HITS PR. **LEFT** LOCAL PRO BRIAN TOTH CHARGES A SLABBY LEFT IN THE AGUADILLA AREA.

DJ STRUNTZ

WHEN TO GO: November to February.

AIRPORT: Most international flights land at San Juan (SJU), but you can fly direct to Aguadilla (BQN) from US cities such as Orlando and New York.

ACCOMMODATION: Rent an apartment in Isabela, Aguadilla or Rincón.

RUBBER: You'll only need boardies.

BOARDS: Take a selection of boards, including a step-up or semi-gun if the forecasts show a booming swell heading for the island.

WATCH OUT FOR: Crazy drivers, heavy localism at certain spots, car break-ins, shallow reefs.

AFTER DARK: The nightlife in Puerto Rico is mental with thumping rhythms and sweaty clubs.

ALTERNATIVE EXCITEMENT:
It's not all about the parties, waves and beaches; Puerto Rico also offers fantastic golf, hiking, diving and more.

SAMOA

UPOLU AND SAVAII

QUALITY REEFS, CONSISTENT SWELL

The small South Pacific nation of Samoa is located about halfway between New Zealand and Hawaii. The two main islands, Upolu and Savaii, are similar in size to the Hawaiian islands of O'ahu and Maui. From the palm-fringed white sand beaches to the countless small rural villages, the pace of life here is unhurried and laid-back.

To keep everyone on their toes, the Government has made a few changes to the status quo in recent years. They've changed the name of the country (from Western Samoa to plain Samoa), they've changed the side of the road cars drive on (from right to left), and they've changed the country's time zone (from -12 to +13). In order to accomplish the latter, they simply abolished Friday 30 December 2011 altogether!

Happily, one thing that hasn't changed is the quality of the surf that pounds Samoa's numerous reefs. The islands have a virtually unimpeded 360° swell window, and there are some truly world-class waves when everything comes together.

Most of Samoa's best spots lie on the south coast of Upolu, along a string of fringing coral reefs. These reefs are often 500 to 800 metres offshore, so it's best to get a boat out to them (no problem if you're staying at one of the local surf resorts as they usually include boat rides in the package). Incoming open ocean swells break hard and fast on these shallow reefs, producing hollow crystal-clear caverns. Pretty obviously, these are best suited to advanced-level surfers.

During the wet season (November to April) the trade winds blow from the northeast, so the south coast spots are either beautifully glassy or bang offshore. However, the swells coming up from the Roaring Forties at this time of year tend to be on the small side, typically from two to five feet. In the dry season (May to October) larger groundswells hit the south coast, but they're accompanied by southeasterly trades so you need to be a committed dawn patroller to score clean waves.

The imaginatively named Main South Coast Road allows easy access to the villages and bays along the south coast. At the village of Salani you'll find a short barrelling left plus a hollow right just across the channel. Both are consistent, top quality waves... just don't try to surf the left at low tide.

Eight kilometres (five miles) to the west you come to Devil's Island (Nuusafee), a tiny islet which is home to one of Samoa's most challenging waves. The wave peels around the side of the island so it's offshore when the southeasterly trades are blowing. On a big swell the three sections link up to create a long, world-class left which gets hollower and faster the further you ride it around the reef. Shallow and intimidating (you can see the reef right underneath you), this is a spot for experts only. High tide only.

Continue west another eight clicks and you come to Boulders, a chunky left which means business on a decent swell and is reasonably protected from the wind.

Further along the coast you'll find more quality spots like Sales (another hollow left reef) and Coconuts (a hollow right which wraps beautifully around a horseshoe-shaped reef).

Upolu's north coast receives beefy northern hemisphere winter groundswells from November to April, but the breaks here are often onshore at this time of year due to the trades. If the wind direction is favourable, however, head for Tiavea Rivermouth (lefts and rights breaking over cobblestones) or Laulii (a hollow right near the island's main town, Apia).

Over on the 'big island' of Savaii, there's a classic A-frame reef on the southeast corner of the island at Aganoa. When it's on, this serves up a long barrelling left and a short hollow right; it's situated close to a family-run surf camp. There are many more spots to be found along this stretch of coast, including a heavy reef called The Leap which will hold sizey waves and can get really good.

Samoa has a strong Polynesian culture and it's important to respect the local traditions and way of life. Drive slowly, dress appropriately (always wear a t-shirt, unless you're at the beach), and don't eat or drink while walking through a village. Christianity is also a key part of Samoan life; be aware that it's frowned on to do any kind of sports, including surfing, on a Sunday.

– Rob Barber

OPPOSITE OZZIE WRIGHT SCREAMS THROUGH A SAMOAN SHACK.

WHEN TO GO: May to October for solid swells on the south coast; November to April for small, fun, glassy waves.
AIRPORT: Apia (APW).
ACCOMMODATION: There are several good surf camps—The Surf Travel Company offers packages to Coconuts and Sinalei resorts.

Traditional fales (thatched huts) can be rented cheaply if you wanted to go your own way.
WATCH OUT FOR: Sharp shallow reefs are the main hazard. There are mozzies but Samoa is malaria free.
RUBBER: You'll only need boardies.

BOARDS: Take a quiver of boards apropriate for the season you go.
AFTER DARK: Don't miss the amazing fire dancers.
ALTERNATIVE EXCITEMENT: Check out the amazing coastal scenery, or go snorkelling, diving or hiking.

SCOTLAND

THURSO AREA

REEFS, SLABS AND WHISKY GALORE

Just glance at a map and you can see the potential of Scotland – points, bays and breaks facing in every direction provide a surfer's perfect environment. Couple this with the relentless march of pressure systems across the northern Atlantic throughout the colder months, and you've got the dream setup.

The heart of the Scottish scene is the area around the town of Thurso, on the far northeast coast of the Highland region. Unlike the rest of Highland it's not a mountainous wilderness – low peat moors make up the bulk of the landscape and these remote areas are among the few untouched examples of this kind of environment in the world. The whole area is pretty spectacular really – ancient castles haunt the cliffs, Neolithic remains are dotted around, and there's a pervading sense of wilderness. And amongst all this are some of the most sublime breaks in the United Kingdom.

SHARPY

Historically the Vikings have had more influence in the area than the Scottish clans, hence the Scandy names – Thurso meaning 'Thor's River' and Brims Ness meaning 'Surf Point'.

Surfing and hardiness go hand-in-hand north of the border and, as well as having some of the most challenging waves in Europe, Scotland also presents one of the most challenging environments. There can be few other places on the planet where recent advances in wetsuit technology are more appreciated. The idea of slipping into a 6/5/4 confident that you'll last a couple of hours in mid-February is a relatively recent phenomena, and one of the reasons that more and more surfers are willing to drop everything and hit the road if conditions look good.

If you bite the bullet and commit for a few days then you'll need somewhere to stay. The hotels and guest houses in Thurso are cheap and surfer friendly. Alternatively, caravans which overlook the bay are available from April to October.

The summer months are generally worth avoiding as there's usually not much swell around. Like most of Europe, autumn is the prime season as the water is warmest, the days are still long, and the swell plentiful. Any swell from the west, northwest or north will provide waves somewhere along the coast, and any size too. Brims Ness, a shallow reef a few miles west of the town, will pick up any swell going, although it's got to be clean to be good. Melvich, a rivermouth with rights and lefts, can be a delight on small to medium swells. And as the waves get bigger, the options just keep opening up. Sandside can sit alongside Europe's best left-handers on its day... although its proximity to the Dounreay nuclear plant tends to put many off. Slab hounds can get their fill if they do some exploring but beware the photogenic watery accidents are very shallow, remote and dangerous.

There is, however, one wave that rolls off the tongue, Tourette's like, when you mention surfing in Scotland—Thurso East. Even before the O'Neill Coldwater Classic brought us streamed images of this iconic wave, its reputation was massive. To really light up it needs a chunky west/northwest swell and gentle southeasterly breeze; luck into that rare combination and you'll see why so many well-travelled surfers place Thurso East right at the top of the tree. Another big plus is the fact that, even in this age of instantaneous surf forecasts and readable swells, the commitment required to get up here keeps crowds to a minimum (compared to other classic European waves). Even on truly classic days, if you play your cards right and respect the hardy local crew you should snag at least a couple. But don't be too precious about it – within an hour's drive there are a hatful of almost-as-classic waves that you can probably have all to yourself. That's Scotland for you.

– Roger Sharp

SHARPY

LEFT NELSON CLOAREC AND COLD, SLABBING, SCOTTISH PERFECTION.
RIGHT CLASSIC THURSO.
ABOVE THE FAMOUS CASTLE RUINS

NORTH ATLANTIC OCEAN

WHEN TO GO: September to March.
AIRPORT: Fly to Inverness (INV) or Glasgow (GLA).
ACCOMMODATION: Caravans, guest houses and hotels are all available.
WATCH OUT FOR: Nuclear debris and deep-fried confectionary.
BOARDS: Pack a couple of standard shortboards, and something to get you into and out of thick, cold barrels.
RUBBER: A 4/3 and boots will keep you warm from late summer to autumn.
AFTER DARK: Grab some scran in one of Thurso's eateries, then try your luck in one of the pubs. Or if it's the weekend enter the legendary Skinandis nightclub.
ALTERNATIVE EXCITEMENT: Hit the road and check out the stunning scenery. Go for a round of golf at Thurso's spectacular course. Or tour the Pulteney whisky distillery at Wick.

SOUTH AFRICA

JEFFREYS BAY AREA

STILL SOUTHERN AFRICA'S BIGGEST DRAW

Where do you start, and where do you stop, when talking about Jeffreys Bay, universally known as one of the best waves in the world? This wave (in fact a series of interlinking waves) has everything any surfer could ever need, with the possible exception of warm water. A tantalising mix of sand and reef, tubes and open face, consistency and length, J-Bay really is one of those waves that every surfer should surf before they die.

The town of Jeffreys Bay lies about an hour's drive from the city of Port Elizabeth, halfway between Cape Town and Durban. The wave itself has been surfed since the early '60s, when South Africa's pioneer longboarders discovering that the end section was perfect for their heavy logs. As time progressed and surfboards became shorter and more manoeuvrable, the focus moved up the point to the aptly named Supertubes, the barrelling 400-metre section you've seen in countless videos and photos, or more recently in webcasts from the World Tour event, which is held there every July.

Ideal conditions for Supers are six to eight-foot waves and light southwest offshores, a magic combination which occurs with ridiculous regularity through the months of May to September. When this happens, Supertubes throws up some of the most

perfect, powerful and paciest tubes on the planet. And if you time it right paddling through the keyhole (a big 'if', granted) you can even reach the lineup with dry hair. A few minutes later a six-wave set will roll in, each wave a mirror image of the last, with six-second tubes the norm. It's also a known scientific fact that you'll never travel as fast on a surfboard as you will if you manage to catch a six-foot wave at Supers.

If the action at Supertubes is too intense for you, there are plenty of other sections offering world-class waves and a mellower vibe. After Supertubes, comes Impossibles (named with good reason), before sections known as Tubes, The Point and Albatross, which all offer fewer crowds and long rippable waves.

To the south there are yet more quality waves; check out the underrated Magna Tubes just around the point, and Kitchen Windows about a kilometre further. Continue 25 kilometres down the road and you reach the Cape St Francis area, where you'll find another cluster of quality breaks, among them Hullet's Reef, Leftovers, Bruce's Beauties and Seal Point. All these spots can fire under the right conditions, with Seal Point picking up the most swell.

However it is J-Bay that will ultimately break your heart and make you deliriously happy. And if all the planets align and you have Dalai Lama-like karma, it's possible to ride a wave from Supertubes all the way through to The Point, by which time you'll have legs like jelly, a heart beating like a hummingbird's, an 800-metre paddle back out and a sense that no matter what happens in the rest of your life, you can die happy. **– Ben Mondy**

ALAN VAN GYSEN

ABOVE THE CLASSIC J-BAY DAWN SESSION.
LEFT A RARE WATER SHOT OF THE PERFECTION.
THE SHARKS KEEP WATER PHOTOGS AT BAY.

WHEN TO GO: May to September.

AIRPORT: Port Elizabeth (PZE).

ACCOMMODATION: Jeffreys Bay has plenty of options, from backpackers to luxury guest houses. Ticket to Ride offer holidays and surf adventures for gap year students.

WATCH OUT FOR: The chances of encountering a shark are remote, but use common sense. Don't go in the water during the sardine runs, and avoid surfing at dawn and dusk.

BOARDS: You'll need a full quiver: fish, shortboards and guns, all aimed at down-the-line speed.

RUBBER: In winter a 4/3 with booties is a minimum requirement.

AFTER DARK: Good bars include the Moroccan Lounge and The Greek Wine Bar.

ALTERNATIVE EXCITEMENT: Go on a safari to the Addo Elephant Park, the Eastern Cape's biggest game park.

SOUTH AFRICA

CAPE TOWN

WHERE OCEANS COLLIDE

The first thing a surfer will find out when visiting
Cape Town is that it is the place where two oceans
meet. There is warm water Cape Town and there
is cold water Cape Town. The warmer Indian Ocean
coastline gets warm enough to surf in boardshorts
in summer, while the colder side can get down to 10
degrees at the same time of year. So equipment varies
from boardies, to 5/4 steamers with boots and hoods,
gloves optional. Once you get your head around the
water temperatures, then you need to work on your
wave sizes.

There is a variance from the timid Muizenberg
learn-to-surf waves, to the mind-blowingly ferocious
waves of Dungeons, one of the premier big wave

locations in the southern hemisphere. Dungeons has
been the home to many big wave awards, from 'Ride Of
The Year', to 'Biggest Wave', to 'Tube Of The Year'; and
if you're that way inclined, bring your big wave A-game
along if you're visiting.

The Atlantic beaches offer a variety of tube options,
with a few beach corners like Llandudno, The Hoek,
Glen Beach and Scarborough forming these perfect
wedging right-hand barrels. They all like smaller swells
and southeast winds are offshore. The southeaster is
the predominant summer wind and it can be a curse
at times, blowing at gale force for weeks on end.
It is known as The Cape Doctor because no smog
or pollution can stick around when she blows. The

ALAN VAN GYSEN

ABOVE DUNGEONS MADNESS.

ALAN VAN GYSEN

drawbacks of the wind are that it makes the water unbearably cold and blows the swell flat.

When the northerly winds blow, then it's offshore in False Bay, on the Indian Ocean side. Generally there are less waves of consequence on the Indian Ocean side, except for one or two lesser-known reef breaks in the Cape Point Nature Reserve – but they both need a fairly rare east swell to come alive. In False Bay there is the notorious Kalk Bay Reef, a left-hand shallow slab that breaks boards and bodies.

Cape Town has so many waves and so much coastline that there are totally independent enclaves that exist independently; you could live in the deep south and surf the big wave spots there, while someone else could be living on the far west coast and surfing the beaches there, and these two groupings might surf five days a week but never, ever meet. **– Craig Jarvis**

WHEN TO GO: Summer is windy, winter is rainy. Early season is March – May or late season September – November.
AIRPORT: Fly to Cape Town International Airport (CPT).
ACCOMMODATION: Surf Life run lessons, trips and rentals. Surfer's Corner in Muizenberg near CT have rad

apartments. In Mossel Bay, Waves School of Surfing run camps and tours. There's loads of options as you'd expect in a big city.
WATCH OUT FOR: Hijackings, petty crime, and some seriously crazy traffic.
BOARDS: Your standard shooters, and your step-up.

RUBBER: Hooded 5mm and all the bits.
AFTER DARK: Cape Town has a rocking nightlife. Try Harringtons, District or Jordy Smith, Twiggy Baker and Reg Macdonald's triple bar/club set-up under one roof called SurfaRosa.
.ALTERNATIVE EXCITEMENT: Go shark cage diving at Gansbaai.

SOUTH ATLANTIC OCEAN

DURBAN

South Africa's
vibrant surf
city offers
waves aplenty.

For any surfer travelling to South Africa, Durban is the go-to city. You'll see why if you take a stroll along 'The Golden Mile', which takes in the promenade from South Beach up to Suncoast Casino & Entertainment World. Beaches, smoking-hot chicks, African culture and a whole range of fun waves, all in a relatively small area.

Durban is the third largest city in South Africa, with a population of more than four million when you include the sprawling suburbs. The city is the commercial centre of KwaZulu-Natal province and its container port is the busiest in the country. Blessed with a subtropical climate and superb beaches, Durban is also a hub for tourism and boasts a great selection of attractions. Durban's consistent warm-water waves have produced some of the world's best surfers, among them legends Shaun Tomson, Mike Esposito and Martin Potter, as well as present day stars Davey Weare, Antonio Bortoletto, Warwick Wright, Travis Logie and Jordy Smith.

Durban's most popular surf spot is **Dairy Beach (1)** famed for its low tide 'backline barrels'. From April to September, whenever there's a morning low tide and a solid south or east swell running, the competition for tubes here will be fierce. But if you manage to snag a super fast right-hander from behind New Pier, the high-line barrel will be one of your all time best. Make use of the rip current next to the pier for an easy paddle out and don't leave valuables on the beach, as petty crime is rife.

Further along, **North Beach (2)** usually has plenty of good peaks

ALAN VAN GYSEN

and there's a fun rip bowl next to the pier at the southern end of the beach. The lifeguards here operate a blackball system — you can surf as long as the blackball is up, but stay out of the bathing area. Continuing north, **Bay of Plenty (3)** is the next beach, then **Snake Park (4),** named after a reptile park which has since closed down; both offer fun, rippable waves on a clean swell.

Crowds are a factor at all these spots. The local crew rip and they won't let a good wave go unridden. Having said that, there's quite a bit of space – this long stretch of beach is separated by piers and breakwalls, so if one area is particularly crowded, just head to the next one along.

Although sharks are a concern elsewhere in South Africa, Durban's beaches have had shark nets since 1962 and the toothy fellas are no longer a problem in the vicinity. If you're interested in sharks (or just

ALAN VAN GYSEN
CAVE ROCK

awed by them), pay a visit to the **Kwazulu-Natal Sharks Board (5)** at Umhlanga Rocks, just north of the city. You'll learn a lot.

On the south side of the city you'll find **Cave Rock (6),** one of South Africa's heaviest and

hollowest reefs. On a good day it serves up Backdoor-style chambers which break onto a shallow and gnarly rock ledge. The local crew are a tight-knit bunch so only paddle out here if you really know what you're doing.

Durban has plenty to offer if the waves are flat. For starters, visit the Gateway Theatre of Shopping on Umhlanga Ridge. It's home to Durban's **Wave House (7),** which has an amazing twin-peak flowrider plus a 4,000-square-yard skatepark designed by none other than Tony Hawk. Or, for a real rush, go bungee jumping at the awesome **Moses Mabhida soccer stadium (8),** one of the venues of the 2010 World Cup.

CHRIS VAN LENNEP
THE WAVE HOUSE.

After a long day's surfing, there's no better way to reward yourself than with a cold beer on the deck of **Joe Cool's Bar (9)** at North Beach, which also serves great food. Other good places to eat are **The House Of Curries**, for giant-sized roti and the best bunny chow in the area; and **Taco Zulu (10),** a Mexican joint favoured by the local surf crew which gets pretty raucous as the night wears on. **– Rob Barber**

CHRIS VAN LENNEP
"YEE-HA!"

CHRIS VAN LENNEP
SCARY

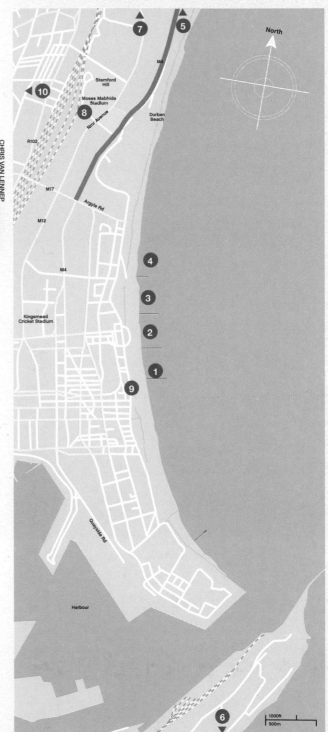

SPAIN

THE BASQUE COUNTRY

MAGNIFICENT MUNDAKA, AND MORE...

The Basque Country is a largely self-governed region of Spain, situated in the northeast of the country. As an 'autonomous community', it has its own flag, its own language (one of the most ancient in Europe), and its own culture and traditions. Inland the landscape is dramatic with mountains, forests and craggy hillsides. The coastline – which stretches from Bilbao to the French border – is mainly cliff-lined and rocky, but a number of large rivers have carved wide valleys for themselves, creating rivermouths and beaches here and there. Among these are a handful of Europe's best surf spots.

The local surfers are passionate, friendly and fiery in equal measure. They are warm and welcoming, yet protective if crossed.

The Basque Country ('Pais Vasco' in Spanish, 'Euskadi' in Basque) is a tough area – industrial, proud and respected. Bilbao and Donostia (San Sebastian) are major cities and surfing is just a summer sport to most beachgoers. The region's pro surfers are respected as modern Basque ambassadors; they include big-wave charger Natxo Gonzales, the Acero brothers and Aritz Aranburu. When the summer pro contests come to Zarautz and Bakio the crowds follow, yet the real Basque beauties don't show themselves until the late autumn or deep winter.

The jewel in the crown of the Basque Country is, of course, Mundaka. On its day, this fabled rivermouth left will serve up freight-train barrels which rifle along the sandbar for 300 metres. It's a like a wave formed in your dreams. But it's an elusive spot. It only breaks on the biggest of swells and consequently it's often flat for months. If you're lucky enough to score perfect conditions here, expect the session to be as dramatic and as tense as anywhere else with truly world-class waves. The locals at Mundaka will not let a wave go unridden, so if you manage to snag a couple of screaming barrels you'll have a surfing story to last a lifetime. Mundaka was a World Tour venue throughout the '00s, and Kelly Slater was crowned World Champion here in 2008. But its fickle nature eventually resulted in it being dropped from the Tour. All the same, it's a special

place and worth a visit in its own right, swell or no swell.

The region has plenty of other waves too. There are dozens of quality beach breaks, many of which are suitable for beginners and intermediates, especially during the summer months. Check out Sopelana, Barrika and Bakio to the west of Mundaka, and Zumaia (which you'll recognise if you watch Game of Thrones), and Zarautz to the east. At the other end of the spectrum, Menakoz is a thundering big-wave spot which looks more Hawaiian than European. It's strictly reserved for experienced chargers. Yes, the Basque Country literally has something for everyone. **– Gabe Davies**

SHARPY

ABOVE THE BASQUE SUPERHIGHWAY HAS MANY MOODS AND IS ALWAYS BUSY. BUT IT'S WORTH IT FOR THE WAVE OF YOUR LIFE.

WHEN TO GO: The prime season for Mundaka is winter, but summertime is fun for beaches and parties.
AIRPORT: Bilbao (BIO).
ACCOMMODATION: Plenty of options in resort towns. In Mundaka there are cabins up on the hill at the campsite or a couple of nice hotels right in the market square.
WATCH OUT FOR: Mundaka is a heavy wave so respect it.
BOARDS: Bring a quiver if you plan to charge Mundaka at size.
RUBBER: Boardies for the summer, a shortie for early autumn, and a fullsuit for the colder months.
AFTER DARK: Hit the pintxos bars for food and drinks, it's the best way to eat and meet the locals. The bars stay open very late so remember to set your alarm for the dawn patrol!
ALTERNATIVE EXCITEMENT: Visit Bilbao's Guggenheim Museum.

SRI LANKA

ARUGAM BAY AREA

SMALL-WAVE FUN IN LAID-BACK SRI LANKA

The Indian Ocean island of Sri Lanka has endured turbulent times in recent decades. It's been scarred by a vicious civil war which raged for 26 years, and in 2004 it was hit by the most destructive tsunami in modern history. The Boxing Day tsunami had a particularly devastating effect on the east coast. Thousands died when towns and villages were inundated by the violent surges; bridges were washed away and fishing fleets wrecked. The country needed to respond quickly to the disaster, and it did, thanks to a massive influx of foreign aid. Roads and bridges were rebuilt and new buildings went up, allowing the vital tourist trade to quickly re-establish itself. Five years later the Tamil Tiger rebels were finally defeated too, and some much-needed peace and tranquillity was restored to this beautiful part of Sri Lanka.

The surf scene on the east coast is centred around the village of Arugam Bay, home to a superb right point of the same name. It's one of several user-friendly points in the area which break consistently from May to November, with July usually being the best month. This period also sees a high proportion of offshore days. The east coast is serviced by frequent Indian Ocean swells which march up from the Roaring Forties.

While advanced-level surfers tend to see Sri Lanka as a 'stop-off' destination between Europe and Australia, the island is a tropical heaven for intermediates. Whatever your ability, you're certain to score some fun waves here. And with friendly people, a laid-back vibe, plus a fascinating ancient culture, you're guaranteed a cool trip.

Arugam Bay (often called A-Bay) rarely breaks over six feet, yet it's unquestionably a world-class wave which peels mechanically down the point for hundreds of metres. "It's a really fun wave," says Brit pro and regular visitor Alan Stokes. "When it's good you can get really long rides and sneak into a few cover-up sections. The reef can be a bit shallow at low tide, but it's nothing too sketchy."

In recent years, as word has spread about its quality, A-Bay has attracted more visitors and begun to suffer from crowding. The fact that it's a very inviting-looking wave means that many beginners are game for a paddle out, and consequently drop-ins are rife. Some of the less experienced locals also lack basic wave etiquette. All this can sometimes leave you feeling frustrated in the busy lineup. So if you want to experience A-Bay at its best, hit it early to beat the crowds. "If you set your alarm and score it without the zoo, you'll be laughing," says Stokesy.

Either side of Arugam Bay there are more breaks to sniff out. Just north of the village, near the new bridge, there's a lefthand slab which can liven things →

OPPOSITE SRI LANKA HAS BEEN A FAVOURITE DESTINATION FOR BRIT SURFERS FOR DECADES. LEE BARTLETT DRIVES OFF THE BOTTOM AT ARUGAM BAY. **RIGHT:** OKANDA'S SHORT BUT SWEET RIGHTHANDERS.

up for advanced surfers. It doesn't break often though, needing a huge swell to work. Further up the coast is Pottuvil Point, another long righthand point with waves breaking over a sand bottom. It needs a big swell to come to life, but on a good day it'll serve up an endless supply of small racy waves which peel down the point for hundreds of metres. The waves break close to the beach and at the end of a ride you just step off onto the

sand and jog back up the point. Be aware that there's not much shelter around here, so take plenty of water and head for the rocks in the middle of the beach to find some shade between sessions. To get to Pottuvil, hop in a tuk-tuk (three-wheel taxi), they're cheap and fun.

To the south of Arugam Bay there are more good spots to explore. The coastline further south, in the Yala National Park, has good potential for discovery although

you need to get access permission from the rangers. There's no shortage of wildlife in this remote jungle region – including leopards, snakes, elephants and lethal crocs.

Any trip to Sri Lanka can't just be about surfing as there's so much culture and history to soak up, and if you're there in the European winter then you'll need to be on the west side. Kandy, Ella, Kumana National Park and the world heritage city of Galle are all worth exploring **– Rob Barber**

ABOVE ARUGAM BAY OCCASIONALLY HOSTS INTERNATIONAL PRO CONTESTS.

WHEN TO GO: May to November.
AIRPORT: Colombo (CMB).
ACCOMMODATION: Plenty of guest houses and cheap hotels in Arugam. Check out Dylan's Surf Co if you need lessons or gear. If in Galle check out the Elysium Collection boutique hotels. Surf School Sri Lanka offer coaching

across the south.
BOARDS: Bring a fish to make the most of everyday small waves, plus a regular shortboard for decent swells.
WATCH OUT FOR: Crowds at A-Bay, nasty bites from mozzies and other insects (get your inoculations sorted). Crocs.
RUBBER: You only need boardies.

AFTER DARK: Check out the local curry restaurants, some are excellent. For a snack, try a roti – a pastry with curried meat or fish inside. They do sweet ones too, like coconut and honey.
ALTERNATIVE EXCITEMENT: Visit Yala National Park (south of Arugam Bay) for amazing scenery and wildlife.

Elysium Collection
Galle, Sri Lanka

ELYSIUM - 48 LIGHTHOUSE STREET - SATIN DOLL

" These magnificent boutique hotels sit discreetly amongst the best in Asia and are located in Galle, Sri Lanka. "

TAHITI

TAHITI, MOOREA AND HUAHINE

AWESOME TEAHUPO'O AND A WHOLE LOT MORE

BEN THOUARD

In many ways it's unfair that Tahiti and Teahupo'o have become inextricably linked. When we think of Tahiti it seems our brains are now hardwired to contemplate those beautiful but deadly turquoise bombs that detonate with almost unimaginable force, juxtaposed against a stunning South Pacific backdrop. From Laird Hamilton's 'Millennium Wave' to any of the action beamed live from the epic 2011 Code Red swell Teahupo'o has grabbed the surfing world by the testicles and simply won't let go.

Yet Teahupo'o is not always death or glory. To paddle out on a clean four- to six-foot south swell, with the sun piercing down from a cobalt sky and the lush green mountains in the distance... well, it's pretty close to surfing nirvana. The waves, while still packing the power of Mike Tyson on horse steroids, are predictably perfect and eminently makeable. It's almost possible to have fun out there.

Of course, as the swell builds, the brown boardshorts likelihood increases exponentially. At eight feet, Teahupo'o seems to double in thickness, and beyond 12 feet you're into cartoon territory.

Julian Wilson, on his first trip to Tahiti in 2011, witnessed the epic tow session on day eight of the Billabong Pro from the channel. "I had sore butt muscles from clenching them all day," laughed Julian. "And that was sitting in the channel. When I finally grabbed the rope, I was saying my goodbyes."

But maybe, just maybe, Teahupoo is giving Tahiti a bad name. You see, it's possible to stay with a family in the village, eat fresh fish and fruit, and live like a king in paradise for $50 a day. Just next to Chopes are waves like Big Pass and Little Pass that are great hotdogging waves suitable for most experienced surfers. And 20 minutes' drive away is Papara, a black sand beach with consistent, super fun waves. Up on the north coast there are more fun waves to be found at Matavai and Pointe Venus.

Elsewhere the neighbouring islands of Moorea and Huahine offer more visions of Pacific paradise, a huge variety of waves, and generally friendly locals. Haapiti, on the west coast of Moorea, is a superb left for experienced surfers; if it's solid, beware the strong current here. Over on Huahine you'll find a cluster of consistent breaks near the town of Fare on the west coast.

The mingling of French and Polynesian culture and cuisine, coupled with the island's natural beauty, means a trip to Tahiti is more than just a surf trip; it's a glimpse into a way of life that is quite possibly the best on earth. **– Ben Mondy**

TIM JONES

TIM MCKENNA

LEFT THE MOST RIDICULOUS WAVE IN THE SURFING UNIVERSE: TEAHUPO'O. **RIGHT** BENJI SANCHIS AT MALIK'S POINT, A FICKLE AND SHALLOW SECRET SPOT.

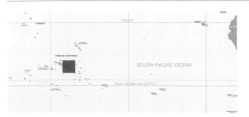

SOUTH PACIFIC OCEAN

WHEN TO GO: May to September has consistent swell and light winds.
AIRPORT: Papeete (PPT).
ACCOMMODATION: Everything from luxury resorts to family-run lodges and pensions. The Surf Travel Company offers a range of packages to suit all budgets.

WATCH OUT FOR: Powerful waves, sharp coral, and the odd shark.
BOARDS: Take as many as your airline will allow. Boards break all too often in Tahiti and are expensive to replace.
RUBBER: Boardies or a shortie.
AFTER DARK: If you've surfed and survived Teahupo'o, a few cold cans of Hinako will be all you need.
ALTERNATIVE EXCITEMENT: Take a drive in the mountains, the scenery is mind-blowing. If you have money to burn take a boat trip out to the Tuamotu Islands —77 atolls with waves aplenty.

USA

SAN DIEGO COUNTY

OFTEN CLASSIC, ALWAYS BUSY

San Diego County epitomises what the stereotypical Californian surf scene is all about. Long golden beaches, lined-up waves and warm offshore winds. From Oceanside to the Mexican border there are hundreds of top breaks fawned over by tens of thousands of surfers who make the pilgrimage every day, come rain or (usually) shine.

Among SoCal's many natural assets are the Santa Ana winds – hot dry offshores that blow from the inland deserts during the autumn and early winter. These clean up the swell lines that march relentlessly down the coast, and they also enhance San Diego's superb climate which averages 300 sunny days a year.

SoCal receives swell from a variety of directions. Northwest swells, generated by Aleutian lows tracking across the North Pacific, pound the coast during the winter months. In spring and summer the juice arrives in the form of long-period groundswells from the South Pacific. Late summer is also the time to catch unpredictable but beefy south swells, generated by hurricanes formed off Mexico.

Oceanside, 40 miles (65 kilometres) north of San Diego, offers a long stretch of quality beach break with reliable banks next to the pier and harbour jetties. Hit it early on a summer south swell to score lush glassy waves, but expect the lineups to be busy. Down the coast, a range of fun waves can be found around Carlsbad and Leucadia; these range from rippable cobblestone breaks to slower beachies, ideal for intermediates and longboarders.

Continue south down the San Diego Freeway and you come to Encinatas, home to one of the best right points in the county, Swami's. This classic point works best on a solid northwest swell so it tends to be a wintertime break. When it's firing, the outer Boneyards section offers steep takeoffs and a few barrels. It'll hold waves up to 15 feet, and then some. When it's on, Swami's is always packed; the ultra keen crew will endure the thickest fog or the dimmest twilight conditions if there's a chance of getting a wave.

A couple of miles further south is Cardiff Reef, a reliable spot with well-shaped lefts and rights, popular with longboarders and riders of all manner of retro craft.

Seaside Reef, adjacent to San Elijo Lagoon, is one of the best spots for advanced surfers along this stretch of coast. A punchy reef with hollow sections and bowls, it breaks on all swells but is best on a west swell at lower stages of the tide. If the waves are good it's guaranteed to be crowded, so keep a low profile and

wait your turn for waves.

South of Cardiff you enter the Del Mar area which can offer good peaks from the rivermouth down to 15th Street. Nearby, Torrey Pines State Park is a good place to escape the crowds; on a medium sized swell it offers fun waves around mid tide for intermediate level surfers.

When the freeway swings inland it signals that you're close to another classic SoCal surf spot – Black's Beach. Tucked away beneath a two-mile stretch of tall cliffs, this world-class beach break packs a heavyweight punch due to a submarine canyon which amplifies the power of incoming waves. Access is via the sketchy trail →

LUCIA GRIGGI

DJ STRUNTZ

OPPOSITE A GLASSY PEAK UNLOADS AT BLACK'S. IN THE BACKGROUND IS SCRIPPS PIER AND LA JOLLA. **FAR RIGHT** NATE TYLER ENJOYING A SUMMER SWELL.

WHEN TO GO: September or October for clean swells and Santa Ana winds.
AIRPORT: San Diego (SAN).
ACCOMMODATION: Plenty of hotels, motels and apartments available. Check out the famous family run Paskowitz Surf Camp, the longest running in the US.
WATCH OUT FOR: Localism at some of the prime spots, crowds at most of the others.
BOARDS: Bring at least two or three boards, their size dependant on the type of waves you want to surf.
RUBBER: A 3/2 will keep you toasty all autumn; you'll want a 4/3 and boots for the winter.
AFTER DARK: For live music check out The Casbah or the House of Blues.
ALTERNATIVE EXCITEMENT: Head for The Wave House at Belmont Park where you'll find the daddy of all flowriders, Bruticus Maximus.

UNITED STATES

ABOVE FUN WAVES AT OCEANSIDE PIER, UP
IN THE NORTH OF SAN DIEGO COUNTY.

behind Torrey Pines Gliderport. Time your paddle out
to coincide with a lull, and watch out for hellish sneaker
sets, they'll do more than just wake you up.

Scripps Pier, next to the Oceanographic Institute of
the same name, doesn't pick up south swells but it can
provide fun, mellow waves on a clean west swell. Aim
for midweek to avoid the crowds.

The upmarket suburb of La Jolla is home to an
array of good waves, as well as some very crowded
lineups. First up are the soft peaks of Shores, popular
with beginners and longboarders. At the western end
of the bay, La Jolla Cove is a big-wave spot which
periodically serves up epic lefthanders for the local
hellmen on macking winter swells. Around the corner
you'll find an assortment of reefs and slabs, including
Horseshoe, Rockpile, Hospital Point and the excellent

Windandsea. These rocky spots are fickle and heavy,
and the locals can be aggressive, so only paddle out if
you really know what you're doing – preferably with an
invite. Just south of Windandsea is one of the heaviest
reefs in the county, Big Rock. It breaks left over a
shallow ledge, gets really hollow, and will happily slam
you into the seabed if you get complacent. Again, it's a
heavily localised spot and always crowded if good.

Around the coastal bulge of La Jolla you come
to a couple of popular longboard hangouts, Pacific
Beach Point and Tourmaline; these mellow waves are
also ideal for beginners and intermediates. A three-mile
stretch of average beach break continues down to
Mission Beach and South Mission Jetty.

Across the mouth of Mission Bay is Ocean Beach,
where you'll find yet more fun breaks around the pier

and jetty. Avoid surfing here during periods of heavy
rain, the water can get pretty polluted.

South of Ocean Beach you reach the sprawling
suburb of Sunset Cliffs where the topography becomes
hilly again. The cliff lined, west-facing coastline is home
to a number of top notch reefs including Ab's, Sub's,
Garbage and Chasm; all work on slightly different
conditions and involve a fair hike across the flat rocky
ledges. Around the tip of Point Loma you'll find the
elusive Ralph's, a quality right point which breaks
over cobblestones on a big south or southwest swell.
Access is only feasible by boat as the adjacent land is
a military base.

To the south of San Diego Harbour are Coronado
and Imperial beaches, which work well on south swells
during the summer months. **– Owen Pye**

SURFING IN SOUTHERN CALIFORNIA IS ALL
ABOUT PERFORMANCE, THE HIGHER THE BETTER.
ALEX GULLETT BUSTS OUT AT SALT CREEK.

SANTA CRUZ

Deep roots, classic points.

The original Surf City USA, Santa Cruz is located at the northern end of semicircular Monterey Bay in Central California. One of the oldest surfing centres in the country, it's renowned for the quality of its breaks, notably Steamer Lane, where the men really are separated from the boys on a big swell. The city is also home to surfwear giant O'Neill, as well as numerous board labels including Santa Cruz Surfboards, Strive and Pearson Arrow.

Unfortunately, the SoCal warmth many associate with the Californian surf scene doesn't extend up to Santa Cruz too often, although it is relatively sheltered from the chilly winds knocking on its northern door. The water is cold throughout the year due to upwellings from the Monterey submarine canyon – so bring a fullsuit (3/2 in summer, 5/3 in winter).

Although Santa Cruz faces south, most of the incoming swell is generated by low pressure systems tracking across the North Pacific. Chunky lines of west and northwest groundswell wrap in and light up the two prime point breaks – Steamer Lane on the West Side, and Pleasure Point on the East Side. Santa Cruz also laps up south swells produced by hurricanes spinning off the coast of Mexico in August and September, as well as

THE WHARF, LOOKING EAST.

long-range southwest groundswells coming out of the South Pacific. This surf city is never short of a wave for long.

Steamer Lane (1) is the heart of Santa Cruz's soul, and plays host to a number of annual events such as the O'Neill Coldwater Classic. Founder Jack O'Neill himself used Steamer Lane as a development centre for wetsuits and new products. Most days you'll find yourself waiting for waves at one of four peaks, depending on the swell size and direction: The Point, The Slot, Middle Peak or Indicators.

When things get serious there's also the outer Third Reef. Of course, with the quality and consistency of the waves come crowds – indeed some days it seems every one of the college town's 60,000 inhabitants is jostling for position in the lineup. The thick kelp can also be a bit of a hassle, especially on small days. The Lane works best on a solid west swell; at mid tide, a good ride can go on 'til your legs give way.

Further around the bay you'll find learner-friendly **Cowell's (2)** and the rare but sometimes punchy beach break peaks of **San Lorenzo**

THE CATALYST ROCKS.

STEAMER LANE'S ICONIC LIGHTHOUSE.

CHRIS BURKARD

CATALYST

CHRIS BURKARD

Rivermouth (3). The next spot is the **Harbor Breakwall (4)** which sometimes provides sucky right-hand barrels at dead low tide on a big swell (although surfing here is technically illegal). Across the boating channel and past a cluster of sheltered spots (Twin Lakes, Blacks and 26th Avenue) you enter the East Side. The focus here is another long right-hand point break, **Pleasure Point (5)** which offers a series of takeoff spots depending on swell size and direction: Sewer Peak, First Peak, Second Peak and 38th. The waves here are consistent, but don't expect to surf here on your own, it's always crowded when good. Sewers can hold waves up to 12 feet; it's best on a southwest swell when it can get hollow. First Peak breaks wider than Sewers and is accessible from the stairs at the end of 30th Avenue; it's less intense than Sewers but can provide excellent rides, which occasionally link up with Second Peak. 38th is predominantly a cruisy spot but can get hollow on a south swell. Further down the

point you'll find a series of inside spots (The Hook, Shark Cove and Privates) which offer fun peeling rights on virtually all swells.

If you're out of luck and you find yourself staring at a flat ocean, check out the **Santa Cruz Surfing Museum (6)** situated in the lighthouse at Steamer Lane. Although small, it houses a fascinating range of boards. The history of surfing in Santa Cruz goes right back to 1885.

The city has loads of great places to eat. For the best pizza in town, head for **Pizza My Heart**

(7); they have boards and surf memorabilia on the walls, and local legend Wingnut does their TV ads. Paula's Cafe at Pleasure Point and Aldo's Cafe next to the Yacht Harbor are both great for breakfast (and lunch).

For live music, head to **The**

Catalyst (8) on Pacific Avenue. The Beastie Boys, Beck, Ben Harper, Bad Religion, BB King, Black Rebel Motorcycle Club, Blue Oyster Cult, The Byrds, The Buzzcocks... they've all played here over the decades, and those are just the 'B's! – **Owen Pye**

A TYPICAL SCENE AT THE LANE.

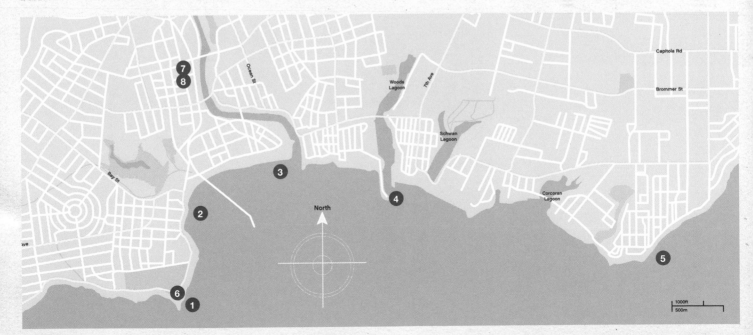

HUNTINGTON BEACH

Southern California's summertime swell magnet.

Huntington Beach, California. Surf City USA! That says it all. It's where pro surfing took off in the States in the early 1960s, and it's still the place to surf during those fairytale summers in Orange County, where the surf is king, and surfers are the slaves.

Huntington Beach is a seaside community of around 180,000 people, which sits about a half hour south of the Los Angeles city border. Though close in proximity, HB is in a world all its own. Some would call it a sheltered city. Others might say its residents are trapped in their own little bubble. But considering how violent, dirty, polluted and stressed neighbouring LA is, maybe it's the truth. In fact, it's gotta be the truth. HB is a lovely town. And if you're a surfer living here, you're in love 24/7, 365 days of the year. 'Cos that's how often you can surf around here. Even in January the water is a bearable 57°F (14°C) so you don't need gloves or a hood. It's the perfect place to live if you live to surf. Sure, other areas of SoCal might have better quality waves, it's just that HB is so bloody consistent.

There's surf almost every day of the year. On a clean swell there'll be fun peaks as far as the eye can see from **Huntington Cliffs (1)** past **Huntington Pier (2)** along **Huntington State Beach (3)** and down to Newport Beach. Throw in nearby coastal towns like Laguna Beach and San Clemente (home of world famous Trestles), and you've got California's equivalent of the North Shore, O'ahu's seven-mile miracle. Only longer. Huntington Beach alone is eight miles long.

Huntington Beach isn't known for tubes, or big waves, it's known

THERE'S NO SHORTGAE OF ACTION AT HUNTINGTON PIER.

JOE FOSTER

LUCIA GRIGGI

for small wave, high-performance shredding. Very exposed to south swells, it's a summertime swell magnet. Hit it early to score glassy conditions in the summer months; onshore sea breezes usually kick in by mid morning.

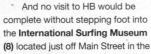

Neighbouring **Newport Beach (4)** is a surf town in its own right with almost as many different spots as there are streets. If you're in HB you'll want to check it out. Next to Newport's harbour entrance is a world famous freak wave called The Wedge. Incoming waves rebound off the jetty and almost double in size before slamming straight onto the sand. It's mainly a bodyboard spot but a few daredevil surfers take it on.

HB's most famous stop for breakfast is **The Sugar Shack (5)** on Main Street, owned by the Turner family. Timmy Turner is an adventurer and filmmaker, while brother Ryan holds it down on any given swell at the Pier. **Sancho's Tacos** is a good call for lunch. After dark **Duke's** or **Sushi on Fire** are both popular places to eat along with Ruby's on the end of the pier.

And no visit to HB would be complete without stepping foot into the **International Surfing Museum (8)** located just off Main Street in the Downtown district. It's crammed full of surfing artefacts that spell out the history of surfing, in California and around the world.

In a nutshell, Huntington Beach has it all. Waves, sunshine, girls, heritage and a huge surfing community. Which explains why they hold the US Open of Surfing here every summer, an event every person should have on their bucket list. A trip to HB during the US Open of Surfing in August is what it's all about. Make that trip. Write about it. Call us in the morning. We think you'll have a clear understanding of why they call it Surf City USA. But then again, if you're hanging Downtown every night, with the three kazillion girls trying to meet 'a surfer', you might just call it Party City USA.

– **Skip Snead**

A BIG DAY AT THE WEDGE.

3

SURF
TRAVEL
INFORMATION

Every destination and every surf break has its own set of hazards, some pretty innocuous, some potentially serious. Here are a few tips to stay safe and healthy when you're away from home.

TRAVEL INSURANCE

One thing easily forgotten (at your peril!) when going abroad is travel insurance. Make sure that you organise this well before you go, and confirm – in writing if necessary – that the policy covers you for surfing. Also check it covers travel delays, cancellations, curtailments, legal expenses, legal support, personal liability and the financial backup of missed and cancelled departures.

Research companies that have good reputations, and if you need to make a claim keep the receipts of everything you needed to buy (especially medicines or other medical supplies). Get the receipts signed by a doctor or other official person if possible, keep them safe, and send them off by recorded delivery within the allocated time stated in your paperwork, so your insurer can't wriggle off the hook on a technicality.

TROPICAL DISEASES

Arrange to have vaccinations at least six weeks before you leave, as they may need time to become effective. Your doctor will tell you which jabs are needed for your destination. See the Resources section on page 222 for a list of useful websites.

Diseases such as malaria and dengue fever can be contracted via mosquito (and other insect) bites, and these can become life-threatening illnesses if left untreated. Some species of mosquito have built up a natural immunity to DEET products, so alternative repellents such as Incognito (which uses powerful, natural ingredients such as citronella and bergamot oil) are becoming more popular.

Use the following tips to avoid being bitten in the first place:
• Always sleep under a mosquito net at night; get one with as fine a mesh as possible.
• Wear long, light-coloured clothing (mozzies are attracted to darker clothing).
• Avoid hanging around near bodies of still water, especially in the evening.
• Wash thoroughly and be as odour-free as possible.
• Olive oil works as a good alternative if you run out of mozzie spray.

The chances of catching tropical diseases and ailments can be greatly reduced by practicing good hygiene and sanitation. Only drink bottled or boiled water, or use water purification tablets. Only consume food that you're certain is safe to eat – if in doubt, stick to the old adage, 'Boil it, cook it, peel it, or forget it'. And keep your food prep areas, water supply, clothing, sheets and living areas clean.

SUNBURN

Nothing sucks more than arriving at your dream destination, paddling out for a long session, getting the most intense sunburn you've ever had, then spending the next week sitting in the shade with your head in a bucket of ice and aloe-vera leaves while you go through the hideous stages of the post-burn spiral.

Follow these tips to protect your skin and maximise your time in the waves:
• Surf early and late to avoid the hottest part of the day, from 11am to 3pm. Many places are affected by onshore sea breezes during this period anyway, so you probably won't be missing much.
• Be aware that you still need to use suncream on cloudy days. Thin clouds do nothing but scatter the sun's UV light and you can still burn easily.
• Bring a decent pair of sunglasses and a hat. Bring long-sleeved shirts and lightweight trousers if you expect to be exposed to the sun for a prolonged period.
• Beware of suncreams that claim to be waterproof and aren't – stick to established brands if you're unsure. If you're fair-skinned go for the maximum protection factor, and consider putting sunblock / zinc cream on top to make sure you're fully covered.
• Think about the areas of your body that get exposed. It's not just your face, neck and arms that get blasted by the rays on a sunny day in the waves, you should also apply suncream to your lower back, your legs (especially the calves), feet, ears and hands.
• Re-apply suncream after a session to replenish any that was washed or rubbed off while you were in the water.
• If you do get burned, apply aloe vera (available as a gel, liquid or straight from the plant!) onto the areas

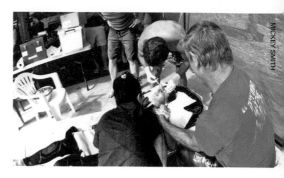

which are most affected. Wear loose-fitting clothing over the redness, take cool showers, and use a cool damp cloth moistened with cold water and skimmed milk (in a 4:1 ratio) to soothe the burn.
• Remember, there's no such thing as a healthy tan, it's just the body's response to skin damage.

SUNSTROKE

Sunstroke – or heatstroke as it's also known – is a serious condition you can face when dealing with extreme or prolonged heat. It happens when your body struggles to regulate its temperature at normal levels, leaving your major organs at risk; in extreme cases it can prove fatal. If you feel weak during or after a surf, replenish lost fluids straight away. Failure to do this can lead to heat exhaustion, which in turn can result in heatstroke.

Sunstroke is defined by a body temperature in excess of 40°C (104°F). Reducing your core temperature is critical in this situation. This can be done by removing clothing, immersing yourself in cool water, using ice packs, drinking lots of water, and finding the shade and ventilation necessary to drop your body temperature back down to normal.

CUTS AND ABRASIONS

In tropical countries, it's vitally important that you treat cuts carefully since there's a higher risk of infection (bacteria love warm environments).
• Clean the wound thoroughly using plenty of fresh clean water, and carefully pick out any pieces of dirt or coral using tweezers. Dry the wound with a sterile pad and apply antiseptic liquid or ointment such as Bacitracin.
• Dress the wound with gauze and keep it clean.

- Change the dressing at least every three days.
- Yellow pus, soreness or redness indicate that the wound is infected. Clean it out again and apply antiseptic. If the infection persists, go to a doctor or hospital.

HAZARDOUS MARINE ANIMALS

Sharks Many of the world's best surfing locations are home to sharks of one species or another. The good news is that we humans aren't the kind of food sharks like to eat and attacks on surfers are extremely rare. In fact you're ten times more likely to be killed by a lightning bolt than by a shark. All the same, no one wants a close encounter of the toothy kind. So if you're heading for a region where sharks are present, here are some common sense ways to avoid them:
- Don't surf near seal colonies or rivermouths.
- Don't surf at dawn or dusk.
- Never surf alone.
- Don't paddle out if you see bait fish jumping and splashing around in the water.

Stonefish These venomous tropical reef fish may be encountered in many parts of the Indo-Pacific including the Maldives, Sri Lanka, Indonesia, the Philippines and Papua New Guinea. Incredibly well camouflaged, stonefish laze around all day on the seabed doing very little. But if you step on one you'll know about it – their dorsal fins are equipped with venomous spines and the intense burning pain inflicted can last for several hours. If stonefish are known to be present in the region you're visiting, avoid walking where they might be lurking. Paddle, rather than wade out across reefs or lagoons; and try to avoid putting your feet down after a wipeout – instead, swim over to retrieve your board and pull yourself onto it. If you are unlucky enough to be stung, soak the foot in non-scalding hot water for ten minutes to deactivate the venom; then clean the puncture carefully and rinse it out thoroughly with water. Take painkillers, and if there are any symptoms beyond localised foot pain and swelling, seek medical attention.

Weeverfish Another type of fish with venomous dorsal fins are weeverfish, which may be encountered at beach breaks throughout Europe during the summer months. Although considerably less venomous than stonefish, weeverfish can still inflict quite a painful sting – if you step on one it feels like you've trodden on a sharp nail. Treatment involves soaking the foot in

a bucket of non-scalding hot water for ten minutes to deactivate the venom.

Sea snakes Venomous but thankfully highly visible, sea snakes may be encountered in many tropical parts of the Indian and Pacific Oceans, including Indonesia, Fiji and southern Mexico. They are generally non-aggressive, and they only have small mouths and short fangs, consequently they're rarely able to deliver a venomous bite. Their venom is highly poisonous, however, so they're well worth avoiding – don't tread on them and don't mess with them. If someone is bitten and begins feeling unwell (with symptoms such as slurred speech, weakness, aching muscles or blurry vision), seek medical assistance immediately so that sea snake anti-venom can be administered. The victim should lie down and keep absolutely still, and the bitten limb should be immobilised by using a splint and bandages.

Stingrays Stingrays may sometimes be encountered at beach breaks or sand-bottom points in tropical or semi-tropical regions. They are non-aggressive fish which feed on molluscs and worms; however, if stepped on, they'll defend themselves by whipping their tails which are equipped with a venomous barb. If stingrays are known to occur where you're surfing, paddle rather than wade out to the lineup; or shuffle your feet along the sand. If you are unlucky enough to be stung, rinse the wound very thoroughly with water (stingray stings are highly prone to bacterial infection), then soak the foot in non-scalding hot water for ten minutes; this will deactivate the venom.

Saltwater crocodiles These large dangerous reptiles inhabit swamps and estuaries in tropical regions such as Costa Rica, Indonesia, Sri Lanka and parts of the

Well before you head off, make sure you meet the country's entry requirements and have the necessary visas.
- Write your emergency contact details in your passport. Make a photocopy of your passport and keep it somewhere safe in case something happens to your original.
- It's important to let your family / friends know where you're going and where you'll be staying. Leave them your contact number, insurance policy numbers and travel itinerary.
- Check with the Foreign Office or State Department as to potential threats in the areas you wish to visit (such as natural disasters or violent political instability). It may be worth checking where the nearest embassy is located, and making a note of its phone number and opening times.
- Bring some spare US dollars in case corrupt foreign cops or checkpoint officials demand impromptu payments – US dollars are universal currency.
- If you're travelling to a third world destination where crime is a problem, it's worth carrying a spare wallet and stuffing it with business cards, old defunct credit cards and some loose change. If you do get held up, hand over the dummy wallet.
- Don't forget your driving licence if you want to hire a car on your trip, and familiarise yourself with local driving laws, which are likely to be different to those used to at home.
- Check for emergency medical evacuation on your travel insurance. If you're doing boat trips or going deep off the beaten track far from medical help. Some boat co's insist on proof of it before taking your booking.
- Make sure you know where you stand with your mobile when abroad, some networks like Three, let you use your phone for no extra cost in Europe, the US, Indo, etc. Others charge you the earth. Don't get caught out with a four figure phone bill on your return.

Caribbean. Avoid surfing (or camping) near estuaries or rivermouths in these regions.

Jellyfish Many types of jellyfish can inflict painful stings, and one or two species are particularly hazardous. The box jellyfish, *Chironex fleckeri*, is a highly venomous creature whose agonising stings can sometimes prove to be fatal. Box jellies may be encountered in a number of tropical Indo-Pacific regions (including northern Australia, western Indonesia, Papua New Guinea and the Philippines) with October to May being the period

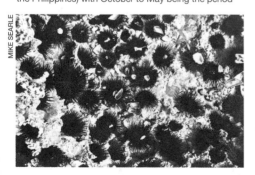

of highest risk. For most types of jellyfish sting (except blue bottle / Portuguese man-of-war stings – see below) the recommended treatment is to apply vinegar, and plenty of it; the vinegar disables the nematocysts (stinging cells), although it won't alleviate the pain. If a box jellyfish is suspected, seek medical help immediately.

• Remove any tentacles by rinsing them off with seawater, or carefully pick them off with your fingertips.
• Douse the affected area with vinegar (except in the case of blue bottle / Portuguese man-of-war stings, when you should instead bathe the sting in non-scalding hot water for ten minutes).
• Use a credit card or blunt knife to scrape off any remaining nematocysts.
• Seek urgent medical help if there are any additional symptoms such as vomiting, difficulty breathing, dizziness or lethargy.

Sea urchins These spiky seabed nuisances are rarely poisonous but they're really painful to step on. Booties or reef shoes will protect your feet if there's an abundance of them. If you step on one, here's what

to do:
• First immerse the foot in hot water to relieve the pain and soften the skin.
• Remove as many of the spines as you can using tweezers.
• Apply antiseptic and keep the wound clean. Any embedded spines should dissolve after about three weeks, but if there's pus or persistent pain visit a doctor.

HYPOTHERMIA

Hypothermia occurs when the body is exposed to cold water (or air) for a prolonged period, and when the core temperature falls below 35°C (95°F). If you're going somewhere cold, make sure you have a really good wetsuit, plus a hood, gloves and boots. And have everything in your car or van ready so you can warm up again as quickly as possible after surfing.

The symptoms of hypothermia include uncontrollable shivering, having cold and pale skin, slurred speech, having trouble coordinating basic functions, and acting irrationally. In severe cases the

victim's pulse will slow, their breathing becomes shallow and they can slip into a coma. Hypothermia becomes a life-threatening condition if the core temperature falls below 32°C (89.6°F).

If someone is suffering from hypothermia, it's important not to expose them to too much heat too quickly; the trick is to gently warm them up, and allow their core temperature to creep back up to a safe level.
• Get the person out of the wind – get in a car, a house, a tent... wherever.
• Leave their wetsuit on, but quickly dry the outside. Then wrap the person up (in blankets, towels or clothing), making sure that extremities covered (especially the head). Share your own body warmth by hugging.
• Offer a high-carbohydrate (sugary) drink, cold or hot, but not alcohol.
• Seek urgent medical help if the victim is suffering from severe hypothermia.

MINOR INSECT BITES AND STINGS
While many insect bites cause nothing more than

an itchy red lump, some bites and stings can trigger allergic reactions due to chemicals released in the insect's saliva or venom. If bacteria gets into the bite or sting it can cause a localised reaction, reddening further, becoming sore, filling with pus and leading to swollen glands and flu-like symptoms, so try not to scratch the bite too much and clean it with antiseptic creams or wipes. If there is a sting left in the wound, scrape it out with a card or your nail, don't try and pincer it out or you may squeeze more venom out of the sac.

Allergic reactions are caused when your body's immune system mistakes a harmless substance as harmful, and releases natural chemicals such as histamine that can lead to swelling and itchiness. These treatments can help reduce pain and swelling:
• Local anaesthetic spray to reduce pain.
• Hydrocortisone cream applied to reduce swelling and inflammation.
• Soothing cream such as calamine lotion.
• Antihistamine cream or pills.
• Some bites or stings may require antibiotic cream or tablets depending on how bad the reaction is.

Serious allergic reactions, or anaphylaxis, will require urgent medical attention.

FRENCH

If you're planning a trip to a non-English speaking country, it's cool to learn some of the lingo. You'll find it loads easier to get by, and the locals will appreciate your efforts to communicate in their mother tongue, even if your pronunciation is a bit sketchy.

Today's language courses for travellers make learning quick and easy. Buy an app a fortnight before you travel and learn some phrases as you're on your way into work or college. Even a bit of last-minute cramming on the flight is better than nothing. If you're stuck modern phones can now help out with basic translations on the fly. Just ask Siri. Good as they are, language courses and phrasebooks don't include much surfing terminology. So here's a selection of surf-specific words you might find useful (plus a few absolute essentials) translated into French, Spanish, Portuguese and Indonesian.

ENGLISH	FRENCH
aerial	aerial
bad	mauvais
barrel	tube
beach	plage
beer	biere
beginner	débutant
big	gros
boardbag	housse de surf
boardshorts	boardshorts
boat	bateau
boots (neoprene)	chausson en neoprene
bottom turn	bottom
breakwall	digue
channel	channel
choppy	agitee
coral	corail
cutback	cutback
ding	reparation
doctor	docteur
duck-dive	canard
expert	expert
fibreglass	fibre en verre
fin	aileron
fin key	clef d'aileron
flat	flat
forbidden	interdit
glassy	glassy
gloves (neoprene)	gants en neoprene
good	bon
good morning	bonjour
goodbye	au revoir
grom	grom

heavy (serious)	sérieux
help!	au secours!
high tide	marée haut
hollow	creuse
hood (neoprene)	capuche
intermediate	intermédiaire
island	ile
jellyfish	méduse
jetski	jetski
leash	leash
lefthander	gauche
legend	légende
lifeguard	maitre nageur
lime	citron vert
lineup	line-up
lip (of wave)	levre
local (surfer)	locale
low tide	marée basse
mid tide	mi-maree
no	non
ocean	océan
offshore wind	offshore
onshore wind	onshore

peak	pic
pier	wharf
please	s'il vous plait
point	pointe
reef	récif
reef pass	passe
righthander	droit
rip current	courant
rivermouth	emboucheure
rock	rocher
roof-rack	straps racks
sand	sable
sandbank	banc de sable
set (of waves)	série
shallow (reef)	peu profonde
shark	requin
small	petit
sorry!	pardon
stoked	ravi
surf camp	surf camp
surfboard	planche
swell	houle
swell forecast	prévision houle
takeoff	take-off
thankyou	merci
top turn	roller
tube ride	tube
urchin	oursin
water	eau
wave	vague
wax	wax
weather forecast	prévision météo
weeverfish	vive
wetsuit	combinaison
yes	oui

ENGLISH	SPANISH
aerial	aéreo
bad	malo
barrel / tube	tubo
beach	playa
beer	cerveza
beginner	principiante
big	grande
boardbag	funda
boardshorts	bermudas
boat	barco
boots (neoprene)	escarpines
bottom turn	bottom
breakwall	muelle
channel	canal
choppy	picado
coral	coral
current	corriente
cutback	cutback
ding	ding
doctor	medico
expert	experto
fibreglass	fibra de vidrio
fin	quillas
fin key	llave de quillas
flat	plato
forbidden	prohibido
glassy	liso
gloves (neoprene)	guantes
good	bueno
good morning	buenos dias
goodbye	adios
grom	peque
help!	socorro!

high tide	marea alta
hood (neoprene)	capuche
intermediate	intermedio
island	isla
jellyfish	medusa
jetski	moto de agua
leash	amarradera
left-hander	izquierda
legend	leyenda
lifeguard	socorrista
lime	lima
lineup	lineup
lip	labio
local (surfer)	local
low tide	marea baja
mid tide	marea media
no	no
ocean	mar
offshore wind	viento en contra
onshore wind	viento terrestre

peak	pico
pier	muelle
please	por favor
point	punta
reef	arrecife
righthander	derecha
rip current	corriente de resaca
rivermouth	boca del rio
rock	rocas
roof straps	cinchas
sand	arena
sandbank	banco de arena
set (of waves)	serie
shallow (reef)	poca profundidad
shark	tiburon
small	pequeño
sorry!	lo siento!
stoked	contento
surf camp	surf camp
surfboard	tabla de surf
swell	marejada
swell forecast	previsión de las olas
takeoff	take-off
thankyou	gracias
top turn	rebote
tube ride	tubo
urchin	erizo
water	agua
wave	ola
wax	cera
weather forecast	previsión del tiempo
weeverfish	pez araña
wetsuit	traje
yes	si

ENGLISH	PORTUGUESE
aerial	aéreo
bad	mau
barrel	tubo
beach	praia
beer	cerveja
beginner	iniciante
big (wave)	grande
boardbag	capa para prancha
boardshorts	calções de banho
boat	barco
boots (neoprene)	botas
bottom turn	bottom
breakwall	paredão
channel	canal
choppy	picado
coral	coral
current	corrente
cutback	cutback
ding	mossa
doctor	médico
expert	experiente
fiberglass	fibra de vidro
fin	quilha
fin key	chave para quilhas
flat	flat
forbidden	proibido
glassy	glass
gloves (neoprene)	luvas
good	bom
good morning	bom dia
goodbye	adeus
grom	aprendiz
help!	socorro!

high tide	maré cheia
hood (neoprene)	capuz
intermediate	intermédio
island	ilha
jellyfish	alforreca
jetski	mota de água
leash	cordinha
lefthander	esquerda
legend	lenda
lifeguard	nadador-salvador
lineup	line-up
lip (of wave)	lip
local (surfer)	local
low tide	maré baixa
mid tide	meia maré
no	não
ocean	oceano
offshore wind	vento offshore
onshore wind	vento onshore

peak	pico
pier	pontão
please	por favor
point	pico
reef	recife
righthander	direita
rip current	agueiro
rivermouth	foz (do rio)
rock	rochas
roof straps	correia de bagageiro
sand	areia
sandbank	banco de areia
set (of waves)	set
shallow	raso
shark	tubarão
small	pequeno
sorry!	desculpe!
stoked	contente
surf camp	surf camp
surfboard	prancha de surf
swell	ondulação
swell forecast	previsão da ondulação
takeoff	take-off
thankyou	obrigado
top turn	snap
tube ride	tubo
urchin	ouriço-do-mar
water	água
wave	onda
wax	wax
weather forecast	previsão do tempo
weeverfish	peixe-aranha
wetsuit	fato de surf
yes	sim

LINGO
INDONESIAN

ENGLISH	INDONESIAN
aerial	terbang
bad	jelek
barrel	gulungan ombak
beach	pantai
beer	bir
beginner	pemula
big	besar
boardbag	tas papan selancar
boardshorts	boardshorts
boat	kapal laut
boots (neoprene)	sepatu bot
bottom turn	belokan bawah
breakwall	dinding pemecah
channel	saluran
choppy	bergelombang
coral	batu karang
cutback	penyok
ding	penyok
doctor	dokter
expert	ahli
fibreglass	gelas fiber
fin	sirip
fin key	kunci fin
flat	rata
forbidden	terlarang
glassy	berkaca-kaca
gloves (neoprene)	bagus neoprene
good	bagus
good morning	selamat pagi
goodbye	selamat jalan
grom	anak kecil
help!	minta tolong!

SIMON WILLIAMS

high tide	air pasang
intermediate	menengah
island	pulau
jellyfish	ubur-ubur
jetski	jetski
leash	tali selancar
lefthander	kiri
legend	legenda
lifeguard	Penyelamat Pantai
lime	jeruk nipis
lineup	barisan
lip (of wave)	bibir ombak
local (surfer)	lokal
low tide	air surut
no	tidak
ocean	laut
offshore wind	darat
onshore wind	angin laut
peak	puncak

pier	dermaga
please	minta
point	tanjung
reef	karang
reef pass	passe
righthander	kanan
rip current	arus pasang
rivermouth	mulut sungai
rock	batu karang
roof-rack straps	tali atap mobil
sand	pasir
sandbank	gundukan pasir
shallow (reef)	dangkal
shark	hiu
small	kecil
sorry!	ma'af!
stoked	sangat senang
surf camp	pondok selancar
surfboard	papan selancar
swell	gelombang
swell forecast	perkiraan gelombang
takeoff	meluncur
thankyou	terima kasih
top turn	putaran atas
urchin	bulu babi
water	air
wave	ombak
wax	lilin papan selancar
weather forecast	perkiraan cuaca
wetsuit	baju selancar
yes	ya

INFORMATION

FURTHER READING

OTHER TITLES FROM ORCA PUBLICATIONS:

BOOKS

SHOP.CARVEMAG.COM

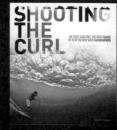

AMAZING WAVES
by Roger Sharp
ISBN 978-0-9930383-1-0
£24.99

INCREDIBLE WAVES
by Chris Power
ISBN 978-0-9567893-3-4
£24.99

**SURF TRAVEL –
THE COMPLETE GUIDE**
by Sam Bleakley
ISBN 978-0-9567893-4-1
£17.99

**THE SURFING TRIBE:
A HISTORY OF SURFING
IN BRITAIN**
by Roger Mansfield
ISBN 978-0-9523646-0-3
£22.99

SHOOTING THE CURL
by Chris Power
ISBN 978-0-9523646-8-9
£22.99

**THE SURF GIRL HANDBOOK
SECOND EDITION**
by Louise Searle
ISBN 978-0-9567893-8-9
£17.99

**THE SURF GIRL GUIDE
TO SURF FITNESS**
by Louise Searle
ISBN 978-0-9567893-7-2
£17.99

**ADVANCED SURF FITNESS FOR
HIGH PERFORMANCE SURFING**
by Lee Stanbury
ISBN 978-0-9567893-9-6
£19.99

**THE COMPLETE GUIDE
TO SURF FITNESS**
by Lee Stanbury
ISBN 978-0-9523646-6-5
£19.99

**THE BODYBOARD TRAVEL
GUIDE**
by Rob Barber
ISBN 978-0-9567893-0-3
£16.99

MAGAZINES

CARVE SURFING MAGAZINE || CARVEMAG.COM

SURFGIRL MAGAZINE || SURFGIRLMAG.COM

INFORMATION
RESOURCES

USEFUL WEBSITES

Once upon time info came from prized maps with annotations, photocopied Surfer mag guides and the Stormrider bible. These days it's all in your phone.

windy.com
A new addition to the surfer's information arsenal is the fascinating Windy, available as an app or online. Wind is displayed graphically and you can zoom around to see whole oceans or just your local area. It's super useful and def worth bookmarking.

coastalwatch.com
Big Australian resource and forecast site with surfcams, information, news, photos and more.

surfline.com
The main US site chock full of features, news and forecasts. The basic info and cams are free but you need to spend a few bucks to access the full range of HD surfcams and the lonfg range detailed forecasts.

windguru.cz
A pure swell forecast site, usually very accurate. The free info is enough for most surf travellers but you can upgrade to a pro version if you want more detail and longer outlook.

magicseaweed.com
International site for surf forecasts, photos, info, historical swell data and loads more.

lonelyplanet.com
Excellent travel site with loads of free info and advice written by journalists and travel experts. Covers hundreds of locations around the globe. There's also a useful forum called Thorn Tree on which you can post questions and search for info from other travellers who've been to certain places.

lowpressure.co.uk
Online shop window for the immaculately researched Stormrider guides, now available in digital formats as well as print.

carvemag.com
Europe's leading magazine Carve keeps you in the loop with all the latest happenings.

surfermag.com
Website of the iconic US magazine, stuffed full of features, pics, information and news.

worldsurfleague.com
The WSL site home to the webcasts of the big league world tour events and heaps of other content.

surfersjournal.com
Website of respected US travel and lifestyle mag The Surfer's Journal, crammed with classic photos and videos, although access to the cream of the content is restricted to subscribers.

HEALTH INFORMATION

Contact your doctor (at least a month before your trip) to find out which vaccinations are required for your specific destination. If you want to do a bit of additional research, check out these medical sites:

traveldoctor.co.uk
A really useful, well-laid out site rammed with info about vaccinations and health advice.

mdtravelhealth.com
A good US site offering general information and advice.

travelclinic.com.au
An established chain of Australian clinics offering vaccinations.

GOVERNMENT INFORMATION

The first port of call for general info about travelling abroad (including visas and travel advisories) is your own government, so visit the relevant travel and health websites. If you're journeying to an obscure or potentially unstable part of the world it's important that you check the very latest information. Also, make sure that your passport is up to date, with at least six months left before it's due to expire; many countries will refuse entry if it needs renewing sooner than that. Also be aware that your driver's license expires. It's not for life, so check if it needs renewing before any big trip.

UNITED KINGDOM
fco.gov.uk – Foreign and Colonial Office.
nhs.uk – National Health Service.
fitfortravel.nhs.uk – NHS information for travellers.

UNITED STATES
travel.state.gov – State Department.
cdc.gov – Centre for Disease Control and Prevention
esta.cbp.dhs.gov – You need a current ESTA to get into the US apply here, it lasts for two years.

AUSTRALIA
smartraveller.gov.au – The Australian Government's travel advisory and consular information service.

NEW ZEALAND
safetravel.govt.nz – The official source of advice for Kiwi travellers.

SOUTH AFRICA
dfa.gov.za – Department for International Relations.

IRELAND
dfa.ie – Department for Foreign Affairs.
tmb.ie – Tropical Medicine Bureau.

WORLDWIDE
who.int – The UN's World Health Organisation provides the latest information on global health matters.

ENVIRONMENTAL TIPS

We all know the ocean is in trouble. Overfishing, pollution, habitat destruction, warming and acidification are just a smattering of the issues facing the big blue. As surfers we're responsible for protecting our playground as much as possible and encouraging others to do the same. Leading by example, especially when travelling, is key.

We all need to reduce, reuse, recycle where possible. Of course it's not always easy to do so when you're faced with the option of a plastic bottle of clean water and no safe option for mains deep in the middle of nowhere but the more we try the better the world will become.

An ocean full of plastic is not the heirloom the next generation really want.

If at all possible: use a proper shopping bag and discourage vendors from plastic